SCHOOLING? I don't want to go to school!

The Author on "Why Argue" at the Dressage Club Grounds, City of Adelaide Parklands. "Why Argue" raced, and is now owned by Mrs. D. Manson-Gray.

Painting by Miss Cathleen Edkins   Photo: I. Roddie

HORSE CONTROL —
THE YOUNG HORSE

THE HANDLING, BREAKING-IN
AND EARLY SCHOOLING
OF
YOUR OWN YOUNG HORSE

•

TOM ROBERTS

HORSE CONTROL—THE YOUNG HORSE
© TOM ROBERTS 1974
Second Edition 1977
Third Edition 1979
Fourth Edition 1985

ISBN 0 9599413-1-2

Should be read in conjunction with:

"HORSE CONTROL AND THE BIT"
First Edition 1971
Second Edition 1973
Third Edition 1975
Fourth Edition 1977
Fifth Edition 1979
Sixth Edition 1982
Seventh Edition 1985

"HORSE CONTROL—THE RIDER"
First Edition 1980
Second Edition 1982

Published by T. A. and P. R. Roberts,
241 Richmond Road, Richmond, South Australia 5033.

Printed at Griffin Press Limited,
Marion Road, Netley, South Australia

ACKNOWLEDGEMENTS

In addition to the fine horsemen I have named in HORSE CONTROL AND THE BIT, it gives me pleasure to thank two expert coltbreakers — Mr Webb McKelvey of California, U.S.A., and Mr Maurice Wright of New South Wales, Australia.

Both these horsemen, like Mr Danny Fitzgerald, are expert in the handling of wild untouched horses and are also remarkable for gaining the confidence of a completely wild 'brumbie' in the matter of minutes only. Little if anything they teach and practise clashes with the principles set down in this book which is written for the novice.

There are several others mentioned in the pages that follow, not the least of these is Mr Herman Heyer of Kingston, South Australia, author of "Reflections on the Art of Horsemanship." To Herman and the many others too numerous to list, I would like to record my thanks. All these people, confident and proved by success, remain exceptionally open to new ideas — and it could be this trait that has led to their success.

The series of first-class photographs of Webb McKelvey are from the camera of his son Mike, who remains in Australia. Danny Fitzgerald has helped again with both photographs and discussions. To each of these and to all who have helped with illustrations, I send my warmest thanks.

For her splendid sketches and line drawings I am again indebted to Mrs Norah Boncey of Salisbury, South Australia. Thanks again, Norah, and particularly for your conception of the attitude of the young horse when finishing this, the first part of his schooling. It's cute.

My warmest thanks I again reserve for my wife Pat — cheerful and bright and always ready to listen or make suggestions, the finished work is certainly as much hers as mine. Pat takes on the role of sub-editor, and although I have often resisted fiercely she sees that we always laugh over it later on! To Pat, my warmest thanks for keeping the task fun.

CONTENTS

Introduction

Chapter		Page
1	THE BASIC TECHNIQUES OF HORSE CONTROL	1
2	A LESSON IS ANYTHING YOU TEACH YOUR HORSE — GOOD OR BAD	6
3	AT WHAT AGE CAN YOU START TO EDUCATE YOUR FOAL OR YOUNG HORSE?	12
4	HANDLING THE FOAL AND THE VERY YOUNG HORSE	17
5	SAFETY OF HORSE AND HANDLER	31
6	HOLDING THE YOUNG HORSE FROM THE GROUND	41
7	INTRODUCING THE YOUNG HORSE TO THE TIE-UP	52
8	BRIDLING A HORSE 'BAD ABOUT THE HEAD'	69
9	CAVESSON HEADSTALL — MOUTHING GEAR — SIDE REINS	80
10	FOR THE HORSE — THE "GO-FORWARD" LESSON: FOR HIS TRAINER — A LESSON IN TEACHING	86
11	LUNGING ... AND HANDLING	99
12	LUNGING ... AND MOUNTING	113
13	THE FIRST FEW DAYS UNDER THE RIDER	121
14	GETTING AND KEEPING A LIGHT MOUTH AND HAND	130
15	TRAFFIC, SHYING AND GENERAL 'SPOOKINESS'	138
16	MAKING PROGRESS: THE PACES — THE WALK, THE TROT	145
17	MAKING PROGRESS: THE PACES — THE CANTER	155
18	REIN EFFECTS	164
19	IMPULSION	175
20	LOADING A HORSE ON TO TRANSPORT	181
	CONCLUSION	205

LIST OF ILLUSTRATIONS

FRONTISPIECE: The Author on "Why Argue," Adelaide Parklands

Fig. No.		Page
1 to 6	Introducing the halter to a young horse	20
7	Yielding to the rein — stepping forward	22
8, 9	Yielding to the rein — stepping back	25
10	A round yard	32
11	A colt-breaker's stirrup iron	34
12	Nylon rope — before and after 'conditioning'	36
13	A section of Mr Gillivray's Round Yard	40
14	Mr Jeffery's "Magic Lunj"	43
15 to 23	A wild bush youngster is yarded, taught to tie-up, stand still while being handled, and to lead quietly — all within an hour	(47 to 51)
24 to 29	The Tie-Up — Tying to bags of sand	(57 58)
30	Spreading the pull over a larger area	59
31, 32	Tying to a folded bag	60
33	A "Dally" in use	62
34, 35	Rope Loop Tie, through halter dees	(63 64)
36	Bowline Knot	64
37	How to tie a Bowline	65
38	A Body-tie	66
39, 40	Bridling a horse difficult about the head	(69 71)
41	Colt-breaker's halter-bridle	72
42	Accustoming a difficult horse to the bit	73
43	Home-made bit designed to prevent the "Tongue-over-the-Bit" habit	78
44	Cavesson and side reins	81

45	Colt-breaker's mouthing gear	82
46) to) 50)	The "Go-Forward" Lesson	(90 (91
51) to) 57)	Teaching the horse to lunge	(100 (to (102
58) 59)	Early preparations for mounting	108
60) 61)	Providing a "distraction" while a hind leg is handled and picked up	(109 (110
62) 63)	Driving from Over the Saddle	114
64	"He shall stand still while mounting..."	115
65) 66)	Preparing the horse for the rider	118
67	Mounted for the first time	119
68	Keeping the horse relaxed	123
69	Revert frequently to a loose rein	127
70	Introducing the controlled walk	135
71	Traffic, Shying and Spookiness	139
72	Seeking the engagement of the hind legs	149
73	Rein Effects — Right 'Open' Rein	165
74	Right 'Direct' Rein	166
75	Neck Rein	167
76) 77)	'Indirect' Rein in use	(168 (170
78	Left 'Indirect Rein of Opposition'	172
79) to) 83)	Difficulties met when loading a horse into transport — Forcing the hand	186
84) to) 86)	— Turning the hindquarters	188
87) to) 90)	— Misunderstanding	191
91) to) 106)	The "Loading Lesson" — How to teach a difficult horse to load into transport quietly and calmly	(199 (to (204

INTRODUCTION

The horse has come into his own again after a gap of some two generations.

When I was a boy, a child couldn't avoid learning something about horses. Horses were everywhere and we were as familiar with them as the child of today is with motor-cars. Without realising it, one grew up with a knowledge of horses and their characteristics, good and bad.

But today there are scores of people buying a youngster or breeding one, and then setting out to break-in and train "their own young horse." I strongly advise "Don't" — unless there is someone very close to the family with experience in schooling young horses.

Horses have to be taught to do every single thing we want them to do — and just as a child is handicapped if he misses a grade at school, so too with the young horse. Each stage prepares him for the next. If his early schooling is not properly handled, he will not make the progress that is expected of him or of which he is capable.

It is the nicest, gentlest, and quietest horse that most frequently suffers from this treatment. The owner does not realise that no matter how quiet, gentle and willing a young horse may be, he will not be able to do what is wanted until he *knows* what we want.

To give a young horse or pony to a child who has only just learned to ride is also most unwise. The quite nice idea that "They will grow up together" is almost invariably impracticable. It generally results in a spoilt (and sometimes dangerous) pony — and often takes all the fun out of the child's future riding. I MOST STRONGLY ADVISE AGAINST THIS NOT UNCOMMON PRACTICE.

Read at least the first two chapters of this book before you make your decision. They are short, but give you a good idea of some of the basic facts you should know.

Although I am writing primarily for those who have not previously attempted to break-in and school a young horse and for those faced with some specific difficulty, I say without hesitation that what is set down on these pages should be known to ALL who ride, drive, own, breed and handle horses.

I leave the book to speak for itself. When writing it I have assumed you have read my first, "Horse Control and the Bit." Those of you breeding your own foal are advised to read both books before the foal is dropped — if that is possible.

Good luck and many happy hours with your friend the other side of the saddle.

I am confident that what you read here will help you both.

(Signed)
TOM ROBERTS

CHAPTER 1

THE BASIC TECHNIQUES OF HORSE CONTROL

Training Procedures:

"That will profit you" — "That will profit you not";
Quiet persistence;
"End-of-Lesson", what it means;
"Old Hat";
Use of voice in training.

Training Procedures

Few people who set out to train and educate a horse give any thought to the great difficulties that face the horse.

How many of us setting out to teach him have given serious thought or study of HOW to teach him: how to establish a system of signals or aids that most riders grow up with and accept as being natural, but of which the horse has no knowledge whatsoever?

I am going to ask you a question, and before you read on I would like you to answer it clearly — to yourself.

Question: "Why does a horse stop or go slower if you pull on the reins ?" If you answer: "Because it hurts his mouth," I am sorry to have to break the news to you — you have failed.

But no, I'll give you another chance: "Why do you jump up instantly if you sit on an upturned tack or drawing pin?"

If you answer again: "Because it hurts" — you really do need to read every word in this book!

The horse stops — and you jump up — not just because it hurts, but to stop it hurting. By no means the same thing.

And there isn't any doubt: if jumping up didn't stop the pain, *you* would try doing something else. So, too, eventually does the horse. *These are not trick questions.* If you really believe in and act on the answer you gave to the first, then you think that all you have to do is to hurt your horse's mouth and he will stop.

On the contrary, the important thing is to let him know — to teach him — how, by doing what you want of him, he can *avoid* any pain, irritation, inconvenience or discomfort the bit (or whip or spur) might otherwise cause. Good trainers do everything they possibly can to avoid hurting the horse or even letting him hurt himself. Our real goal should be never to have to hurt our horse.

Reward and Punishment is often cited as the secret of successful horse training and undoubtedly both rewards and punishments have their place. But — we should seldom, if ever, resort to punishment when teaching our horse anything new. Punishment, when we use it, should be reserved for exceptional occasions. Don't think "Reward and Punishment."

Encourage and Discourage is a better guide, as it drops the term 'punishment.' When riding a young horse we alternate from encourage to discourage very frequently and quite often change from discourage to encourage several times in a matter of seconds.

But the term 'discourage' still has the drawback that it *can* include punishment; and we should discard any term that could include punishment as a normal training procedure. Punishment and teaching are "divorced."

It is to avoid using any expression that could possibly include punishment as a normal teaching procedure that I suggest you think in the terms:

"THAT WILL PROFIT YOU" — "THAT WILL PROFIT YOU NOT"

These terms mean exactly — EXACTLY — what they say.

"To Profit" is to benefit or gain: to be better off. The profit to the horse can be any reward or encouragement the trainer may think his pupil should receive — and it must, of course, be available to give.

"To Profit Not" means that the horse will gain or benefit not at all. Just that. It certainly does not mean he will suffer a loss or be worse off — as he would be if he were punished.

This is what is important about these expressions — and why I use them. By no stretch of the imagination can "Profit you not" be construed as punishment.

It consists of the withholding of any gain, reward, encouragement or profit. That, and only that.

Quiet Persistence

'It will profit you not' means that the horse will not be encouraged to follow a line of conduct other than that we have in mind for him. We withhold any gain — which means we quietly continue with our demands, whatever they might be.

We persist. We quietly persist with our demands.

This gentle discouragement of 'quiet persistence' is something that horses seem to find irresistible. Whenever you are in doubt as to what course to follow, mounted or dismounted, revert to "Quiet Persistence." Your quiet persistence is the real 'That will profit you not.' It discourages the horse *without punishing him.*

Punishment does have its place in the training scheme, with some horses more clearly than with others — but even then it should be used only occasionally. Do not revert to punishment when you are trying to teach the horse something new. It upsets the horse and destroys the calmness so essential to his taking-in a new lesson. So punishments are 'out' when teaching any new lesson.

END OF LESSON

End of Lesson is the best, most effective and most convenient of all rewards and encouragements.

WHAT "END OF LESSON" MEANS

When teaching a horse almost anything at all — no matter what it is, "End of Lesson" means a pause, a break, a rest for a while — or even, on some occasions, completely finishing work for the day *at the moment* the horse has made or is making progress in a lesson.

At the very instant of the action that constitutes progress, the teacher ends the lesson — for a while, at least.

Ending a lesson constitutes a reward, an encouragement, an incentive to the horse to try to follow and understand what is being taught him.

THE "END-OF-LESSON" TECHNIQUE IS PROBABLY THE MOST IMPORTANT PROCEDURE IN THE SCHEME OF HORSE TRAINING

We use the End-of-Lesson Technique from the first day our young horse is yarded and continue using it to the last day of his schooling.

"End-of-Lesson" is always available for use.

Because it is easy for the horse to understand, it keeps him calm and so leads to the greatest progress. When the horse is calm, the most permanent impressions are made on his mind.

"End-of-Lesson" is of equal value to the trainer. It keeps him looking for and recognising progress as the horse tries first one thing and then another. He looks for progress to encourage — rather than 'stupidity' to punish.

IT'S "OLD HAT"

"Old Hat" is another expression I will repeatedly use to indicate the horse's attitude to a previous experience. He (I pretend) says: "Old Hat!" whenever he is asked to do, again, something he has already proved to be not objectionable.

The "Old Hat" technique is used in literally hundreds of ways — as you will read later on.

It means we do something (or get the horse to do something) new — and then before anything can go wrong or he becomes upset, we *'End-the-lesson.'*

Next time he is in a similar position he remembers nothing unpleasant resulted from the first occasion, and he remains calm. A few repetitions and he accepts it (whatever it is) as, "Old Hat."

An instance: we separate a foal from its Dam for a few moments. Before the foal has time to become very excited at finding itself alone, we put them together again. Tomorrow or on some other occasion, we separate them again and once more put them together after a short period. We do this several times and after a while the foal ceases to worry. "It's 'Old Hat' — nothing to worry about, we'll get together again later on!" seems to be the reaction.

This is a characteristic of the horse. Recognise it and keep it in mind. From it we learn to repeat lessons rather than to prolong them — particularly if what we are doing or getting the horse to do is exciting or frightening to him.

USE OF THE VOICE IN TEACHING

The use of the voice can also help in training. You want the horse to do something, it might be to lead forward or step back — anything. So you do something you hope he will eventually come to understand — but you will be very lucky indeed if he happens to try the right thing straight away. Until he does, you quietly persist with your actions.

By quietly persisting with your aids or pressures (whatever they may be) you aim to show him: "Not that, Boy, not that," and your voice can help by you quietly saying, "No", "No", as he tries the wrong things.

You will be teaching him many things in the coming months and if you quietly say "No" each time he tries *other than what you want* he will come to recognise that "No" means he has tried the wrong thing.

This can be most helpful in dismounted lessons as well as in early lessons when mounted. Use any monosyllable for the sound, any short single sound will do just as well: "Hey," "Now," "No." It is the *sound*, not the word, that matters.

The use of the voice helps, too, with the encouragements you want to give the horse when he does or tends to do what you want of him. Here again the words you use mean little; it is *how* your voice sounds that is important. When he tends to do right or to do better, change to a "purring" type of sound. Say anything you like as long as your voice sounds pleasant and 'purring': "That's right; he's clever . . . he's a clever boy" — and let him associate that kind of sound with your End-of-lesson reward.

The use of the voice can be very useful at times to let the horse know when he is on the right track, particularly in the early work dismounted. There are scores of things you do not want him to do on any occasion and he may try quite a number of them. To each attempt you gently say: "No," "No," and you quietly and gently persist with your demands.

Think and act gently and kindly — for he is trying. Say 'No,' 'No,' gently and quietly, but in a manner he could not possibly confuse with your "Purring".

The voice can convey to him "Approved" or "Not Approved" almost simultaneously with his action, and under all circumstances — mounted or dismounted.

There's no end to the number of things you do NOT want him to do and he may try a few of them or all of them. To each attempt you should gently indicate to him: "Not that," "Not that." Or better still, think: "Not that, Boy;" think gently, think kindly; he is trying.

Most important of all, when he does show the slightest tendency to do the ONE thing you *do* want you must instantly change your 'tune' and substitute: "That's right", or "That's better, clever Boy ... clever Boy." Then "End of Lesson"; have a rest.

The really important thing is your ability to show approval or disapproval instantly.
Two seconds later will be too late. Sometimes the youngster will have tried so many things that if your approval is late he will have difficulty in knowing what *did* please you.

If you use the same purring tone always — and instantly — and only to show approval, you will find he relaxes the instant you begin to use it. When mounted you can FEEL him relax under you, and you'll be able to imagine him thinking: "That's good. Struck it at last. Now, exactly what DID I do that pleased the man?"

More about the Use of the Voice in Chapter 11.

TO SUM UP

Think and act in the terms, "That will profit you" or "That will profit you not."

Although "Profit you" includes rewards, "Profit you not" *does not include punishment.*

Punishment should play no part in the teaching of a lesson, but rewards should be constantly used in all our teaching.

Encourage and reward all behaviour you would like the horse to continue — particularly when he has been difficult.

To discourage the horse if he does other than what is wanted, quietly persist with your aids or actions. When you want to convey to him, "That will profit you not" — just fail to let-up with whatever you are doing: *gently persist.*

"End of Lesson" is the best, most effective, and most convenient of encouragements. To be of maximum effect it must *instantly follow* the act we wish to encourage.

"Old Hat" is an expression used to indicate the horses's attitude to any previous experience that has not proved to be upsetting.

The use of the voice can be very helpful in training. It will never take the place of the "It will profit you — it will profit you not" actions — but it can augment.

CHAPTER 2

A LESSON IS ANYTHING YOU TEACH YOUR HORSE — GOOD OR BAD

*How you teach your horse what you don't want him to learn: A Warning:
What constitutes a lesson — and "End of Lesson";
Breaking a lesson into parts;
How does a horse think?
The horse that has already formed a bad or dangerous habit.*

HOW YOU TEACH YOUR HORSE WHAT YOU DON'T WANT HIM TO LEARN — A WARNING

Every experience the young horse has, becomes a lesson. If what he learns is useful, we like to call it 'training' or 'education.' But if what he learns is a nuisance or dangerous, we often brand it a 'vice.'

Do not deceive yourself: the horse's faults indicate the degree of his trainer's failure. Every vice, every bad habit he learns or acquires, has to be laid at the door of the person who, by lack of knowledge or care perhaps, permitted him to gain that harmful experience.

Training horses consists not only of influencing them in the direction we have in mind, but also in guarding against the formation of tricks and habits that are disagreeable, annoying or vicious.

I have explained how "End of Lesson" — making a break in a lesson, pausing during a lesson, terminating a lesson — is used to encourage a horse to repeat what he last did before the break. As the horse's training progresses and we consistently utilise this to encourage him, he comes to watch for every little concession we make. Every pause or interruption becomes an encouragement no matter what causes the interruption.

Unless we are very careful and very watchful when things are going wrong and we are either not sure what to do or perhaps a little frightened to do what we know we should be doing, then we are likely to look for an excuse to pause or not to go on immediately. We may excuse ourselves afterwards, "But I had to stop — or get off — and alter a stirrup leather or tighten his girth."

So, if during a period of opposition or resistance you 'let up' for a moment or two, say to re-gather the lunge rein or if you are on his back to alter your stirrup leathers perhaps, you will have encouraged him in his opposition, resistance or misconduct, whatever it might be.

You did not mean to, of course, but you will have done so. He notes: "Resistance pays. It profits me. It is a good thing to do."

The horse does not know what is going on in *your* mind but he does notice that what he was doing had profited him. By the unwitting "End of Lesson" encouragement *at the wrong time*, you have given him a clear lesson in wrong-doing.

In any instance where the horse is resisting and you are compelled to stop and put something right, see that he does not rest while you are doing it. Keep him doing something — bustle him in some way or other — but on no account let him have a rest or 'peace and quiet,' which would encourage him to repeat his wrong-doing.

The advice of the great horseman James Fillis should be taken to heart:

> "The lesson should never be interrupted and on no account should it be terminated by reason of the resistance of the horse."

To that I will add:

> "Or for any reason that the horse could construe that way."

If you are at a disadvantage for a moment, don't pause unless you really are compelled to do so — rather continue on a reduced note.

I will stress again and again that "End of Lesson" is one of the best ways of getting through to a horse. Watch to see it does not follow on wrong-doing. It is by this means that he most often learns bad or dangerous habits.

WHAT CONSTITUTES A LESSON?

— An Instance

A young horse is yarded and is so frightened that you cannot get near enough to touch him. Eventually with quiet persistence you are able to touch him. The moment you do so, you walk away — "End of Lesson;" period.

That, at that moment, is a complete lesson for the horse: that there is nothing to fear from you. Indeed, on the contrary, you show him that standing still brings relief from your advances and the moment he lets you touch him, you walk away.

It must be *you* leave the horse — not he that bolts away from you. If he darts off then again you follow the advice of James Fillis: "The lesson should never be interrupted and it should on no account be terminated, by reason of the resistance of the horse."

You quietly persist with your advances until the horse stands for a moment. When he stands, you quietly leave him.

A minute or so later, longer perhaps if you have something else to engage you, you repeat the lesson. It may take almost as long or even longer this time, as he may not yet have 'caught on' to the idea.

Again, *you* leave the horse as soon as you touch him. Again, you "End the Lesson."

As a rule, after some three or four approaches the horse grasps the idea and will let you touch him to get rid of you. He is learning a most important lesson: *that you persist when he resists and you desist when he learns to acquiesce* — at least in this stage of his education. Each approach and acceptance is a complete lesson.

One lesson leads to the next, and the next lesson is that he must bear your company for a second or so before you leave. Then several seconds. Each stage is progress, and you 'do your act' — End of Lesson — and leave or back away. Next you only move your hand off him and do not leave him every time: and so it goes on.

'End of Lesson' — Another Example — Answering the Rein

Later on you are riding your horse and want him to stop. You lightly stretch the reins and he stops. You should then immediately relax or lighten the reins again; you reward him by ending the lesson. You relieve his mouth of any additional pressure you may have put on it. You are showing him, letting him learn by experience: "I want you to stop so I slightly tighten the reins, if you stop, or even go slower at first, I will take the extra pressure off the reins." End of lesson.

The horse is learning by the End-of-Lesson technique that: "To stop or go slower when the bit presses more is a 'Good thing to Do'."

(You are recommended to practise the horse in this basic requirement before you ride him, see "Driving from over the Saddle," Chapter 12).

BREAKING A LESSON INTO PARTS

I have just given instances of what may constitute a lesson, and many lessons may advantageously be broken into several minor lessons.

Again take teaching the horse to stop as an instance. Imagine you are walking at, say, 4 miles an hour and you slightly stretch the reins to ask the horse to stop. He isn't yet clear what the tighter rein means and instead of stopping, he moves his jaw or his head, or for a while resists the bit or 'drops it' — but continues on at 4 m.p.h.

The rider quietly persists with the slightly stretched rein.

After a few paces, finding that what he has done or is doing has not profited him in any way, the horse may either by accident or design try going slower. He drops to 3 m.p.h. *Immediately* you should encourage that line by "End of Lesson." You lighten the reins again.

Don't think: "I wanted him to drop to a halt so I will keep at him until he does." If you do so, the young horse will see it like this: "What CAN I do about this thing that is worrying my mouth? Turning my head, tossing my head, bringing my nose in — doesn't improve things. I'll try going slower." And he drops speed a little.

If he finds the additional bit pressure still persists, "That is no good, either," he observes and then goes on to try something else. Perhaps he begins to fret or jig. He has proved — *you* have proved to him — that going slower, like tossing his head, "profits him not."

You have missed your chance.

The young horse must be encouraged — at first — even if he only *tends* to do what is wanted. The pressure on the reins should be lightened immediately, if only for a moment. Try to tell him, through the reins, *"That's the idea! That will profit you."*

And then, a few seconds later, you can ask for another slowing down.

The lesson in mind in this instance is to teach him that a slightly tightened rein — by no means tight enough to hurt him — means "Stop," or "Go Slower." And any and every tendency to do what we want *must* be encouraged.

We may break this lesson into four or even more minor lessons: from 4 m.p.h. to 3 m.p.h.; from 3 m.p.h. to 2 m.p.h.; from 2 m.p.h. to 1 m.p.h.; stop.

I have more to say about this matter of rein tension in Chapter 4.

※ ※ ※ ※

Only while it is still a lesson do we end it as a reward. Once something being taught has been grasped — understood by the horse, once he understands what is wanted of him in a particular situation, it ceases to be a lesson. It becomes part of his knowledge.

He is then expected to do what he knows is required of him, and as he responds to our actions or aids we convey to him: "Well done," "Very well done" — or "Not so good; repeat that last movement." We congratulate him rather than reward him.

Our approval is his reward then, his profit. And it is really wonderful what a horse will do to gain our approval — if we do not resort to force but ask for his co-operation.

The "Go-forward" lesson of Chapter 10 gives instance after instance of this training procedure.

HOW DOES A HORSE THINK?

He *can* think in certain ways but in a very much different way from ourselves. He seems to be quite unable to think ahead like we do. Almost all his actions are based on his past experiences — not by working things out, as we do. If you and I are hurt we are not only conscious of pain but we immediately think ahead: "Will this injury incapacitate me? And if so, for how long?" "Will it be a permanent handicap? Will it prevent me taking Irene to the ball next week? Could it kill me?" — and so on.

Not so the horse; he is conscious only of what he is experiencing now — the pain. He will not be in the least concerned about the most frightful injury if it does not hurt much or if it has been treated with painkiller. He knows nothing and thinks nothing about cuts, bruises, broken limbs and disablements, bleeding or arterial bleeding.

He will quickly notice what leads to trouble or pain — and also what leads to its discontinuation. He thinks hardly at all, but he does notice and reflect. He takes notice of and remembers his experiences. He reflects and anticipates rather than plans.

The horse learns remarkably little beyond his experiences.

I will repeatedly *stress*, "Horses learn from their experiences" — and if they are permitted to gain anything from a certain action they will naturally try to repeat it. The horse knows of no such thing as 'vice'; he only sees it as a "Good thing to Do."

Let me give you an instance from my own and quite recent experience. The horse concerned had learned to run under a low branch and leave his rider, as Jorricks said: "Hanging there like a Cherub in a tree." Surely we might call that trick a 'vice'?

"No such thing," the horse would surely have pleaded. "I do that to get the weight off my sore back. It's a tremendous relief."

And so it proved to be; for the moment I mounted I found the horse showed signs of the greatest discomfort under the rider. A broken front arch of the saddle-tree with its jagged steel edges biting into his wither was the cause. Of course going under a low branch was a "Good thing to Do" — as the rider immediately 'dismounted' and so made an End-of-Lesson period — and the discomfort ceased.

The horse knew nothing of the fact that the rider might be hurt; he only knew "Running under low branches brings relief." You will understand his attitude and viewpoint better having read about the use of the "End of Lesson," period or pause technique.

Each horse starts off in life knowing nothing whatever of what will be expected of him. *Nothing whatsoever.* Each and every thing that we want of him has to be taught him. No matter how quiet, how gentle, how willing a horse may be, he cannot do what is wanted until he knows what we want — until he learns what our actions mean.

If he has a vice, as we call it, it means that we have shown him, taught him by the experiences we have given him, that that 'vicious' trick will bring relief from our demands.

THE HORSE THAT HAS ALREADY FORMED A BAD OR DANGEROUS HABIT

This is a task for an experienced rider. Discretion, apropos and tact are essential and also the skill and courage to put them into effect. And the last requirement is hardly an advantage without the other qualities.

These habits or tricks are usually the result of pausing or resting the horse — ending the lesson — at the wrong time, for instance after he has reared or bucked or jibbed, or whatever the vice may be that he has picked up or tends to pick up.

I only mention punishment here, as if I do not do so I may lead some to think it is wrong ever to become punishing.

A quick tap with the whip, a light but threatening jolt of the bit or whip at the right moment, will check many a budding rogue — if you know *when, how, and to what degree to act.* (Read what is said about punishment in Chapter 4).

If you are not sure, withhold punishment and keep to quiet persistence — "That will profit you not." *But do not 'back out'* or he will be encouraged to repeat his bad behaviour.

Be sure, too, that you always remain ready to reward every tendency the horse shows to behave better. Even in the worst cases when punishment is clearly necessary and appropriate, reward should be instant and clear, even lavish, when he shows signs of better conduct. Remember that the trick, whatever it might be, is something someone has allowed the horse to learn, something he has been 'taught'. Be firm and resolute. He has to be stopped — but try to feel sorry for him too.

Do not forget the great value of encouragement and the End-of-Lesson rewards, even in your discipline: "THAT will profit you," you have to show him as soon as he gives you the opportunity to do so.

I have read or heard: "Fear and anger never exist together in a horse," and that could be so. Certain it is with humans, that fear — when what causes it has disappeared — often changes to anger and uncontrolled brutality.

Do all you can to control *yourself;* particularly when any fear is relieved. In the case of a difficult horse this will usually be when he starts to behave better.

TO SUM UP

These first two chapters will give you an idea of the basic techniques and principles of horse training.

I have placed them first because you should be following their general lines from the very first time you approach your foal or young horse.

In assessing the trainer, the horse's good points and his bad points will be put in the balance. One really bad point can make a horse dangerous and practically worthless.

A lesson, remember, is ANYTHING the horse learns from you — anything, and everything.

CHAPTER 3

AT WHAT AGE CAN YOU START TO EDUCATE YOUR FOAL OR YOUNG HORSE?

When to start: Education begins before breaking-in;
Age at breaking-in;
Shoes before breaking-in?;
"Nursing" the young horse's legs.

> "A colt that's backed and burden'd,
> Being young
> Loseth his pride, and never maketh Strong."
>
> Shakespeare

WHEN TO START

Young horses are wonderfully strong in some ways and even foals only a few days old can gallop, kick and jump with astonishing strength and ability.

Nature has given the horse only one real defence against the wild animals that otherwise would have destroyed the breed. This defence is speed — the ability to escape. Even the youngest foal is capable of escaping with its mother from most animals that might attack them.

These attacks would occur only occasionally, however, which meant that after such an effort and strain on the foal's young legs there usually followed several days or even weeks of quiet grazing, frolicking and rest that repaired any ill effects the hardly-formed limbs might have suffered.

Experience has shown us that young horses worked regularly at normal work or worked on hard ground, stony, rough, heavy or holding ground develop all sorts of troubles with their legs, and these often lead to damage and blemishes that remain for life.

When we ride a two, three, or four-year-old and feel him strong and lively under us, it is hard to keep in mind that the strength is for emergency use only and that *the youngster is not mature enough to stand a continuing effort.* So, if we use a very young horse, we should either copy nature and give him regular and quite long rests or we should 'nurse' him, i.e. use him with great care and forethought.

On a farm the first course is easy to follow. If he is needed the young horse is caught, broken-in and used for a short while, if that is necessary, and he is then turned out maybe for days or for weeks or months, until he is wanted again. If there has been any trouble coming up, the rest in the paddock gives it a chance to clear up before it develops into anything.

If, on the other hand, the youngster has to be put into regular training and educating after the breaking, there is nothing for it but the most careful nursing of his legs.

Children's ponies are often worked as two-year-olds and many of them are still going sound and strong well into their late twenties. This is because they are usually only lightly ridden and they also get many periods of complete rest — often weeks on end.

Thoroughbreds used for racing are often broken-in and raced as two-year-olds, but many of them are broken down before they are five and their useful life is over. Others, luckier perhaps or in better hands, go on apparently none the worse for their early work. Pre-natal feeding has a big bearing on the structure of the limbs. (A well-balanced diet for the mare before foaling and for both mare and foal after foaling is an important factor and is one that, if neglected, can never be quite corrected in after-years).

In the days of cavalry no-one would consider the purchase, or even the gift, of any horse less than five years of age for military purposes. Experience had proved that younger horses could not be relied on to stand up to the regular training required of them in the ranks. A four-year-old would not be accepted.

EDUCATION BEGINS BEFORE BREAKING-IN

The Foal

Even in the first week of his life we can start to accustom the foal to the handling that will be part of his everyday life later on. As he grows we can get him used to having a halter on, to being led, and also to having his feet inspected.

These lessons can begin as early as you please and go on whenever opportunity offers. But the foal must be kept respectful — he must not be permitted to become cheeky or disrespectful.

Not a Question of Age

"At what age can I start to educate my young horse?" is not a question of age but of what he is intended to be used for — and how constant, regular and strenuous will be his work after breaking-in.

If you are going to take plenty of time over it — and why shouldn't you? — begin as early as you like with your youngster's education, even if you don't intend to ride him for another year or more. Take all the time you have, and you may well leave days, weeks or even months, between lessons. Provided you go back and repeat the last lesson the youngster will go on just the same after six months as after six hours.

THE ACTUAL AGE AT BREAKING-IN

Two years is certainly not too young to have him broken-in — provided he is given only a few weeks very light work under a very light rider. Then out he goes again. No proper work, just let him become accustomed to a rider; let him grow up accepting the idea of being ridden. When next you tackle him it will be "Old Hat."

A three-year-old: give a total of about three months, or less, work for the whole year. Not in one period — and make it a four-day week if possible.

A four-year-old: you may give a total of six months work or more if he is not overworked or stressed. Don't let him become tired or jaded.

At five years, he can be brought into regular work but it should be light at first, and the horse gradually conditioned to harder work. Horses broken-in after five years of age are often quite difficult: they usually have minds of their own after they are six.

You may get away with a good deal more than this, many do; but it is unwise to try it unless pressed.

WHEN BRINGING HIM IN AFTER A REST

Never think to go on from where you left off last time when you bring your youngster in after a rest. Spend a little time the first day to lead up to where you left off. (I'll tell you more about this in later chapters).

If, at any time, when working your young horse you think you can detect the slightest sign of soreness or lameness, *rest him immediately* and back into the paddock. Don't wait for a definite lameness to set in — rest immediately.

Rest BEFORE lameness fully develops, is the answer: "An ounce of preventative is worth a ton of cure."

SHOES BEFORE BREAKING-IN?

No! Not unless the feet are worn or broken and work would damage them more. Have the feet trimmed, by all means, and they should be checked regularly. The fronts should be kept 'paired' both for level and equal length and so, too, should the hinds.

Only put shoes on when it becomes necessary. An iron-shod hoof is a much greater menace to you, to other horses, and to his own limbs if he should strike himself, as so many youngsters do.

When you do fit him with shoes, don't leave them on for more than four or five weeks; after that time I take them off and work a horse without shoes again if his feet permit it. Shoes should not be necessary when the going is soft.

Always — if you turn your youngster out — before doing so *remove his shoes* if he has any on, and cut his feet back, unless the paddock is stony or extremely hard.

Care of the feet is a MUST and requires attention from the earliest days: we should examine his feet every opportunity that offers.

"NURSING" THE YOUNG HORSE'S LEGS

I have spoken of looking after or 'nursing' the young horse's legs.

Nursing his legs begins in the nursery. If a foal does not get a full and well-balanced diet, he may grow big and fat and appear to be as strong as any other. It is when you begin to work him that the effects of any deficiencies show up.

Calcium shortage shows its effects when you start work, as the legs, although they look normal, will lack strength. Bones with a shortage of calcium might be compared with a concrete beam made with insufficient cement in the mixture — they will not stand up to stresses.

See that your youngster gets plenty of lucerne (alfalfa) dry or green, as it contains a lot of lime. Learn something about what constitutes a balanced diet for mare and foal, if you have one. Proper feeding later on may improve the condition, but nothing quite corrects it.

Work him for short periods only. Twenty, thirty or at most forty minutes is enough at any one time, particularly if the young horse is to be worked regularly for a while.

Cantering should be avoided at first and then be limited to short periods. It should only be on soft going: the faster the pace the harder the horse's legs hit the ground. As Jorrocks said in his famous "Handley Cross": "It ain't 'oppin' over the little fences wot nocks 'orses legs about, it's the 'ammer, 'ammer, 'ammer on the 'ard, 'ard road."

Jumping, if you do any, should be mostly on the lunge and on level soft ground. This allows the youngster to get practice and experience with the least possible wear on his legs. Obstacles should be long from front to rear rather than high. Long leaps teach the horse to use judgment in his "take-off" and the angle of arrival lessens the stress on landing.

If the youngster is very lively, let him have fun and games loose in the paddock whenever you can, daily if possible. Otherwise he'll be inclined to do so when you are up — and *that's bad for his legs.*

Holidays — lots of holidays — will correct most leg troubles. Let them be for as long as possible. If your horse is clearly lame, call the Vet. The 'obvious' is not always the real trouble. Remember, you never know how close you are to your horse's limit; you only know when you have passed the limit and overdone it.

I have never forgotten something I read many, many years ago in a book translated from the French: "It is with the horse as with fruit — damage once done can never be corrected."

TO SUM UP

Start "gentling" your young horse as early as you can. Don't leave it until the day you intend riding him. Get him accustomed to being handled, led about, having things rested on his back — before the "breaking-in" period. Think of "gentling" or preparing him rather than "breaking" him.

Take plenty of time.

Take care to have a rider of reasonable weight on his back, particularly when he is first ridden.

Rest him for at least two days in every week while he is at work. Don't tire him physically or let him get 'fed up' — bored.

Avoid fast work. He's still in 'kindy' remember. Most of the work should be at a calm long striding walk, making him use his hocks and shoulders.

Stony, uneven or slippery ground can start sprains and other injuries, and should be avoided even more than hard ground. Holding ground, i.e. soft ground that holds the horse's hoofs, and — worst of all — ground that is very soft *in places* as at some beaches, will start sprains very easily and pull tendons. Such damage is often irreparable.

Shoeing, when necessary, should be regular and the shoes should be removed every four to five weeks. I like to take the shoes off and wear down the foot by working the horse without shoes until they become necessary again. If shoes are left on too long, with the toe growing faster than the heel as it does, additional strain is placed on the back tendons of the leg.

Children's ponies, particularly in country areas, may never need shoeing, but the feet should be kept trimmed level — level when viewed from the front.

Rest should follow immediately on the slightest suspicion of soreness. Let the rest be for as long as possible and always with the shoes off — unless the hoof is damaged.

CHAPTER 4

HANDLING THE FOAL AND THE VERY YOUNG HORSE

*When to start teaching your foal;
Use a small yard for handling a foal or any young horse;
Use a special halter for a foal;
Getting the young horse to accept a halter;
Teaching the young horse to yield to a stretched rein — to lead forward, to step back; the 'relatively still' hand; "Good Hands";
Keep the young horse light in hand;
Discipline begins before Mounting;
Kicking and biting.*

WHEN TO START TEACHING YOUR FOAL

When a foal is bred at home or on a farm, or in any place where the dam is brought into stables fairly regularly, the education of the foal can be more or less continuous from the day it is foaled — and if and when it is convenient.

The younger the horse is when you start him off on a new experience or begin to teach him something, the more readily he will accept that thing, whatever it is. Later on he will look back on it as something that has 'always been.' We should do all we can to see that the memories of new experiences are pleasant, not painful or frightening things that will excite the youngster when he looks back on them — or if something similar happens later on. Do not hurt him or *let him hurt himself.*

When a young horse has been well-handled as a foal, has occasionally been led about in a small yard and perhaps tied up and had other restraints put upon his liberty, he grows up knowing and to some extent accepting that he has to do what is wanted of him. He does not think about it, he just knows it is so and has always been so as far as he is concerned. It is "Old Hat".

Handle the Foal Whenever it is Convenient

Where you have a foal near home, take any opportunity that offers to prepare him for the future. Get him used to having you run your hands over him, particularly if he shows any signs of being itchy — as foals generally are when changing their first baby coat. Rub him and scratch him and occasionally brush him. Let your handling become a pleasure for him. But don't, as so many are inclined to do, continually brush a young horse's tail. Every time you do so you will find a few hairs in your dandy brush: you will be removing hairs quicker than they can grow and you will soon have a tail looking like a worn out whitewash brush. Long tail-hairs take years to grow.

Handle the youngster about the head for short periods only and always stop handling him while he is keeping his head still, not when he is trying to avoid your hand. Young horses almost invariably object to having their ears touched.

Be sure you do not try to hold his head still even when you have a halter on him. Follow his head with your hands; show him that moving his head will not profit him, whereas keeping it still *will*. Use no force on the head and be sure you study Chapters 8 and 11 on 'Horses Bad About the Head' and 'Lunging and Handling'.

Repeatedly stop handling him: always *after* he has let you go a little further.

This applies to all handling; down the neck and along the back, and particularly down the legs. Stop the progress of your handling each time he lets you go a little further *before* he tries to move away from your hand. Go back then, and start again from where you began last time. Each time, *you* stop and go back when he lets you go a little further . . . before he moves away from your hand.

Always maintain a firm frank contact when handling the young horse or foal. Lay the full of your hand on him. You will find horses object more to a very light touch than to a firm contact.

USE A SMALL YARD FOR HANDLING A FOAL OR ANY YOUNG HORSE

An occasional half-hour or so in a small yard with a well-fitting halter and a long rope or lunge rein attached should present no difficulties.

In everything we do, we should follow a policy of letting one thing lead up to the next. This makes for quiet steady progress. Where we have a very young horse and plenty of time, we can continue his lessons whenever it is convenient: it may be this afternoon, or tomorrow, or it may not be until next month or next summer.

It is astonishing how far an experienced horseman can progress with a young horse with only a single half-hour lesson a month. The youngster will not have forgotten the preceding lesson no matter how long the gap — but make a practice of repeating the previous lessons before starting the next.

Do not attempt too much at any one time and don't be too exacting at first. Be gentle, be patient; but be resolute with whatever you ask. Be firm, but only ask for a little progress. No over-indulgence — no nonsense — for your "dear little foal" wrongly handled can grow to be a frighteningly strong brute.

Use no force. This is one of the reasons for recommending a small yard for handling. You may be able to hold a very small foal by force should he try to escape, particularly if you follow the rules given about angles in Chapter 6; but in a very short time he can grow too strong for his handler and if he struggles he may escape — completely break free.

We can prevent this in a small yard if a long rope or rein is used. Even if the youngster pulls away, he does not break free, for the rein will reach to the fence with ease.

We can show him: "That will profit you *not*".

Even in a much larger yard, one up to 60 feet in diameter, if there is a standard 30 ft. lunge rein on the youngster, its end will remain in the centre of the yard to be picked up again whenever we feel like it. He hasn't gained anything. He doesn't have a chance to learn he has broken free, he still has the weight of the rein, 30 ft. of it, on his head. He knows nothing of the rein having been dropped or of it being picked up again. It is a very different story if this happens in a big paddock, where he learns he CAN escape from us.

Avoid handling even a very small foal in a big paddock where he can experience the advantage of using his strength against you if he pulls away. *Horses of all ages learn from their experiences.* What they have experienced, good or bad, they KNOW.

Do all the early handling, if possible, in a small yard or stable.

USE A SPECIAL HALTER FOR THE FOAL

All that is required for handling a foal is a suitably-sized halter, a rope and/or, if possible, a lunging rein.

Do not use a halter designed for a grown horse; you will find the youngster much more difficult to handle with a halter that is too big; it will move and slop about and it will worry the small colt or filly. A closer fit is not only more comfortable for a foal but you will find him easier to hold, partly because it *is* more comfortable.

GETTING THE YOUNG HORSE TO ACCEPT A HALTER

Putting a halter on is a very early task and is usually fairly easily done as nothing has to be passed over the ears.

If there is any difficulty it will probably be in getting the youngster to let you put the noseband over his muzzle. Older and bigger horses often lift their heads too high for the handler to be able to reach (see Figures 1-6).

My line with this type of horse, whatever his age, is to hold the noseband of the open halter under his nose. I stand on the near side with my right

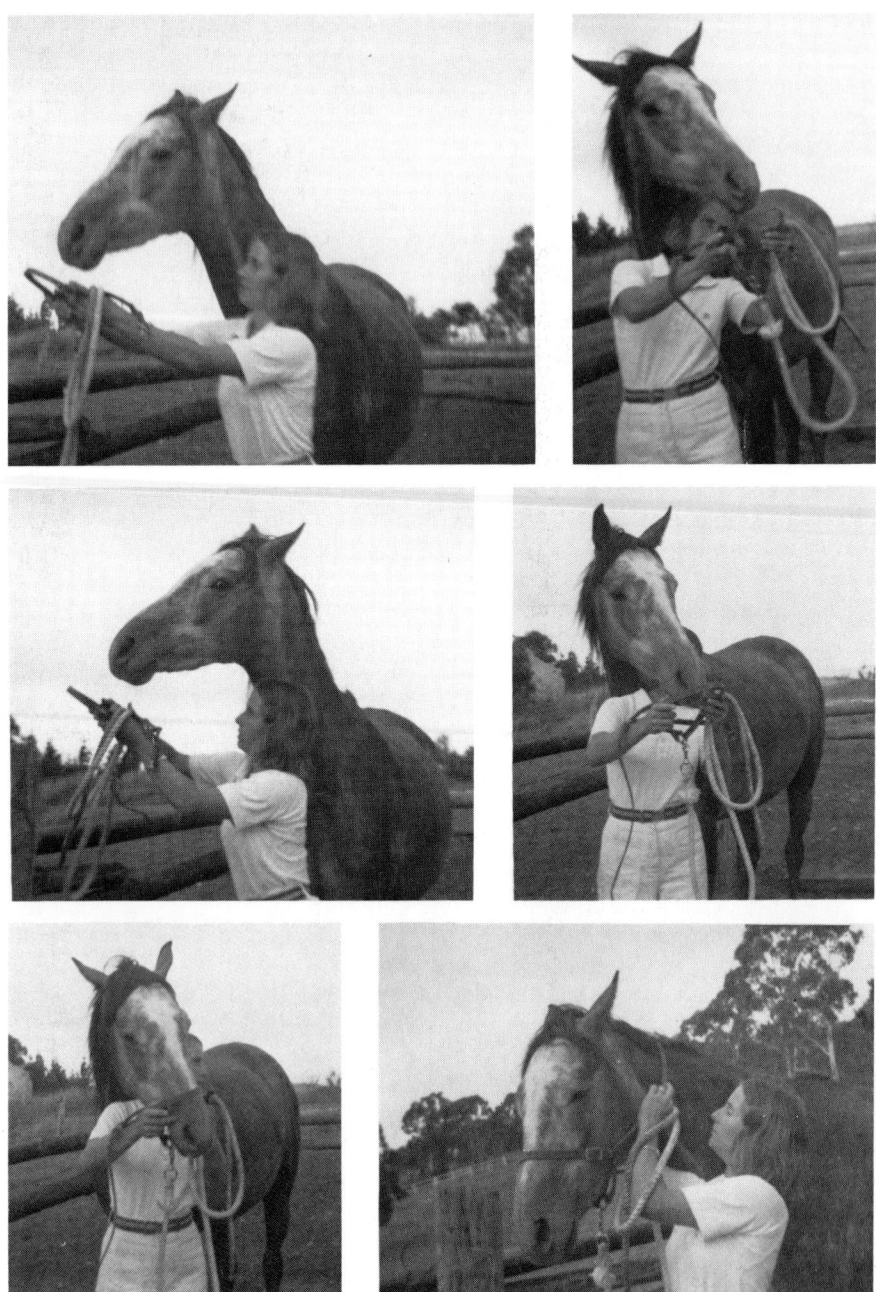

Figures 1 to 6 show how the halter can be introduced to the horse. This youngster had been quite "difficult about the head."

shoulder under his neck (if he is big enough), facing the same way as the horse. I then keep the noseband under his nose, no matter where he moves his head — up, down or sideways, (I have him in as small an enclosure as possible, a horse-stall or stable, so that he cannot get far from me.)

I don't try to put the halter on him; I wait for him to drop his nose into it. This is a good example of the "It will profit you not" technique, coupled with "Quiet persistence".

Don't be in a hurry and do not attempt to put the halter on the youngster. He will try to avoid the noseband. You do not attempt to interfere with his head — you keep the noseband under his nose. He cannot keep his nose stuck up in the air for as long as you can wait for him to lower it. Make no attempt to put it on his head — just wait for him to lower his nose into it.

When eventually he does drop his nose in or partly into it, don't hurry to buckle the halter on. Remove it at once. Take it away. Show him he has made a lot of fuss over nothing.

Do this several times and only when he lets you put it straight over his nose without worrying about what you are doing, think to buckle it on his *neck*. Pass the headstall around his neck well back from the ears, a good six inches or more at first. Put it on and take it off several times if you like, "Old Hat." Don't be in a hurry, particularly if the youngster is in any way nervous about it.

When the halter is first left on the foal, he should be allowed to run loose with it on for ten minutes or so without a rope attached. You will get quite a lot of fun watching his antics with "that strange thing" on his head. Don't leave it on for long at first; as soon as he is somewhat used to its feel, go up to him and take it off again.

Do not get it on and immediately start teaching him to lead — unless circumstances compel you to do so. Don't let him start off with unpleasant associations, either with the halter or with anything else you may put on him. He's a baby; you have time, why not use it?

Taking the halter off will be something of a relief to the foal that he will associate with you. Take advantage of that angle, too.

TEACHING THE YOUNG HORSE TO YIELD TO A DRAWN OR TIGHTENED REIN

It will be of the greatest value to us and to the young horse if he is taught — as early as possible — not only to lead but to yield to or follow a drawn rope or rein, no matter in which direction it is drawn.

This will include:

>   ... leading forward, when the rein or rope is lightly drawn to the front.
>   ... turning when the rope or rein is lightly drawn to either side.

> ... stopping or stepping back when the rope or rein is lightly drawn to the rear.

He has to be taught these things, and the sooner they are taught, the better.

I want to be sure you realise that even these simple things have to be *taught* the young horse. We will do this quickly and easily if we avoid the use of force and so keep him calm — and give him the chance to learn how to deal with a stretched rope or rein. There is a good deal more to it than just pulling and slackening.

Notice how *often* I will stress keeping the horse calm when teaching him something.

Good Hands

There is no doubt that some riders can use their hands much more effectively than others; they produce better results with less force and less effort. They have what is universally known as "Good Hands".

You cannot start the young horse off in these dismounted lessons by normally using a heavy hand — and then expect him to switch over and become miraculously light later on when you are mounted on his back. It is very much a case of: "The way the twig is bent so shall the tree grow." If you want your horse to be light later on, *you must start off by being light.*

Develop your "Good Hands" and your horse's "Good Mouth" from his earliest days.

Figure 7:
The young horse stands and wonders what the best way is to deal with this suggestion. After trying several alternatives 'without profit' he eventually yields to the slight tension of the rope and steps forward. "That will profit you" I instantly show him, for the rope immediately slackens.

Don't get tough, heavy or forceful when TEACHING this or any other new lesson. It will produce the opposite effect to that required, for horses resist force until they have been taught to yield to it.

Later on, if he is slow in his response when he KNOWS what is wanted, we can give the rope or rein a few very light short tugs.

22

TEACHING THE HORSE TO LEAD FORWARD

To lead forward is the first lesson; or rather the first lesson is to teach him to step forward ONE STEP, no matter how small, when the rein or rope is tightened. The lesson is not to GO forward but to yield to a stretched rein and COME forward. The "Go Forward" Lesson (Chapter 10) is quite different.

If you pull hard on the rope or rein when you first put a halter or bridle on your young horse, the horse will almost always either resist you — fight you — or move in the opposite direction. This will start him off associating head pressures with resistance and pain.

Don't pull — don't use force — *just lightly stretch the rein and then keep the same light contact on it until he yields by moving forward;* whereupon you immediately allow the rein to become light or slack. You are showing him, giving him a chance to learn by experience: "Yield to a drawn rein or rope and it will become slack again. It will cease to worry you."

A few horses step forward almost immediately, particularly if you are gentle with them. But most just stand there at first (see Figure 7). You may think he is being stubborn; but it isn't that. It is that he does not yet know what to do about it. He doesn't even know that he is required to do anything.

What you want him to do is so obvious to you that it might not occur to you that he doesn't understand. So be ready to be patient with him. Put a light feel or tension on the rope and keep that same feel on it until he moves as you want him to move — in this case, forward.

After he has been standing there for a while he will probably try moving his head in one direction or another: forward, backward, up or down, or to either side.

Just keep the same feel on the rein, for he is trying to find out if there is some way of dealing with this new experience. Show complete unconcern by quietly maintaining the same contact — you don't want him to move only his head, you want him to step forward, no matter how small a step at first.

By quietly persisting, you are showing him: "That will profit you not". But the very instant he shows the slightest inclination to move his weight or his feet forward, then you show him, "THAT will profit you — *yield to the rein and it slackens*".

You do not pull. A pull is a continuing action, like a person pulling a branch of a tree along the ground. With a pulling hand the weight stays on the rope even when the branch moves. So, too, with the horse if you pull. The weight stays on his mouth or head even though he yields to it — whereas you have to show him that the slight tension on his head CAN be avoided if he yields to the rein or rope.

The 'tension' I refer to is somewhat similar to what the horse would feel if you shortened the rein a single hole. Your hand after that initial shortening, keeps "relatively still," i.e. still *in relation to the horse's head*, while you wait for him to step forward.

Your hand must not move back even a fraction of an inch even when he yields, for that would be pulling. If anything, you should exaggerate the lightening of the rein when he moves forward: then, "End of lesson," pause.

While he is having his end-of-lesson rest, let me remind you again — do not let your hand get appreciably heavier when the youngster fails to move forward as you want. Do not make things worse for him if what he tries is not what you want. He will be experimenting to find out what to do to get rid of this pressure he cannot understand.

Neither in this nor in any other lesson think to punish or penalise the horse when he tries the wrong things. Rather encourage him to try something else until he gives you the chance to say, to show him, "*THAT'S it!*"

After he has had his End-of-lesson rest, begin again. Don't expect him to yield immediately, for he will not have learned from that single lesson. Don't be disappointed if he more or less repeats the first performance, although the second lesson seldom lasts as long as the first. The third time — after the second rewarding pause — he usually does what you want almost immediately.

Repeat the lesson perhaps two or three times more and then finish for the day. You will seldom have this trouble again, but if you should, don't hesitate to repeat the lesson.

Never let this — or any other — lesson go on until it becomes boring, and do not get *heavy handed*. Remember, we are aiming at good hands for ourselves and a light response from the horse when his training is finished.

> One of the most valuable features about this lesson is what it can teach *you*, the horseman and aspiring horse trainer. It gives you an opportunity to discover the effectiveness of a 'relatively still' hand when used on a young horse: a hand that remains still *in relation* to the horse's head. A hand that lightly follows the movements of his head and so maintains the same 'feel' until the horse yields to it.

TEACHING THE HORSE TO STEP BACK

The rein-back, at this stage of his life, is just another lesson in yielding to a drawn rope or rein. This time he has to learn to take a step back whenever you ask it of him by stretching the rope or rein to the rear.

This, too, is something you can teach the horse long before he is mounted. It can be taught using a halter, a cavesson, or with a bit in his mouth, and it will help to prove to you how effective this 'relatively still' hand can be. (It is just as effective, later on, when he is first ridden).

Figure 8: The author demonstrates the 'yield to the rear' lesson. This horse would move forward when being mounted and we were unable to get him to step back again — so the "step back" lesson was given and as usual we found that the horse merely did not understand.

Figure 9: Mrs Erica Jarvis teaches "Narilla Beverley" to yield to the halter and step back. Notice the calm attentiveness of each of these horses.

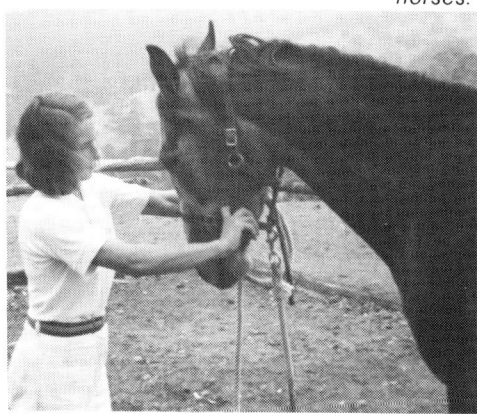

The lesson is: "If, when you are standing still, I put a light backward pressure on the bit or noseband, I want you to yield to that pressure. Again it is not your head I want you to move back, it is your weight, your body, your feet."

Place yourself either in front of the horse or stand on one side, by his shoulder. From either position you can take hold of the noseband or the rings of the bit and then put a light and even feel on each side.

Again, be light, and be quite clear in your own mind as to what you want the horse to do: what action on his part will enable you to show him: "THAT will profit you."

If he moves only his head at first, as he generally will, behave again as you did in the 'yield to the front' lesson. Quietly follow his head movement with your hands so that you keep a gentle and even feeling on each side of the noseband or bit. Again you maintain your 'relative stillness'. You quietly persist with the even contact and gently show him, "That will profit you not" (see Figures 8 and 9).

The more you hurry him, the longer he will take to find the correct answer.

The more force you use the more the horse will resist the pressure.

But, *the moment he moves his weight or even tends to displace weight to his rear,* you should instantly cease the contact. "End of Lesson," pause. Show him "THAT'S what is wanted" by instantly ending the lesson.

After his End-of-lesson reward, you can repeat the lesson as you did in the 'yield forward' lesson.

THE "RELATIVELY STILL" HAND

The relatively still hand is most effective with everything you will be teaching the very young horse before he is mounted. You use it repeatedly in his very early days under the saddle when you meet resistance to the hand. In particular, its effect on older ridden horses that have resisted every effort to get them to step back quietly and easily is often astonishing.

It is this "feel" of the hand with its quiet persistence, that makes a horse yield — eventually — without you having to revert to force. Learn the value of it and the "feel" of it dismounted. It shows the horse that although you will not fight or use force — at this stage — neither will you give in.

Use the same feel on the reins if you meet opposition to a single rein when you want the horse to turn. Remember this is the "Yield to rope or rein" lesson; when it comes to just getting the horse to go along with you, you will find the "Go-Forward" Lesson (Chapter 10) to be the answer.

Teaching the horse to yield to a drawn or tightened rope or rein is a first lesson. It does not hurt, hurry, worry or excite him, and so he keeps calm. After a few more lessons it becomes "Old Hat".

I often pretend to my pupils that I listen to the young horse's conversation when he gets back to his Dam and the others in the paddock — and this is the gist of what they say: "Oh! They make me sick," he protests. "They really make me ill. They can't *make* a horse yield to that light tension, you know. They can't!" Old Prince, the draft horse, very drily asks: "Then why do you do it?"

"That's it!" chirps the infant — "That's just it. They can't make you do it, but they won't let you do anything else until you do..."

KEEP THE YOUNG HORSE LIGHT IN HAND

The young horse has to learn — you have to teach him — that he has to walk along, or stand, light in hand. Such a lot of mouths are partially spoilt before mounting by the people who have been leading the youngster.

So many young (and sometimes older) horses drag one about by the halter or bridle when they are being led. This should not be permitted once the horse has been taught to lead. You must not permit him to ignore your feel on the halter or bit when you are dismounted — and expect him to respect it when you are mounted.

If he does not stop lightly *once he knows* that what you are doing means 'stop,' you should show him you can become sharper as well as milder. Shake him off the noseband or bit if he repeatedly drags you around when you are leading him — but make sure, first, that it is *not you just 'hanging-on' to his head.* Shake or vibrate the rope or rein, and after each few vibrations or shakes see if he will go slower without you having to hang on to him. Check repeatedly that it is not *you* hanging on to him.

I seldom find it necessary to repeat the vibrations more than two or three times at the most. Situations like this must not be permitted to deteriorate into a sort of tug-of-war, but don't get angry either. He is just trying something (if it is him) and it is for you to show him "That is not allowed: get light. Stay light."

Failure to keep the young horse light in hand can give much trouble later on, as you may find out when you have to load him on to a transport (see Chapter 20). He has to learn to lead *and* stand "light in hand" — you should not have to hang on to him or use force to hold him.

DISCIPLINE BEGINS LONG BEFORE MOUNTING

Any cheeky youngster who 'walks all over you' when being led or who pushes you away as though you were another horse — or who in any way starts to show disrespect — should be checked immediately.

Act instantly rather than sharply. Cheekiness, lack of respect, should be reproved instantly, much as later on you will check and perhaps punish open disobedience.

I stress this matter, as time after time I see the results of mistakes made by inexperienced people who are prepared to take all the time and care their horse may need — but who are reluctant to check what they should (and usually do) recognise as being a lack of respect on the part of the horse.

Horses do not take offence. Their 'feelings' are not hurt by a smack. Their attitude is more: "Goodness me! I must remember not to do *that* again."

And you must not take offence either. Correct the youngster but immediately he behaves well again, show him all the care and affection you can — for as long as he behaves in a manner you approve.

The young horse must respect you *and show it.* Many of you will be more afraid of doing the wrong thing than of anything else... DOING NOTHING IS THE MISTAKE MOST COMMONLY MADE.

Study Your Horse

Always watch for the effect of your actions. Don't become sharp suddenly; at least, not at first. At first your actions should be more in the nature of warnings; but when the youngster clearly knows and takes a chance, *then* you can be clear and decisive. Don't overdo it, of course; remember you are only dealing with a cheeky baby horse now — merely checking something that *MIGHT* develop into a much more serious habit.

Much of the success of good handling depends upon the ability to recognise the causes of resistance and 'playing up.' The speed and readiness with which the handler recognises a change of attitude will determine to a great degree his skill as a trainer. The old proverb: "A stitch in time saves nine," is never more applicable than when handling a horse at all stages of his training.

A sharp word, accompanied at times by a shake of the rein or rope, if given at the first sign of deliberate resistance by a horse that up to that time has had only pacifications from his trainer, will do more good than real severity a little later on. This applies equally to the yield-to-the-rein lesson if it becomes necessary.

KICKING AND BITING

Kicking is often not vicious but nevertheless the youngster has to understand it is not allowed; at least, not as far as humans and other animals are concerned. However, we ought always to keep in mind the horse's view of what he is doing.

Very early in life he will have learned that if he kicks at certain irritations (flies etc.) he can often get rid of the irritation. He registers: "Kicking at things that irritate is a good thing to do: it gets rid of them." His experience has taught him this.

He will also have found that some irritations cannot be kicked away; he has tried kicking at the spot, finds kicking produces no relief and sooner or later learns to rub, bite or scratch the spot, perhaps against a tree.

If he kicks or bites at us, we can try dealing with him as Mother deals with Imp at this family table. Mum, Dad and the family are sitting at the table with lively talk proceeding. Thinking he might not be noticed, young 'Imp' reaches out to take something he knows he should not touch.

Mother, without interrupting her conversation, gently taps his fingers. Not a word is said, and the other youngsters just grin.

The act may be repeated several times, in which case the final tap may prove to be quite sharp and the 'Imp' dissolve into tears. There may not be a word said — and there need not be.

The 'act' is played in two distinct parts. First the 'Imp' is given a quiet tap while in the actual act of reaching out. Its repetition clearly means, "That is not permitted."

When the lesson has been repeated several times however, and there is no chance that 'Imp' misunderstands, then his Mother takes the second step and shows him: "Persistent and deliberate wrong-doing will not be tolerated and will receive sharp correction."

We should behave somewhat similarly with our kicking or biting young horse.

Dealing with Kicking and Biting

Colts and stallions are much more given to biting than mares; but mares on the other hand are much more prone to kick. Although all do not conform to these tendencies, most do.

If you have a youngster that tends to bite or kick at you, treat him exactly as Mum treated the Imp: smack the offending part — the muzzle or the hindquarters — quite lightly at first, so that he comes to recognise: "Biting (or kicking) brings a light smack." If he continues, persists, then you should get progressively tougher and eventually smack really hard if it should prove to be necessary.

If you have followed the course suggested, he will know what he is getting it for.

Bad and persistent biters and kickers should eventually be sharply corrected, and I suggest a noisy flat thin lathe for kickers, using it quite high up where he is well padded with meat. Bad biting horses are not suited for children: I have seen a man's nose almost completely severed by a bite from a horse.

(When I say 'biting and kicking,' I don't mean the little nips and kicks at nothing that so often go with grooming and saddling — but anything in the nature of an attack should be dealt with *immediately*).

Do not deal sharply with the youngster at first. The early smacks on haunch or muzzle should be light until he recognises what action on his part causes them. Light taps at first are more effective than sharp ones, as they do not alarm the offender. Light taps leave him calm and he is able to connect cause and effect more readily. Once he recognises what action of his provokes your reprisal — then, as your smack becomes progressively sharper, he will know what to do or cease doing, to avoid it. He will recognise that biting or kicking, or whatever it is he indulges in, is "NOT a good thing to do."

In subsequent lessons the preliminary light taps will eventually be unnecessary, and this is where the trainer's tact and skill show up. With slight modification and perhaps more caution, I follow this same course with the more dangerous tricks and habits of the adult horse. But we are not dealing with dangerous horses in this work!

I merely want *not* to mislead you when I say: Think in the terms "It will profit you not" rather than punishment. Although we occasionally revert to punishment, *do not think of it as a normal procedure.* But if, going back to the 'Imp,' the horse should say when he gets a sharp rap: "It didn't hurt, See...!" then we may make it hurt next time.

KICKING AT WHIP OR SPUR

Later in life the horse may feel a different sort of irritation, such as the tap of a whip, the pressure of a rider's heel or spur, perhaps, and it would be a surprising thing if he did not at some stage try to get rid of it by a light kick or two. It worked with the flies, remember.

If you discontinue with your tapping with the whip or leg when he kicks, the horse will register: "That fixes that! Kicking at the whip (or whatever it was) is a good thing to do." By "ending-the-lesson," that is what you will have shown him.

What we should do in such a case is not to become upset at his kicking but to show him by quietly persisting with the taps: "That will profit you not." And we then go further to get him to understand — *"Moving forward* is a good thing to do and will stop the whip, leg or spur." (More about this in Chapter 10 "Go-Forward" and Chapter 20 "Loading into Transport").

That sort of kicking, however, is quite different from his kicking (or biting) at us.

TO SUM UP

Handle the foal early but carefully, whenever it is convenient.
Let as much of your hand, your arm and even your body contact him — not just the tips of your fingers.
Use a well-fitting halter.
Give any young horse his first handling and leading lessons in a small yard.
Use a long rope or rein that will more than reach from the centre of the yard to the side so that he cannot escape from you even though you cannot hold him.
Do not expect a young horse or foal to yield to rope or rein until you have taught him to do so. Teach him very early in his training to yield to rope or rein in whatever direction it is drawn, to the front, to the side, or to his rear.
Do not lead the youngster outside the yard without a halter or while he is still inclined to try his/your strength.
Do not let the young horse become cheeky or disrespectful. Deal with kicking and biting: Kicking or biting at humans is to be checked from the start.
Keep him light in hand at all times and don't let him drag you around when you are leading him.

CHAPTER 5

SAFETY OF HORSE AND HANDLER

*A good stockyard makes for ease, speed and safety in handling and breaking-in;
A round yard has many advantages;
If you have other than a proper yard: Some important safety precautions;
Nylon reins and ropes recommended;
Lunge rein makes for safety and good habits;
How to construct a Round Yard.*

HAVE YOU A STOCKYARD?

The small man, the amateur, the inexperienced person, handling a young horse without proper facilities is at a great disadvantage to the man on a farm or station. Without proper facilities he has to be much more careful, take more precautions and generally go slower.

Not one in a hundred of those who read this book will have the advantage of a proper stockyard. This is a very real handicap. A young horse pulling or breaking away from his handler while in a small stockyard from which he cannot escape, is certainly very little, if at all, better off as the result of his efforts. If there is a long rein or rope attached to him he will not have gained a thing, for as he moves around, the rein pulls into the centre of the yard and his handler can easily pick it up again immediately. The horse doesn't have a chance to realise he has been free.

This is very different from the man working a youngster in a paddock, large or small. In such a case the young horse that breaks away has definitely profited by his resistance or fighting, as he gets free: he then has an experience that often leads to further trouble.

Proper facilities and proper tools are essential to any task: even more so if the person doing the job lacks experience. So the people for whom I am writing here need to be much more cautious than the professional colt-breaker with tested gear and suitable horse-proof stockyards.

The Round Yard has Many Advantages

There is much to be said for a round yard (see Figure 10) for handling young horses. If you are thinking of building a special yard,

Figure 10: A round yard at Noarlunga, South Australia. The top rails have not yet been placed in position and the bottom rails are rather lower than is necessary for horses only. The long panels have additional posts in the centre for strength.

you might like to follow the instructions of how to construct Mr D. McGillivray's Round Yard given at the end of this chapter. But this cost is not warranted unless many horses are to be handled.

It is almost certain that you will not have a proper yard, either round or any other shape; so from now on I am assuming that you will not have an ideal breaking-in yard.

Do all you can to avoid handling or trying to hold your young horse in an open paddock, particularly when he is no longer a foal and if he has not yet been taught to lead. A nearby fence makes all the difference when it comes to holding a young horse should a tussel develop.

Do as much handling as you can in his stable yard, or in the stable itself if you have one. Use a place that he knows and is familiar with, and so small that he cannot get away from you. (If it is a foal you are handling, he will be calmer and easier to handle if his dam is kept in sight). If the yard or stable is strange to him, let him examine it and become accustomed to it before you start to handle him.

When it comes to lunging or actual breaking to saddle, an enclosure some 30-40 feet across will do very well after his initial handling in a smaller yard. In it you can teach the horse to lead and to lunge, and get him working under a saddle.

SOME IMPORTANT SAFETY PRECAUTIONS

Wire Fences

These should be avoided if possible; but it is not always possible to do so. Most horses, but not all young ones, have a fair respect for a good tight wire fence — but loose wire is a definite hazard. A horse is usually able to free himself without much damage from a well-tightened wire fence if he gets into it, but loose wire can loop completely around a leg. Worst of all is barbed wire with only one end fastened. A horse can literally tear his legs to pieces on it.

Clean up all loose wire before you begin. Move it right away. Loose wire should never be left about anywhere near where a horse may move. Then see that the wires in the fence are tight. The tighter, the more rigid the wire fence the less damage to the horse should he get a foot through it.

Use an enclosure with railing fences — if you possibly can — or at least one with a rail along the top. Low wires in a fence, wires less than two feet from the ground, add to the danger of the horse getting his legs caught up without in any way assisting in keeping him in. Avoid if you can, low wires in the fences of any horse paddock.

Clear the Ground

See that the ground you are to use is reasonably free from tufts of strong grass, stones, glass, sticks or anything else that might interfere with *your* fast and free movement. If the ground is not right in this respect, then clean it up before you begin work on your youngster. You will, on occasion, have enough to engage your attention without having to look where you are putting your feet. Even a loop of binder-twine can bring you down if you have one foot on it when your other strikes the loop.

Avoid All Unnecessary Risks

I have known a rider mount a horse for the first time with a circular-saw and a chaff-cutting machine in the same paddock. What madness — a frightened horse could run or buck into such a machine and permanently disable himself. Remember it is your task not only to break-in the young horse but to have, when you finish, a sound and unblemished one, too. Who wants to be responsible for a well-schooled but disfigured or disabled horse?

The tray-top of a truck or any other such projection can be a great danger to the rider's legs. Even if the horse is successful in avoiding it, he may not leave the necessary margin for *your* leg.

Examine the area carefully and clear it before you start. If you cannot get machinery removed, either fence it off or by bags and old tyres cover any sharp edges and projecting corners there might be.

Your Own Footwear. This might be a good place to mention the footwear you use when handling a young horse. Thongs, slippers or footwear of any kind that hangs loose on your feet can be a handicap, and can lead to trouble and danger. You are sure to need to move quickly at times, and any footwear that is loose or tends to come off or catch up on anything, should be avoided.

Boots, elastic-sided for preference, are recommended; although shoes will do. Leather soles, too, can become very slippery when worn on grass for long — you may have enough trouble at times holding your horse without the additional difficulty of an insecure foothold.

It need hardly be said that whatever type of boot or shoe sole you use before mounting your colt or filly, do not mount with anything on the sole that will prevent your foot leaving the stirrup readily when you leave the saddle, either voluntarily or involuntarily. Even boots that have been half-soled can trap your foot in a stirrup.

The stirrup irons used by a colt-breaker should be both heavy and loose-fitting (see Figure 11), so that the iron will slip easily off your foot if at any time you come out of the saddle. Light stirrup irons tend to cling to the foot.

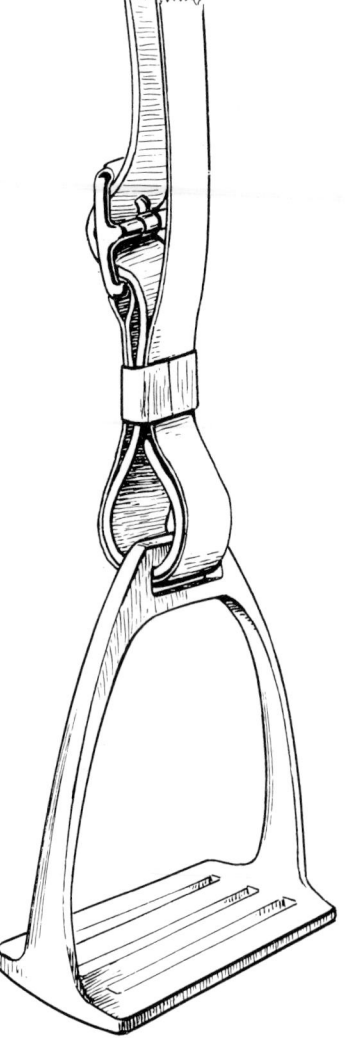

Figure 11:
A STOCKMAN'S STIRRUP IRON
This stirrup and its method of buckling aims at maximum service and safety in the "Outback". The buckle can be raised or lowered without the length of the stirrup being altered, and by this means wear can be transferred from one part of the stirrup-leather to the other (wear is much greater where the leather is doubled back — at the saddle, the stirrup-iron and buckle-fastening). Moving the position of the buckle gives many times the length of wear. The iron is made large and heavy — to shake off the foot easily in a fall as well as give the length or service. The dee through which the leather passes is made deep enough to allow the loose end to pass through a second time, thus letting the unwanted end take the wear. The large keeper is usually made of brass and is big enough to allow the four thicknesses to pass through.

To fasten to the saddle: *place the keeper on the leather first near the buckle. Then drop the iron on and pass the leather back through the keeper. The end of the stirrup-leather is then fitted to the saddle "wrong-way-up" so that the buckle will be away from and the smooth side towards the rider's leg when he is mounted. This method of fastening the stirrup and leather is not suited or necessary for riders who change the length of their stirrups for different types of seat — jumping and dressage, for instance.*

Do not use light small irons for breaking-in — they can bend and trap the foot if an accident happens and a horse falls on them — and they do not shake off the foot easily if the rider falls.

While on the subject of stirrups, if ever you should find yourself being dragged with one foot trapped in a stirrup iron, there is only one course for you to follow — and you should know about it before you find yourself in that very dangerous situation. There is nothing you can do with your hands as you will be hanging head-downwards, unable to reach the stirrup. But you will have one foot free. *With the free foot, kick at the stirrup iron* — usually the slightest jolt will release the other foot.

Have your mind made up as to what you will do *before* the accident occurs and act instantly you find the iron clinging to your foot — before you get dragged. See that every child is taught to do this. Teach it to them early.

Rope Burns. When a rope or anything similar (including a lunging rein) is held tightly in the hand and is forcibly dragged through the fingers, it produces exactly the same effect as would grasping a redhot poker in your hand. It produces great blisters on palm and fingers almost immediately.

Wear gloves. It is because of this tendency of a rope or rein to burn that so many experienced horsemen find it advisable to wear gloves (leather, dogskin) when handling a young horse from the ground. One really good rope burn and you will forget all about gloves looking 'sissy.'

NYLON ROPES AND REINS RECOMMENDED

Nylon is not only lighter and stronger for rein or rope, but it is not affected by weather — water — and so usually lasts longer. It left damp or put away damp, cotton ropes, reins, rugs and tents etc., deteriorate very quickly.

But because nylon is a stronger material, it is usual to make nylon ropes thinner and lunge reins narrower. Nylon is also very slippery, even when dry, and exceedingly so when wet. It is also much stiffer, less pliable, than cotton.

These features make the usual nylon ropes and lunging reins very difficult to hold in the hand, and so until recently I have always avoided using them.

Mr Webb McKelvey, a 'roping' breaking-in expert from California, while visiting us recently, showed us how to overcome all the difficulties and shortcomings associated with nylon ropes and reins — *by the simple process of rubbing the rope or rein with a very coarse sandpaper.*

The effect of this treatment is astonishing. The hard slippery surface of the nylon not only becomes soft and pliable, but it immediately loses its slippery surface. The surface becomes 'woolly,' almost fluffy, and this in its turn causes the rope to increase its diameter by up to one-third. The thicker non-slippery rope now becomes easier to hold than cotton rope or rein (see Figure 12).

A nylon rope or rein so treated becomes a first class tool with a much longer life than cotton.

Figure 12: Mr. Webb McKelvey's 25 ft. rope before and after being "conditioned". In use it is difficult to believe it is the same rope.

When he returned to America, Webb left his 'treated' rope with me, and I notice that in the one place where the rope is wanted to slip easily (near the horse's neck) that part has not received the sandpaper treatment.

If you have, or acquire, a nylon rope or rein, I strongly recommend you to treat it with very rough coarse sandpaper. This was only one of the scores of items of real information Webb McKelvey passed on to us during his visit — and for which we return our most appreciative thanks. You don't know WHAT you don't know until you know it!

USE OF A LUNGING REIN RECOMMENDED

The use of a lunging rein is strongly recommended when handling a young horse. Not only is it best for lunging but its length has other decided advantages in handling a young horse at all times, particularly during the breaking-in period and just after.

A good lunging rein should be about 30 feet (approx. 9 metres) long, and preferably not less than 1¼ inches (about 32mm) wide.

Unless it is very thin, a rope of this length is too heavy for lunging and a thin rope, even more than a narrow lunging rein, is very difficult to hold firmly in the hand when dealing with a resisting horse.

For leading, lunging and handling the young *horse a long wide lunging rein is recommended.*

LUNGING REIN MAKES FOR SAFETY AND GOOD HABITS

It may not occur to you to use a lunge rein on your **young horse** whenever you lead him into the open at first. "Why not an ordinary rein?" you might think.

This is just another instance of playing safe when it is so easy to do so. If the horse gets a sudden fright or shies unexpectedly when he is being led, he has a good chance of breaking free if you have him on an ordinary short rope or riding rein. If you possess a lunging rein, why not use it?

Don't, through sheer thoughtlessness, let your horse learn that he can break away from you.

Danger of Loops. Every lunge rein I have seen has had a loop, usually about 6 inches long, stitched into the rein at the end to be retained in the hand. I have never been able to find any reason for this practice by the manufacturers. Of course you should not put a hand or foot through the loop — but, isn't it just possible *someone* will at some time or other?

Let your very first action after buying a lunge rein be to 'make safe' that loop: tie a knot in its end. You will need the knot anyway, for it **not only neutralises that dangerous loop but it warns when you have reached the end of the rein when, as will happen, it has to be played out quickly.**

I should caution you here that when you have any difficulty in holding a horse either by rope or lunge rein, never, NEVER, wind it around your hand or any other part of your body to prevent it slipping. On the contrary, you should be alert at all times to see that the horse does not draw you into any loop of rein or rope that may have dropped to the ground. Ropes are extremely prone to twist and form loops and you will find it very distracting to feel any part of the rope even touching your legs when the horse itself should have your complete attention.

Coiling the Lunge Rein in the Hand

This is an ordinary, simple precautionary measure — one of many you will do well to know and never fail to practise.

First, check that you have a knot in the end of the rein. Then take up that end in your left hand and hold it at such a length that, as you stand upright, the knot hangs about three to four inches above the ground. If any part of the rein is nearer the ground than this you may find yourself *stepping* on it when the horse is engaging your full attention. Avoid the possibility of such a distraction — and keep in mind that when resisting the horse at a difficult moment, one tends to crouch or bend slightly at the knees.

Now, continue to take up a succession of loops in the left hand, taking particular care that each successive loop is a little smaller than the last. Each loop lays on top of the ones already held in the hand.

Taken up in this way, each loop will play out quickly and smoothly if it proves necessary to do so. Should there be any one loop larger than those already taken up, it can — and sooner or later will — get behind the others. When it comes to playing out the lunge rein you may then find your hand firmly trapped in the centre.

This, too, is a normal and standard precaution to be taken whenever you are leading or holding a young horse on a long rein or rope. Apart from the safety angle: what is the use of having the long rein if you hold it in a manner that prevents you utilising its length at the very moment you need it? You have to gather up the rein or rope one way or another; make a habit of doing it the best way.

TO SUM UP

A proper stockyard is a great asset — use one if you possibly can.
> If you haven't a proper yard, do as much handling as possible in the stable or stable yard.

Let the youngster become familiar with a strange yard or stable before you **start** work on him.

Clean up all loose wire and any rubbish in the yard.

Check that the wires are tight in any fence.

Use strong heavy stirrup irons and know what to do if you find your foot trapped in a stirrup and you hanging head down.

For leading, lunging and handling the young horse, a long wide lunging rein is recommended.

Rub any nylon rope or rein with coarse sandpaper to loosen up the hard slippery surface.

Tie a knot in the end of the lunging rein or rope and coil it in such a manner that will ensure its quick and uninterrupted running out whenever necessary.

Guard against rope burns and never let any rope or rein become entangled about any part of your body.

HOW TO CONSTRUCT A ROUND YARD

(From "Australian Horses — From Paddock to Park" by the noted horseman the late D. McGillivray, first published in Sydney, Australia in 1902).

A round yard is relatively easy to build, is inexpensive, strong, safe and effective. You can build such a yard with farm timber cut off the property, which means the cost will be negligible. Such rails and posts are usually stronger than sawn timber, and, having no sharp edges, are less likely to damage the animals using it. These days, piping is frequently substituted.

Mr McGillivray, whose people still live in the south-east of South Australia, recommended a yard not more than 30 ft. or less than 18 ft. in diameter. He suggested the ideal size to be 21 ft. (6.4 metres) and recommended it to be set out in this manner:

Timber Required

Ten straight round posts, 11 ft. (3.35 metres) in length and not less than 5 inches (12.7 cm) in diameter at the smaller end after de-barking. Forty rails, each 6 ft. 6 ins. (2 metres) long and not less than 3 inches (7.6 cm) in diameter at the smaller end after de-barking.

Setting Out the Yard

The Posts. Drive a short peg into the ground in the centre of the area where you propose to erect the yard. Into the top of the peg knock a nail and hook the end of a 10 ft. 6 ins. (3.2 metres) tape on to the nail. At 10' 6" distance from the centre, drive in another short peg to mark where the first post is to be placed.

Keeping the tape stretched, move in a circle away from the first peg and at every 5 ft. 7 ins. (1.7 metre) knock in a similar peg. If your measurements have been accurate the tenth peg will prove to be just 5 ft. 7 ins. from the first.

If you want the gate to face a particular direction (and you usually have a good reason to do so) you might well begin with your first boundary peg where one gatepost will be. Each peg is meant to mark the centre of a post-hole; the butt of each of the 11 ft. posts should be set 3 feet (1 metre) into the ground, leaving some 8 ft. (2.5 metres) above the ground.

The Rails When the posts are up, start from the first again and either bolt or wire-twitch the rails to the inside of the posts. The height recommended for the centre of the lowest rail is 2 ft. 4 ins. above ground level. There is nothing to be gained from having a rail lower than this and in an emergency (which we hope never occurs) it provides an emergency exit.

The higher rails, bringing the total to four, are set one above the other 20 inches (63.5 cm) from centre to centre, resulting in the top rail being some 7 ft. 4 ins. above the ground. This might seem an excessive height but many a horse jumps out of a 6 ft. high yard. The extra height will put him off having a try, and so the rails for the top should be the weakest you happen to have.

Fix the rails on to the first panel and then miss each alternate panel and repeat. The last panel will be the ninth, and will contact the other gate-post.

You will have noticed the rails are 6 ft. long and the pegs only 5 ft. 7 ins. apart. The excess length of the rail should project, equally each end, *outside* the yard (see Figure 13).

Next, panels 2, 4, 6 and 8 are railed, placing these rails above those already secured. Both for appearance and easy fixing, it will be found best to have the bigger ends of the rails all the same way.

There is something to be said for having the lower rails bolted in position, but the upper rails will be more secure if fixed in position by a Queensland Twitch; the twitching should be done from the outside.

The tenth panel is the gate; and the rails there will be used as slip-rails. Two additional pieces of light timber are placed upright on the inside of the rails at the gate posts.

See that all knots on the timber are removed. A good breaker does not hesitate to take a necessary risk — but will not take any risk that is avoidable, either for himself or for his horse.

Figure 13: A section of Mr McGillivray's Round Yard. See that there are no projections to the inside of the yard — ends of rails, bolt-heads (if used) or wire ties. This precaution is for the benefit of both horse and man.

CHAPTER 6

HOLDING THE YOUNG HORSE FROM THE GROUND

Angle of Rein — Great difficulty in holding the horse from some angles;

> *Most advantageous angle to use;*
> *Holding the horse from the side;*
> *Jeffrey's "Magic Lunj";*
> *The difficult horse.*

ANGLE OF REIN

Before we go further I feel I should be sure that you know the many mechanical and physical advantages the horse's shape and construction give; from where and at what angles our comparatively puny strength can best be applied; and of the many advantages our intelligence can give us when applied to that knowledge.

Experience proves that the position taken up in relation to the horse is of the greatest importance when we have to hold him from the ground and against his will, or when for any reason the horse fights or pulls to get away.

But *experience* is a hard and expensive teacher — and these are things you can learn from the written word.

What I have to say now under this heading is well known to every horse-breaker or trainer and to most horsemen. They know the facts and how to use the knowledge — but I have never known these facts to be set out so that a newcomer to horses can work things out for himself when he meets a situation new to him.

Great Difficulty in Holding the Horse from Some Angles

If we look at the horse we see that his four legs form quite a long base of support for his body: long from front to rear and narrow from side to side. We should also note that his head is set on at the end of a comparatively long neck.

Holding a Horse from Behind

Because of his shape, we find great difficulty in holding a horse should we try to do so from directly behind him. From this position we are not only unable to hold him should he make a sudden and determined effort to break free, but on account of the speed at which he can move to his front we will have no chance of even keeping up with him.

Held from behind, the horse will escape from us if he really tries — so it is for us to see that we do all we can to avoid finding ourselves trying to hold him from this position.

Holding the Horse from in Front

From the front, from directly or nearly directly in front of the horse, we will find ourselves just as powerless to prevent him moving backwards if he makes a determined effort to escape in that direction. Running backwards, however, he is much slower and so not likely to break free as we can run forwards as fast as he can run backwards, and so we can usually manage to stay with him.

To his front:- the horse can utilise both his great strength and speed to maximum advantage.

To his rear:- the horse can also operate at great strength — but with little speed.

In each of these directions, forwards and backwards, the horse is resisting us from his long base, and his limbs are moving in the directions in which they are designed to move most efficiently.

The importance of recognising these facts will not need to be stressed.

We should be most active and alert to avoid being placed in these positions when trying to hold any young horse from the ground.

BUT —

HOLDING THE HORSE FROM THE SIDE

We find that the closer to 90° the angle: lunge rein to spine, or rope to spine, the easier it will be to hold any horse in a conflict of wills.

With the rein at or approaching this angle, we have the horse fighting from his *narrow base*, fighting sideways. His conformation makes moving to the side both awkward and difficult: moving sideways he has neither strength nor speed to help him escape. If we use this knowledge we can deceive him as to his strength, his relative strength.

Another point I should draw your attention to is that the horse's head and neck project forward in prolongation of the line of his spine — and we can use them as a lever. *From the side we can use his head and neck as a lever against the horse.* This is another advantage that should be recognised, and of which full use should be made.

Once this is recognised it will also be clear that where we attach the rope or rein is also very important. The more forward along the neck the rope is attached the greater will be its leverage effect, particularly from the side, and the easier it will be to hold the horse — all other things being equal.

So, too, with the head: the further down the head, the closer to the nose the noseband to which we attach (or through which we pass) the rein or rope, the more effective that rope or rein will be.

Conversely, with a rope passed around the base of the neck near the shoulders, great difficulty can be experienced in holding even a three-months-old foal. We should never attempt to do this, particularly in an open paddock, — for, should we be unable to hold him, the foal can get away and we may not be able to catch him easily. He learns (we will have taught him) not only that we cannot hold him but that he *can get completely free from us.*

Avoid mistakes like this that often lead to years of trouble. Use a halter on a foal — and take advantage of all the leverage his head and neck give you. Although the foal has nothing of the strength of a yearling or two-year-old, and so is not so likely to break away, this situation changes in only a few months and he quickly becomes stronger than man. It is for you to see that he does not discover this fact.

Jeffery's "Magic Lunj"

Mr Maurice Wright, who at the moment of writing is travelling Australia demonstrating "The Jeffery Method," uses what the late Mr Kel Jeffery called his "Magic Lunj."

I quote Kel Jeffery: "...Whenever the youngster tries to jump away, he is by some mysterious force swung back to face you. That," says Jeffery, "is what I call my 'Magic Lunj.'"

Figure 14:
"I make a swinging hold only when a colt is at right angles when jumping away, when his forefeet are off the ground, enabling me to swing him back facing me — with the rope loose around his neck because I 'let go' the instant — the split second — after he has got the jerk that has brought him around to face me. You still appear friendly because, although apparently all-powerful, you are kind and reassuring the moment the youngster is swung back to face you."

Jeffery was well aware of the advantage of the 90° angle. What made his action work like 'Magic' was the fact that he only took advantage of the angle and the leverage at the moment when the horse's forefeet were off the ground — at the moment when the horse abandoned his long base and had only a single point of support — his hind legs.

He used the rope only when the horse had rendered himself for a 'split second' incapable of resisting.

I'll quote Jeffery again:

> "The important thing is to *let the rope slacken* about the horse's neck the fraction of a split second after he moves as you 'requested' him to respond to your gently persuasive 'request' pull."

But note that he only used his 'request' pull at the moment the youngster was at 90^0 to the rope and his forefeet off the ground. He calls it a "Request" pull now, to point out that the horse is at such a disadvantage that the pull you give him would be more appropriately called a request.

Jeffery was dealing most of the time with wild station colts, and these frequently rear and swing away as he describes. He used his "Magic Lunj" when the horse was jumping away — and he always slackened the rope "a fraction of a split second" later as the youngster was forced to face him.

HOW THE HORSE SEES IT

As the young horse grows we are very conscious that his strength is becoming greater than our own — but he does not realise this.

If his earlier experiences have shown him that we can hold him, that he cannot escape — then that is something he KNOWS. He knows it because he has proved it: he has learned it from experience. He knows it for a *fact* unless, or until, we let him learn otherwise.

He knows nothing of what we call strength. What he has experienced he knows, "I can't get away from them." He accepts it and will not question it later on, just as you and I don't keep putting our hands on a hot iron to see if it still burns.

LIMIT THE EXPERIENCES OF A FOAL OR YOUNG HORSE TO WHAT YOU WANT HIM TO KNOW AND REMEMBER

You can see how it is most important that every precaution is taken to limit a foal's experiences to what we want him to know and remember, and not only in this matter of holding him.

Experienced breakers and trainers are prepared for trouble even when they do not expect it. They will not take a risk just for the sake of a moment's effort. Good breakers never take silly or unnecessary risks: if they do, well, they are just not good colt-breakers. It is not fear, it is knowledge, skill and professional pride that motivates. How would you feel if, when you got your colt back from the breaker or trainer, he proved to have the really bad trick of pulling or breaking away from you — and you, perhaps, want him for a child?

The most painful (and permanent) injury I have ever received from a horse was caused by a pony with this trick. I didn't let him get away, but in holding him the tendon was torn from the muscle of my upper right arm.

As a rule the young horse learns these tricks by an accidental experience, certainly not by thinking and scheming.

Be more than usually careful in his formative years. Always take full advantage of the length of his neck and head as well as the full effect gained at an angle of 90⁰ — and have him in a small yard.

THE DIFFICULT HORSE

There is one catch, one snag, about this 'the neck is a lever' knowledge, and that is that nothing is effective as a lever if it bends under the power (weight of the rein) applied. And the horse often bends his neck in two quite different ways when trying to get away from his handler. Each makes him much more difficult to hold.

In the first case the horse bends his neck some 90⁰ at the shoulder, so that his head and neck become a prolongation of the line of the rein while his spine still remains at a sharp angle.

In this case the leverage of the neck has been lost — but he is still resisting on his narrow base and his spine remains at a right angle.

The second case is the more troublesome. In this instance the horse bends his neck to allow his quarters to come around towards you until his *spine* becomes parallel with the rein — and he then has you trying to hold him from his rear. Both leverage and angle have been lost (see Figure 22).

He cannot be held from this angle. If the fight is continued, the horse usually takes his quarters around even further and if the rein is attached to a halter, it then has a complete turn around his neck with the horse again facing your way.

You will be pleased, then, that you have your horse in a small yard — or he would break away — break free.

A horse doesn't know you cannot hold him until he proves it by his experience. A fence nearby hinders him from using his strength — he does not know that and will not realise what has handicapped him. So take advantage of that circumstance and do all you can to have a rein or rope long enough to reach to the side of the area you are working in.

With the rope at a right angle to the line of the spine and the spine parallel to the fence, it is almost impossible for a "wild" or nervous horse to jump out. The handler has him at a great disadvantage and the moment the horse lifts his front feet off the ground, can use Jeffery's "Magic Lunj." The advantage of a round yard in such circumstances is obvious.

Do Not Fight The Horse

By that I mean don't use your strength against his strength — except where conditions put the horse at a great disadvantage. Even then, only use force, or resistance, for as long as these conditions last. The longest this is likely to be is a part of a second — a split second!

Understand this policy and one finds the reasons for the practices of most of the great horsebreakers and tamers of the past and present, starting in the 1850's in America with Rarey — his exhibitions in England and Australia — and on to men like Webb McKelvey today; and here in Australia such men as McGillivray, Jeffery, Wright, Fitzgerald, Wilton, Readhead — and innumerable others I have never even heard of.

I recognise the unfairness of mentioning only some; but what I cannot help but notice are the many similarities in their methods as well as their differences. I was fortunate enough to have Maurice Wright and Webb McKelvey from America, meet at my home. I was able to listen to these two men, each expert exponents of different methods — and I was astonished at the degree of agreement between them. And — also — how each was prepared to listen to the other as well as talk and demonstrate.

TO SUM UP

Recognise the advantage of leverage the horse's long neck gives; use it when you can, but recognise too that when it comes to a matter of using force it is possible for the horse to offset this advantage. Use a small yard and long rope or lunge rein until he has learned to yield to the rope or rein.

The closer to 90⁰ the angle of rein or rope-to-spine, the easier it is to hold the horse.

The further from the shoulders the rope or rein is attached, the easier it is to hold the horse from either side.

Take every precaution to limit the experiences of a foal or young horse to the things you want him to know and remember.

The horse quickly learns to trust us if we can see things from his point of view. Prove to him you are trustworthy.

Figure 15: Trapped in an enclosure from which he cannot escape, the horse finds himself approached by a queer creature of which he knows nothing. "What is he going to do to me? What CAN I do?" he thinks as the man slowly approaches.

He is every bit as fearful as we would be if we were trapped and then 'closed in on' by a wierd "something" from outer space. The unknown creature might well bear nothing but goodwill towards us but how would we know? Would we stand relaxed as it extended something towards us to touch us — a ray of light, a hand, a claw, a hook — anything at all?

How the horse behaves from this point on is determined by what he finds out about us from his experiences with us: how WE behave towards HIM.

Figure 16: The youngster has just been roped and is now really terrified. He screams (see his open mouth) as he feels around his neck the 'something' that to him is obviously an extension of the creature itself.

He tries to fight free — to escape from this strangling tendril; but as the man puts no constraint on him he finds the rope apparently harmless. He is prepared to fight but finds there is nothing to fight.

But even when it is loose as the photograph shows, the weight of the rope maintains contact. The light rope quietly demonstrates to him: "Fighting and trying to escape will 'Profit you not'." The rope is loose (see shadow) to prove to the horse that we are not trying to hurt him.

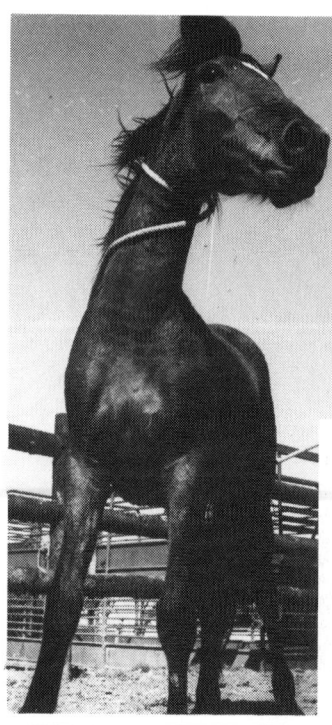

Figure 17:
The horse continues to twist and turn, only to find that not only does the contact from the man remain constant but it spreads to other parts of his body and hindquarters — and that it causes him no hurt or harm. No longer quite so fearful of this creature that so far has not hurt him at all, the wild horse starts off to see if there is any other way of escaping from his captor.

Figure 18: Still hoping to escape from the hold of this creature, the young horse runs around the enclosure and finds not only that he cannot escape but that he cannot get free from the 'extension' reaching from the man.
Webb knows that for the horse to jump out of the yard is almost impossible, for with the rope at the 90° angle and well up around his neck, the moment the horse lifts his forefeet from the ground, he has him at too big a disadvantage (Jeffery's 'Magic Lunj', see Figure 14). Webb is maintaining 'relative stillness' with the rope and is also active to keep the rein at the most advantageous 90° angle.
The horse, not being hurt, gets calmer and calmer and sooner or later turns to face his handler. His first terror is gone. It is now the task of the handler to allay the horse's fears further and show the youngster that if he is co-operative there need be nothing unpleasant between them.

48

Figure 19: Eventually the horse turns and faces the man and at first he is just allowed to stand there and discover that the rope around his neck will not hurt him if he does not resist it.

After a while Webb quietly moves, gently swinging the rope and bringing it into contact with the horse's head — always light and gentle and with many encouraging pauses. He also shortens the distance between them.

Notice in all the illustrations of experienced horsemen their poise and balance and relaxed condition. You see it here with Webb McKelvey and later with Danny Fitzgerald — and they never underrate the danger of a very frightened horse.

Figure 20: Although still very suspicious, the colt is coming to realise that the man is not badly disposed towards him. Having proved he cannot escape he is now noticing what happens if he does not try.

Webb, by avoiding the use of any force or any quick sudden movement, does all he can to reassure the youngster.

Figure 21: The young horse, having found his handler in no way inclined to hurt him and after running back several times, starts to examine the man.

Figure 22: Fear takes over again as soon as the colt feels the constraint of the rope — this time on his head.

Although the angle from which the photo was taken makes the rope appear to be taut, this is not the case. There is no additional resistance from the man, and a few seconds later the horse is moving around the yard as in Figure 18, but to the left this time.

The photograph also shows how the horse can completely void the leverage action of rope and neck by doubling both head and hindquarters towards the handler. In such situations we cannot win if we fight the horse, so we should not fight but quietly maintain 'relative stillness. (See page 23, Chapter 4).

Force should not be used unless or until the horse is at a serious disadvantage; this was done a little later when Webb used a 'dally' around a post as shown in Figure 33 in the next Chapter.

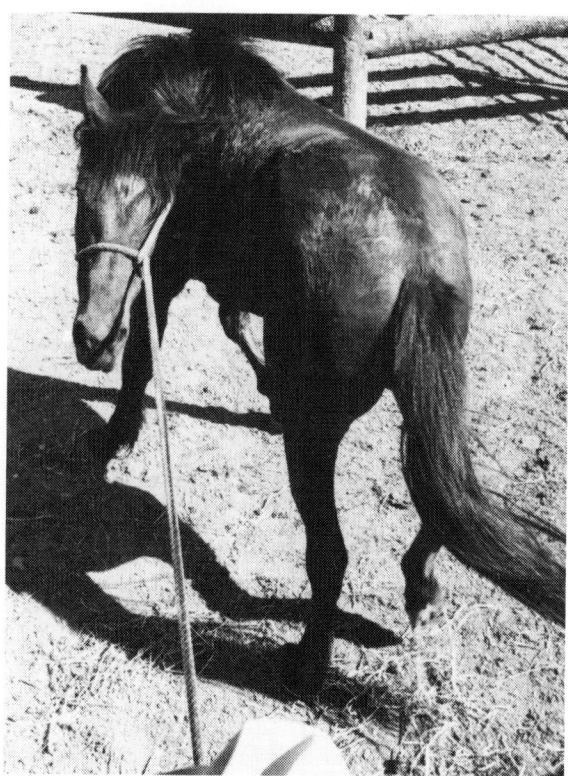

Figure 23: Less than an hour after his first meeting with his handler the young horse has been taught to tie-up, stand still to be handled and to lead quietly. Although quite confident, Webb as ever is ready for the unexpected. His rope is coiled in the way we recommend you to coil the lunge rein in Chapter 10, so that it will run out smoothly and quickly if circumstances should require it.

The experiences of the last hour have shown the horse that he cannot get away from his handler and that we are gentle and kindly if he accepts our superiority. He can still be frightened, though, by sudden movements or painful force — whether the force originates from his end of the rope or ours.

◆ ◆ ◆

I have shown and explained these photographs taken by Mike McKelvey, which with many more, appeared in the Australian magazine "Hoofs & Horns" in January and May 1973, to show how completely different techniques use the same guide-lines and follow the same rules. Rules you will have read about in earlier pages — "Profit you" and "Profit you not;" the neck, and later the head, being used as a lever and the rope at the 90° angle; "Quiet persistence," "End of Lesson" and "Relative stillness of the hand" — and others. Reading J. D. Wilton's "The Horse and His Education" you will see instance after instance of the application of these rules and guide-lines.

These photographs are somewhat out of place in this book — for they are only suited to the experienced and the expert with a completely wild and untouched horse. The point is — to recognise that all good systems follow the same basic rules.

CHAPTER 7

INTRODUCING THE YOUNG HORSE TO THE TIE-UP

Successful experiment in tying up a foal;
Tying up with the reins — mouth injuries possible;
Snubbing post and rope — requirements;
Points in common of different methods;
Spreading the pull over a larger area;
Using a 'Dally';
Other methods may suit other circumstances;
Do not tie-up with a running noose;
Don't let the horse learn his strength.

I repeat — this book is not written for professionals handling the wilder type of untouched colt or filly. I am writing for the scores, hundreds, of people who can ride but who have little or no experience of breaking-in — and whose wish it is to "gentle" and educate their own young horse or pony.

Most of these young horses will be accustomed to being handled. Many of them, handled and led from their earliest days, never need — and never get — a definite tie-up lesson. They learn the constraints of a leading rope and of being led by hand, and are then tied by the halter to a strong fence in their stable yard: often not directly to the fence but via a piece of binder-twine.

SUCCESSFUL EXPERIMENT IN TYING UP A FOAL

If the roughness of a forced tie-up lesson does not appeal to you or if you lack suitable facilities, as many of you will, you might like to see how your youngster responds to a trial I made a few years ago. I reported on it in "The South Australian Rider", the magazine of the Dressage Club of South Australia Inc., and several reports of the successful application of this method have been received since the article appeared. It has much to be said for it and I suggest you give it a trial first.

Here is the report as published in the magazine:

The Foal's Tie-up Lesson

I had been asked to stable a foal for a few days to get it away from its dam to wean it. While I had it at home, I spent a few minutes each day teaching the eight-month-old weanling some of the things that would be useful for it to know later on, the "Go-Forward" lesson, loading into a float, leading and lunging, etc.

I would have given her the usual tie-up treatment, but as I had no post with the necessary margin of strength I made the following little trial on the "It will profit you — it will profit you not" principle. Once before I had tried the same principle in a completely different matter (see Chapter 20) and it had been astonishingly successful. It proved to be no less successful in tying up.

The foal was in no way nervous; in fact, perhaps a little the other way and had to be kept 'respectful' (a foal should never be encouraged to be cheeky).

By the rope attached to her usual halter, I tied her to a single length of binder-twine passed round a post of the fence of her yard (I had previously prepared several similar lengths of twine ready for the experiment).

She had never been tied up before and did not know she was tied up until she moved her head too far; then, of course, she felt the pressure on her head. The moment she felt constraint she snatched at the rope, and broke the twine quite easily.

I had her in a stable yard about 14 ft. x 14 ft., but she did not attempt to move away: she didn't even know there was anything to move away from. If the yard had been too big, the youngster might not have been easily caught again. Had it been bigger than it was, I would have had a second light rope or rein with which to hold her, for she must not be allowed to get away or profit in any way by her action.

The foal was no sooner free than she was tied up again. Again, she stood quietly until by chance she again tightened the rope. She broke the twine immediately. This happened time after time, but as she was not being hurt, she kept calm and began to take notice of what was happening.

Although she broke the twine quite easily when she wanted to, the little thing found it took quite a tug to break it. It did not really hurt her or alarm her, but it was not pleasant — and so was to be avoided unless there was something to be gained from the unpleasantness.

But as she was not allowed to profit in any way from the tugging, she would naturally want to avoid the little discomfort it did cause.

The Foal Checks her Observations

So she began to check on her observations; tried moving her head slowly — and noticed, or checked her suspicion — that it was her own movement that caused the unpleasantness. She still broke the twine, though not with the same startled force of the earlier pulls.

However, not pulling quite so sharply made the twine a little more difficult to break, and so made the jolt a little more unpleasant. She broke it a few more times and then tried letting go after stretching the rope tight.

As soon as she found the rope stopped pulling when she did, she made a few more experiments to prove it and then completely 'gave it away': stood still and appeared to forget it.

"End of Lesson" for the day; she had caught on.

The next day I tried her again. She broke the twine once only and then stood still. She had proved to herself that pulling back or snatching at the rope was unpleasant and totally without gain or profit. The following day she went home again to her Mum, weaned.

It was two years before I saw her again. She had just been broken in and when I saw her she was tied to a fence post by the usual rope and halter, while her owner saddled her. I had told the owner of the little experiment and I was pleased to hear that she had never once pulled back.

One swallow does not a summer make. And this one instance proves nothing; but it is interesting, and the principle or rule behind it may prove valuable. When the little thing found that although it frightened her at first it didn't really hurt when she pulled back, she began to make her own quiet observations and reflected on them.

If hurt too much, horses will not do this. They just **panic**. They become too upset to notice."

TYING UP WITH THE REINS — A WARNING

Under no circumstances try teaching this tie-up with the reins of a bridle. The bit will hurt the youngster's mouth too much. Just use the ordinary halter and rope and a piece of string. No lesson is learned easily if it is accompanied by sharp stabs of pain. Leave tying up with the reins until a much later date — after the youngster has learned with the string, rope and halter.

While on this matter, *if at any time your horse pulls back and breaks the bridle when he has been tied by the reins* you will almost certainly be concerned only for the damage done to your bridle.

Breaking the reins does not usually injure or damage the horse's mouth — it is when the *bridle* breaks and the bit is violently torn from the mouth that serious damage can occur. Be sure you search for damage to the horse's mouth in such a case.

If your horse suddenly becomes difficult when answering the reins or keeps tossing his head, think back: "Has he pulled back at any time and injured his mouth!" Such a tear is often at the side of the jaw, between the jaw and the lip, and on the inside of the lip where it is not easily found.

Raising the bit in the mouth will often keep the bit off this injury — or give the horse a few days rest — or use a half-moon pelham until the laceration heals.

Always search carefully for mouth injury whenever a horse pulls back and breaks his bridle. The injury may be temporary — but the habits it forms may continue long after the injury is healed.

THE SHARPER TIE-UP LESSON

BEFORE YOU BEGIN — THE ROPE AND THE POST

The snubbing (or tie-up) post used, particularly if unsupported by other posts as when it forms part of the yard, should be set solidly into the ground, at least 3'6" (1.2 metres), and should stand 6-8 ft. (2-2.5 metres) above the ground. This height tends to prevent a horse coming down on the post. It should be round and smooth.

You will also need a strong rope some 22-30 ft. (7-9 metres) long, nylon for preference and treated as described in Chapter 5. New untreated nylon rope is not suitable; it is too thin, stiff, and slippery.

If you propose to tie direct to the post, do so at about the height of the horse's withers and leave only 4 ft. (1-1½ metres) of rope between the post and the horse's head. If the horse is tied with less than 3 ft. (1 metre) he can severely injure himself against the post as he lashes his head from side to side in his struggles. If too long, he can give his neck a fearful jolt as he rushes to the rope's limits as he occasionally will.

Caution: When tying a young horse at any time, watch to see that *your fingers are kept clear* of any bends in the knot, or the rope may mangle them should the horse suddenly pull back.

DIFFERENT METHODS OF TYING UP — THE MANY POINTS IN COMMON

It is always a great advantage if a person handling horses understands not only that this or that works, but also understands how, when and why it works.

Most methods of tying up, often in completely different ways, aim to reduce the frantic fight the horse usually offers when he finds himself rigidly tied to an unyielding object. The more he fights the more he is hurt; the more he is hurt, the harder he fights: a vicious circle that all the best methods try to avoid.

A horse does not learn like we do, by thinking and reasoning. He learns by noticing and then reflecting on what he notices. To do this, he has to be kept calm. If, when first tied up, he is hurt and finds he is unable to escape from what appears to him to be an attack, he panics and fails to notice cause and effect. Anything more removed from calmness than a horse when first he finds himself inescapably fastened to a post or tree, is hard to imagine.

We know that the horse is hurting himself — but it is just as clear to him that *it is the rope that is attacking him.*

All the most successful methods of tying-up aim to keep the horse calm. They do so by:

....reducing the strength of whatever force the horse can use;

....reducing the painful effects of whatever force he actually uses; and

....reducing, in some cases, the resistance of the rope and whatever he is tied to.

The Neck as a Lever Again

It has been shown in Chapter 6 how leverage gives us an advantage over the horse. If, with this lever, his neck, you can hold him with, say, 100 lb. weight on the rein or rope, then it becomes equally clear that in such a situation he is only able to apply something less than the 100 lb. Whatever strength will hold him, is more than the strength that he can apply.

Every inch of leverage reduces the strength that the horse can apply. He is still as strong as ever — but he cannot utilise his strength to the maximum advantage. This applies to you and me also; we cannot lift a heavy weight unless we stand quite close to, or over, that weight.

It is quite important that we are conscious of the fact that by limiting the strength the horse can apply, we also limit his ability to hurt himself.

Increase the Area of Contact

Note too, the larger the area over which the pressure of the rope is spread, the less likely it will be to injure or cause pain. A half-inch rope, for instance, will hurt more than will a 2-inch rope; also anything round in shape, as is the section of a rope, will bite in and cause more pain than will a flat surface of the same width — a 2-inch strap, for instance.

So, with the best methods, the shape and width of whatever is passed around the horse's neck to hold him, is recognised to be of paramount consideration.

When it comes to the degree of pain the horse can cause himself, other factors also come in.

If the rope is resting on bone only lightly covered by skin, as are the last two vertebrae of his neck, it will hurt much more than if it rested a little further back from the ears, where the neck is better padded. The more padded the bone with muscle and flesh, the less the rope will hurt — and also the less the likelihood of damage to the vertebrae.

WHAT WE TIE TO NEED NOT BE RIGID AND UNYIELDING

Some methods of teaching the horse to tie-up utilise a certain amount of give in the tie.

Tying to a folded inner-tyre tube instead of the rope going directly to the post is one method advocated. I have never used this idea, as I have heard of a tube being torn apart, which would naturally encourage the youngster concerned to fight again the next time he felt himself tied up.

Should you try this method, use a second rope around the post to limit the stretching of the tube — or to take over from the tube if it should break. With this precaution, an inner tube can be recommended as preferable to a direct tie to the snubbing post.

Tying to Bags of Sand

Another method of providing "give" in the tie-up is used at the Woodlyn Stud of Mr and Mrs Colin Rogers, Clarendon, South Australia (see Figures 24 to 29). Colin ties his youngsters to three nearly-filled bags of sand. The weight of the sand is the limit of the pull the horse can exert and its force or constraint, like the motor tube, is applied progressively — not with the shock that a tie to a rigid post gives. The number of bags (the weight) will vary with the size and strength of the horse. For obvious reasons too much weight will be better than too little — you can always take some off.

I've not used this method either, and I can only pass on Colin's recommendation.

You will need a certain amount of open ground as the horse may move the bags quite a few yards as he backs and finds the bags start to

Figure 24: Mr Colin Rogers, having closed each of the bags with a clove hitch and tied them together with the same rope, now doubles a short length of chain to them as it is sometimes difficult to get a youngster close to the bags. I am examining the neck tie, which consists of a length of fire-hose which is made a close fit around the 7-month-old weanling's neck.

Figure 25: The youngster is not hurt by her struggles as the bags move a little and the fire-hose about her neck spreads the pull over a large area.

move towards him. An additional advantage claimed for this method is that eventually it teaches the horse to stand when the reins are thrown over his head.

If left in the open the bottoms of the bags can quickly rot, and if not replaced can lead to trouble.

Figure 26: She is handled all over in due course of time and although she breaks back into a struggle many times, she is not hurt and so not badly frightened.

Figure 27: She is trying another line: "I'll see what will happen if I just hang on..."

Figure 28: She decides to give it another try.

Figure 29: "If I just stand still, it doesn't worry me at all — but I'll keep an eye on it just the same!"

SPREADING THE PULL OVER A LARGER AREA

Tying to a Folded Bag

In his book, 'From Paddock to Park', the late Mr D. McGillivray recommended tying the rope to a folded wheat or bran bag instead of passing the rope directly around the horse's neck.

This is an excellent method and is practised widely throughout Australia today. It reduces to a minimum the pain or damage the horse might otherwise inflict on himself. By doing so it keeps him calmer and he soon notices that it is his pulling back that causes trouble for him.

Used either in association with a dally or tied directly to a snubbing post, it is a practice I can strongly recommend.

A length of fire-hose is used by Colin Rogers for the same reason.

Preparing the Bag for Tying

Select a wheat bag or sack in good condition and fold lengthways into four. You will then have eight thicknesses of heavy jute, some 6 inches wide.

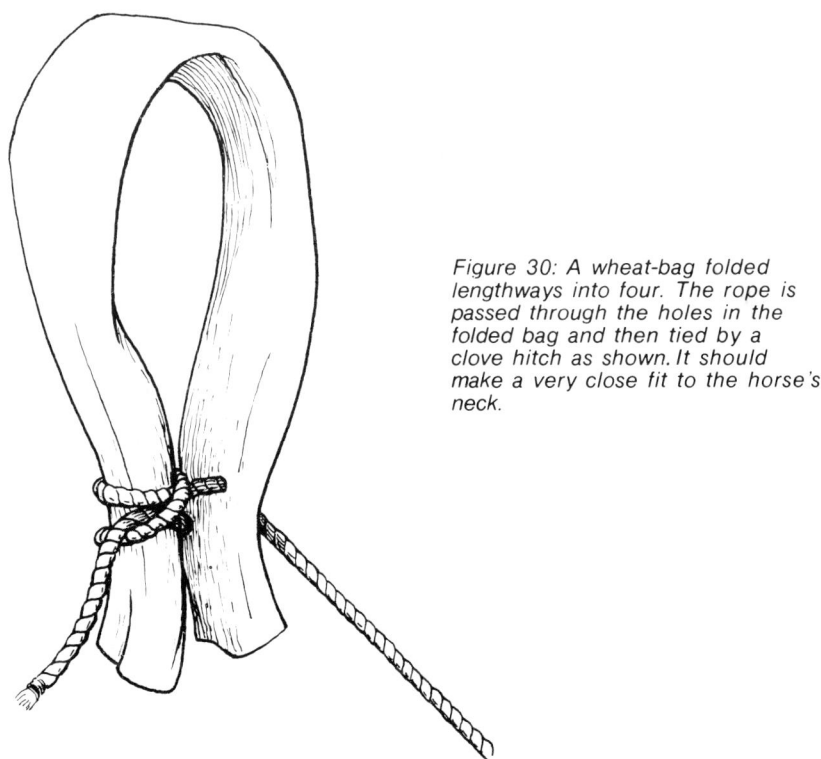

Figure 30: A wheat-bag folded lengthways into four. The rope is passed through the holes in the folded bag and then tied by a clove hitch as shown. It should make a very close fit to the horse's neck.

Pierce through the eight thicknesses at the open end of the bag some 2-4 inches from the seam or turndown at the mouth (if you use a blunt spike you can make the holes without cutting the material). Now pass the end of the rope through the holes in the folded eight thicknesses (see Figure 30).

Put the bag around the horse's neck and tie the end of the rope you have just passed through the holes, to the other end of the bag.

It is better to have the loop of bag around the neck a trifle too small than too large, as it will only remain tight while the horse is actually pulling against it. The rope slackens off again through the holes immediately the horse takes his weight off it.

There is no danger of 'choking the horse down,' as the bag is wide and it releases automatically as the rope slackens. The bag itself also stretches somewhat under the first stresses — much better have it a little too tight than too loose for the first tie-up or two.

The bag should, of course, be placed around the smallest part of the neck to utilise the full leverage of the neck against the horse. The wide soft bag will not damage the bone of the vertebrae near the ears.

 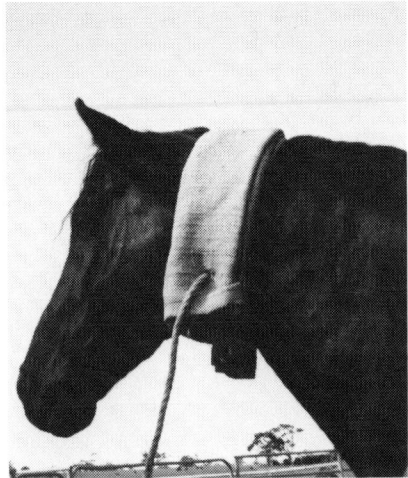

Figures 31 and 32: Bill Reed's "Jerilderie Midnight" acts as a model to show the bag tie in place. It is an advantage if the rope is then passed down through the noseband of the halter before taking it to the snubbing post.

Only a simple clove-hitch is needed to secure the rope to the other end of the bag (see Figures 31 and 32). You can add a third half hitch if you feel it might work loose. However, it is best not to tie the two ends of the bag together until you are satisfied you have the loop the correct size for your horse's neck.

PASS ROPE DOWN THROUGH NOSEBAND

The running end of the rope should always be passed down through the noseband of a strong halter before being tied to the snubbing post.

Do not tie up with the halter as it will break under the strain unless it has been especially made for the task. Tie to the bag and only pass the rope down through the noseband. This not only extends the leverage of the neck to include that of the head but what is more important, it *stops the horse getting his head under the rope* in a struggle. If this happens, and it can if you don't have the rope down through the noseband, the loop around the neck can revolve about the neck until the knot is at the top, at ear level.

From that position the rope will pull over the horse's ears and eyes — no more need be said. Passing the rope through the noseband will prevent this situation occurring, as will the tie and halter used by Mr Bill Reed (Figures 34, 35).

The closer the noseband fits, within reason, the more effective it will be for the purpose.

USING A "DALLY"

By the use of a dally around the post, the handler can limit the weight the horse can put on the rope. (I should say here that the term 'dally' was new to me, but Mr McKelvey — seen here in some of the illustrations — repeatedly used the term which is in common use in the U.S.A. The term is new but the method very old).

Instead of tying the rope to the snubbing post, a complete turn is taken around the post and the handler then holds the running end in his hand (see Figure 33). The biggest strongest horses can be held easily by means of a dally. The rope can be played out during the horse's worst struggles and any slack can be easily taken up when the horse 'lets up,' as he repeatedly does.

The rope can also be completely released should any circumstance require that line of action. Its primary use, however, is to *limit the resistance offered the horse.*

The handler, by means of the dally, uses the rope as an angler uses his reel and line: he plays out when the weight on the line threatens to become excessive, and takes up the slack (reels in) each time the horse slackens off so that he can play out again when the need arises.

The rope must not be allowed to remain long and loose.

The handler must continually and repeatedly take up the slack each time the horse "gives:" not attempting to pull the horse in but just taking up the slack. If the rope is allowed to become long and loose, the horse can give himself a frightful jolt as, using all his strength, he reaches its limits.

The value of the dally lies in its ability to give and take — its ability to slacken off and take in — as the handler requires.

With this in mind, see that the post is smooth and round, that the rope encircles the post at about the height of the wither and that the coil of the rope running to the horse is lower than the end running to the handler. If reversed, the rope can become locked and immovable.

The horse can see that the 'thing' around his neck is connected somehow with us and that he cannot get away. He needs to be very much cleverer than he is to realise the effect of that turn around the post, and he has no chance of recognising how his handler and the rope are associated: where we finish and the rope begins. Remember though, that any pain caused the horse he will also attribute to us — or associate with us.

Figure 33: Visiting Californian horseman, Mr Webb McKelvey, demonstrates a "dally" around a snubbing post. He is playing out the rope at the moment.
The dally allows the handler to play the horse much as an angler plays a fish. By allowing the horse to 'take' to some degree, the strain on the rope and the hurt to the horse is reduced. Each time the horse slackens off for a moment or two as he repeatedly does, the handler takes up the slack — as the longer the rope the greater the jolt the horse gives himself as he again reaches its limit.
In the handling of this young wild horse, Webb was demonstrating that he needed nothing more than a 25 ft. rope for the task. Note his poised and balanced stance as he plays out the rope, and his close attention to the horse.

If you are going to use a direct tie-up instead of a dally, be sure you use McGillivray's folded bag. It is a splendid idea — although if you intend to use a dally the use of the bag is not quite so important. I recommend "Use both" — keep the horse as calm as possible; hurt and frighten him as little as you can. Let him learn your apparent strength by all means, but don't let him know it is something to fear.

ROPE LOOP TIE: THROUGH THE HALTER DEES, OVER THE EARS AND TIED IN THE CHIN GROOVE BEHIND THE JAW

This tie is used by Mr W. V. Reed of "Jerilderie Stud," The Range, Willunga, South Australia, who tells me both he and his brother at Tintinara have used it on hundreds of horses without trouble.

Certainly it is simple and effective (see Figures 34 and 35), and I have successfully used it myself recently.

The front stay of the noseband of the halter should be rather longer than is usual and so permit the dees at the sides of the noseband to lie further back. It should be fitted not more than one inch below the projecting cheekbone — *no lower.* If the noseband is too low it is difficult to keep the knot up in position behind the jaw.

The tie rope is passed through the dee of the noseband and then back again through the upper dee. It is then passed over the head and threaded back through the dees on the off side of the halter. Finally it is tied at the back of the jaw by a bowline knot.

The knot should be tied a little higher than the chin-groove so that the bottom of the encircling loop of rope does not come below the line of the mouth when the horse struggles.

The effectiveness of this tie is due to the maximum leverage obtained by including both head and neck. It is of the utmost importance that the rope passes *through the dees* of the noseband and not just inside the noseband — and that the noseband is fitted higher than usual to allow for the bowline knot.

Figure 34: Bill Reed with a weanling at his "Jerilderie Stud." Note the comparatively high noseband with the bowline knot tied close up under the noseband: these points are important. When the youngster resists, the pull is up the nearly straight rope so that although held firmly, no undue pressure is applied to either the front or the back of the head. The photograph was taken some ten minutes after the rope was first tied.

Figure 35: Miss Andra Eastgate's "Nantawarra" had acquired the habit of breaking the string to which he was tied at shows, and we tried the effect of a second longer tie with the Reed Bros. utilisation of the rope through the halter dees. The rope and halter came into action after the horse had broken the string.
The experiment was successful and 'Nantawarra' has learned to tie without the need of a rope.

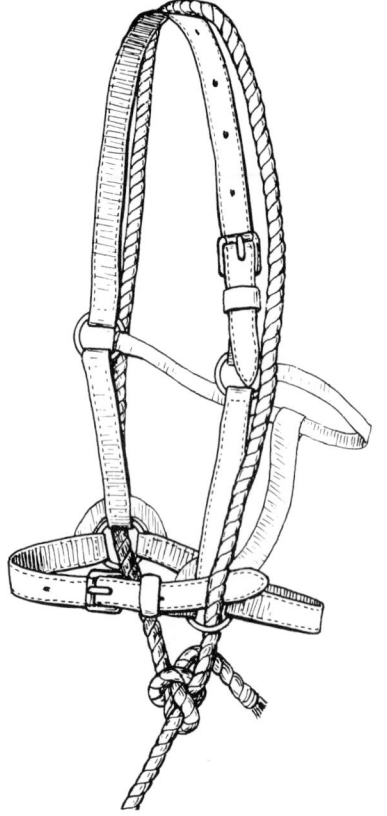

Figure 36: Showing the bowline knot tied very short under the noseband.

Bill Reed strongly recommends passing the rope back through the top dee as well as through the noseband dee.

The noseband is fitted high on the head and the bowline tied close to the noseband.

The rope when stretched is almost straight and controls the head with the least pressure about the muzzle.

Figure 37: TO TIE THE BOWLINE:

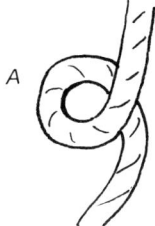 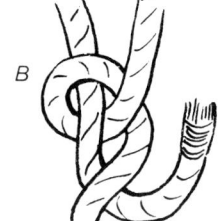 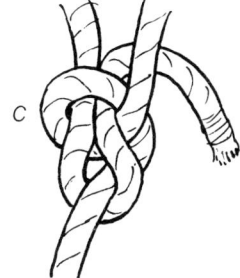

A. First: stand facing the horse and form the loop in the standing end of the rope as shown.
B. Pass the short end (running end) through the loop formed — under — then over — then under the standing end of the rope. Before going on and completing the knot, pull the running end through the loop so that the knot will be close to the noseband.
C. The running end is then taken around the standing end and returned through the loop the way it came at first. There is no need to draw the second loop tight.
Become familiar with this knot, for its main feature is that no matter how much weight the horse puts on it, it will remain easy to untie.

Bill tells me he has never had a rope or halter pull over the ears when using this tie-up; he claims that the passing of the rope through the noseband dees and tying behind the jaw ensures its pull is always directed downwards and therefore cannot pull forward over the ears. Use only a bowline knot (see Figures 36 and 37) — other knots become too tight to untie.

There seems to be no reason for not using a dally when first tying with this or any other gear, as it has its advantages. I recommend you do this.

CHOKING DOWN: DO NOT TIE-UP WITH A RUNNING NOOSE

Although it is usual to use a running noose around the neck of a young horse when he is first handled in a yard, NEVER use one for the tie-up. I saw this done many years ago and the horse "choked down."

It was a shocking sight, cruel, heartless and quite unnecessary. The horse fought so desperately that he broke part of his skull — the bone protecting the eye — and he continued to fight until he dropped unconscious. Nothing excuses such treatment. Horses *will* resist force.

When a running noose is used for handling as described in Chapter 5, the rope is permitted to remain tight only for "a split second." Provision should always be made for the loop around the neck to loosen instantly.

The question of "choking down" does not arise with the halter-type tie-up or when the rope is tied to a bag, or if a dally is used.

OTHER METHODS TO SUIT OTHER CIRCUMSTANCES

There are other ties that are effective and under some circumstances I have preferred to use them.

Horses with the confirmed habit of halter-breaking, can be defeated by passing the head-rope through a tie-up ring and tying it just above the horse's knee by clove hitches. When the horse pulls back, the same movement pulls his fore-leg forward and weakens his base of support. A Police Horse, "Robina" (named after me and you couldn't find a plainer horse!), always had to be tied in this manner. It is not suited for a first tie-up, however.

Tying by a Front Leg. Another effective tie-up for persistent halter-breakers is to tie them by a front leg. A 'shackle' is fastened below the fetlock joint and then a rope passed around a suitable post at ground level with some 2-3 ft. of rope. Once the horse accepts the constraint, the rope can be left quite long. This is useful at times as it permits the horse to graze over quite a large area: valuable if you are not carrying a lot of feed.

Elephants are tied by a front leg, you will doubtless have noticed; they would never stop laughing if you tried to tie them by the head — and they having no neck!

Other Ties: include passing a long rope from the neck through the noseband as described earlier, then around a post or suitable rail. It is then taken back and passed around the horse's body and chest and tied there with sufficient loose rope to pass around the root of the tail, as shown in Figure 38.

Figure 38: A very effective tie-up, but not recommended for the novice without help from an experienced breaker. There are several variations of this type of tie; they all aim at reducing the force that the horse can use (each end of the rope takes half the strength used).

Whenever the rope is returned and tied to some part of the horse's body, only half the force he uses is applied to the head and neck. It reduces the force on each return of the rope to less than 50 percent. I have only tried the tie used on "Robina" and I would recommend you leave these other types of tie until you have an opportunity to work with a person experienced with them.

I mention these ties as they are used and recommended by many good colt-breakers and because each of them, as with all the good methods, prevents the horse using his strength to his advantage. This in its turn prevents him hurting himself and so avoids upsetting him.

The tie-up you use will generally depend upon the conditions and facilities available to you at that time.

DON'T LET THE HORSE LEARN HIS STRENGTH

What happens to the young horse the first time or two that he is tied up can make a big difference to his subsequent behaviour. If, when he fights hard something breaks and he gets free, he does not tell himself that he is strong. He is more likely to register: "I was attacked by this thing near my head. It grabbed my neck when I moved. I couldn't get away — and the harder I fought, the harder it fought too. I was terrified; and I fought, and fought, and fought."

"Just when things were at their worst and I thought I would never get free again — I was free!"

"What a good thing I was able to put up with the pain: and I now know that when things are at their worst I am closest to winning. To win, I must be ready to fight and suffer the pain — fighting is a good thing to do, it profits me."

From then on, your horse faces life KNOWING he can get free if he fights and struggles hard enough. The more he is hurt in a fight that he wins, the harder he will be to correct later on. He will remember that relief came at the moment of the greatest pain from the fight.

To the horse, when he is held by the rope, post and gear, it seems that *we* hold him, if we stand near the post. If he is successful in breaking away, it appears to him that *we were unable* to hold him.

Try to avoid letting the tie-up lesson become a test of strength; put him at a disadvantage and if or when such a test develops, see that you win while doing all you can to avoid hurting the horse.

Snaphooks on Ropes for Young Horses

Do not use any rope with snap-hooks attached for early tie-ups. Unless they are very large the snaphooks will not stand anything like the strain the rope will hold.

If you leave a halter on a young horse at any time, check that there are no projections on which it can be caught. The halter will irritate him at first and he will repeatedly rub it against projections. You can lose your horse by getting the halter caught under a tap, for instance. Even if not injured, such an incident may make him difficult to tie up all his life.

TO SUM UP

- There are many different approved methods of tying a horse for the first time — but they ALL aim at reducing or eliminating the chances of the horse being injured or hurt.
- If repeatedly tied to stout string that breaks without really hurting him, a foal or very young horse gets a chance to notice that it is his own action that causes the trouble and he will usually learn not to pull back. He must not be allowed to break free, however — he must not be allowed to profit from his pulling back.
- Tying to bags of sand, inner tyre-tubes, using a dally — all tend to 'cushion' the force of the horse's struggles.
- Using McGillivray's folded bag takes most of the punishment out of a direct tie-up to post or tree; but if you intend using just a rope around the neck you are strongly advised to use a dally too.
- Do not tie to a stable halter; it will break. Only pass the rope down through the noseband.
- If a young horse tied to a post manages to break free, he is then likely to repeat that action at any time — perhaps every time he is tied up.
- All the best methods of teaching the horse to tie up, although dissimilar in many ways, have this point in common: *they aim at minimising the force that the horse is able to use.*

CHAPTER 8

BRIDLING HORSES "BAD ABOUT THE HEAD"

Never tie the head down;
Getting the bridle over his ears;
Getting the horse to take the bit in his mouth;
Difficulty in removing the bridle:
 — let the horse 'spit' the bit out — don't take it out.

HANDLING THE HEAD OF A DIFFICULT HORSE

Unbroken horses almost invariably object to having their heads handled. I have said something about this in Chapter 4 on handling the young horse or foal and I am assuming now that you have a halter on your young horse before you think of introducing the bridle.

When a horse makes a practice of moving his head away from your hands, he usually lifts it too high for you to be able to do anything about it (see Figures 39 and 40). On no account try to hold his head still and never tie it down to handle it. If you do, he will fight the rope and the rope will hurt him — and this will confirm his fears that you

Figure 39: If he is very touchy about the head, let the young horse become accustomed to having a rope passed over one ear — I always deal with the left ear and eye first. Don't use force; quietly persist (see Ch. 4: 'Putting a halter on a Young Horse').

were going to hurt him. He then becomes even more difficult to handle about the head.

Never tie his head down. Use no force on the head. You will find that the 'quiet persistence' of the "It will profit you not" method much more satisfactory to you both.

You have a halter and rope on your horse, and as you lift your hand to touch his face you should maintain a light even feel on the rope. Don't attempt to hold his head still — you haven't the slightest chance of doing so. Just look at the muscles of his neck and compare them with the puny muscles of your arms. You *can't* hold his head still — never enter a fight you cannot win. It only gives the horse an opportunity to realise his own strength.

Show him, rather, that he cannot get his head away from your hand. Show him: "Moving your head will profit you not". Just maintain the same feel on the rope and let your other hand follow his head. If he raises it beyond your reach, then keep one hand up just below his nose and maintain the light feel on the rope with the other. In a stable or your small enclosure, you should have no difficulty in keeping with him.

Follow the line recommended with the foal in Chapter 4. You keep your hand up knowing he cannot keep his head held so high for long; follow his head around with your raised hand until he lowers it to your hand. *Which he will do eventually.*

When he does — when your hand touches his head for a moment or so — show him *"That* will profit you" and quietly move your hand away again, "End of Lesson"; rest, period, for a moment or so and then start again from the beginning.

I warn again — whatever you do, don't tie his head down. He will fight the rope and in doing so usually lashes right and left to the full extent the rope allows. If your face or body happen to be in the way, you can be really hurt or disfigured. The quiet persistence method is, in every way, to be preferred.

Do as much of this handling of the head as early as you can; don't leave it to the day you want to put a bridle on the horse. If you have time, you can have quite a bit of fun getting the better of him. Have a carrot cut into half-inch pieces in your pocket and give him an interest in the 'end of lesson' breaks. The handling of the head and neck is one of the first things to be tackled.

Horses usually like having their foreheads rubbed and also the space underneath and between the jaws. Take advantage of that, and rub him there whenever you get the opportunity, for the horse cannot rub himself in either of these places. Let rubbing his head, your handling his head, become a pleasure to him.

PASSING THE BRIDLE OVER HIS EARS

It is a good idea to begin preparing the horse for a bridle, of having it passed over his ears, long before you intend using one. You have a halter on and you have been handling his head. Now any time that suits you, start slipping an ordinary noseband of a bridle on him: just the noseband and headstall, but without the browband. Let the headstall out to about the last hole and also loosen the noseband; slip it on over the top of the halter and over his ears.

When you can do this without any trouble and eventually without needing a halter on him, then you can think about putting the browband back on the headstall.

This sort of thing can go on from the earliest days (see Figure 40), long before you are thinking of using a bit. Prepare him for bridling just as you prepare him for shoeing: well before you need to shoe him. In each case you are, perhaps, establishing the habits of a lifetime.

When he is ready, replace the browband and see that it is both loose and low until the headstall has passed over the ears. The more difficult about the head the horse is, the more important is each of these easy steps — or lessons. In this case, the noseband of a bridle is used as a means to an end only — to accustom a difficult horse to having something passed over the ears.

One thing at a time: and there are at least three things we have to introduce in the simple matter of putting a bridle on a horse:

1. passing the bridle over the ears;
2. getting him to open his mouth; and
3. getting him used to having a bit popped into his open mouth.

If you get him accustomed to doing each separately, you will have little difficulty in introducing the whole bridle.

Figure 40:
Erica Jarvis asks: "Is this what you mean?" And it is. Both hands in firm but gentle contact with the horse's head and the left eye in no way interfered with when the hand is raised to pass the bridle over the left ear. Every care must be taken to avoid interference with the eyes, as it is at this moment you will be trying to get him to take the bit in his mouth. He won't attend to the bit if something is worrying his eye at the same time.

GETTING THE HORSE TO TAKE THE BIT INTO HIS MOUTH

Note the wording of that heading. We aim ultimately to get him to *take* the bit into his mouth, not his trainer having to force it on him.

Deal with the bit quite separately if the horse is at all difficult. If he has been troublesome with a bridle without the bit attached, you will face a much more difficult task with the steel bit held close to his nose and hitting his muzzle every time he moves his head sharply.

Firstly we have to get him to open his mouth; or, to put the same thing a different way, to separate his teeth. You may be surprised at me saying anything so obvious, yet it is astonishing how many people try to force the bit into the horse's mouth while his teeth are still firmly closed. It's his teeth we want open, not just his lips.

Don't be rough — and don't hurry. Putting one or two fingers into his mouth from the side (in the space between the incisors and molars) is usually all that is needed; but not always. If he still keeps his mouth firmly closed, as some do, slip a piece of carrot or apple or a 'horse cube' into his mouth from the side. Treat it as fun rather than be grim

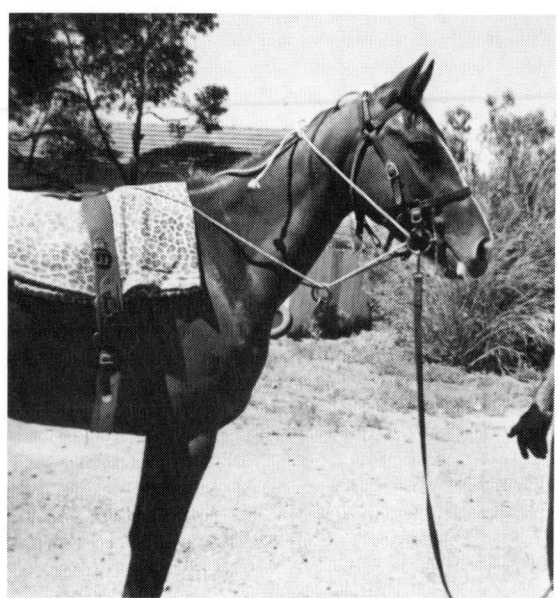

Figure 41: Danny Fitzgerald's halter/bridle especially designed for colt-breaking. The top strap is adjustable so that the browband can be raised, lowered or even removed if that is required. When removed it takes its place at the top and the halter is then used without a browband.

Notice how loosely everything is fitted. The long browband allows the headstall to ride well back from the ears as recommended in 'Horse Control and the Bit'. The browband itself is fitted low so that it does not interfere with the front of the horse's ears. Noseband and throat-lash are both loose-fitting and only the bit is fitted high — well up into the corners of the lips.

This halter doubles as a bridle in the early days. The bit can be introduced to the horse quite separately from having something passed over his ears. Other points of interest: the horse's quiet relaxed acceptance of contact with the bit due to the light weight on the mouthing rein. He neither fights nor 'drops' the bit ('drops' means drawing his nose in to escape contact). He does not let the bit worry him in any way, he just accepts it.

72

about it; and when he does open his mouth eventually, "End of Lesson" and a titbit. Don't put the bit in straight away if he has been troublesome; encourage him by 'end of lesson'.

Allow a little time to get him to take the bit casually; and again, do look to see where the opening between his teeth is — and quietly present him with the bit THERE.

If the youngster proves to be very difficult and jerks his head about a lot so that he keeps striking his mouth against the steel bit, you will find it easier at first to tie or strap the snaffle to the halter, as seen in the picture of Danny Fitzgerald, Figure 41.

It is much more difficult for the horse to strike his nose against the bit when the strap is so short.

With a very bad case I once had to correct, I substituted a short piece of rope for the bit — something softer until he had learned what to do.

First, I tied one end of the rope to the dee on the off side of the *halter*, then brought the other end under the mouth and through the dee on the near side, leaving a loop long enough to put into the horse's mouth. The lower the halter noseband is for this task, the easier it is to pop the rope 'bit' into his mouth when he does open it.

Don't tie the rope to the dee on the near side; just pass it through. You will need to draw it up when the rope is in the mouth. (I used a piece of smooth rope about the thickness of a snaffle bit, see Figure 42).

Figure 42: Showing how you can accustom a young horse to having something passed into his mouth even though you do not have a bridle or bit handy. Let it become "Old Hat" from his earliest days.

Use no force. As soon as you get the rope, or bit, into his mouth, reward the horse with a titbit if possible, and take the rope or bit straight out again; "That will profit you", you show him. Make a fuss of the youngster and give him a let-up for a few minutes. Do something else for a while if it suits you.

Don't "Take" the Bit out of the Horse's Mouth

I have just done something that I try to avoid doing. I put my thoughts into the wrong words, so I hasten to draw your attention to it. Do not think of 'taking' the bit out of his mouth. We do not 'take' the bit out: we should *lower the bit and let the horse "spit it out."* Let him push it out with his tongue.

If you think "take," you will tend to take, or pull, and the bit can get caught on the horse's bottom teeth. This hurts and causes him to throw his head in the air — often with the bit still caught up in his teeth.

"He's hurting himself," you rightly think; but he only knows he gets hurt when the bit comes out of his mouth. If it happens several times, you have another difficulty developing (which I deal with later).

Repeat the exercise from time to time as convenient, until the youngster takes the rope without any difficulty. The time has then come to substitute a light bridoon snaffle. Once he grasps the fact that opening his mouth and having something put into it will not hurt, you are over that hurdle. Don't hurry — and every now and then pop something tasty into his mouth together with the bit. Make it a pleasant experience for him: remember, you may be establishing the habits of his lifetime.

Accept these head difficulties as a challenge rather than just a nuisance. Getting the bridle over the ears with some horses can be a difficult task for an inexperienced person; but putting the bit into his mouth should present little difficulty when not linked with the ears' worry.

Avoid using a big bulky snaffle or one with big rings or long cheek-bars at first. They add to the difficulties; make things easy for him at first.

When you have reached the point where you can tie a snaffle bit to the offside dee of the halter, put it into his mouth and tie or buckle it on the near side of the halter, *the bridle should present little difficulty.* Again remove the browband the first time or so, lengthen the headstall a hole or two, and you should have no difficulty at all; particularly if you have a piece of carrot or dry bread to pop in with the snaffle.

Remember you have lengthened the headstall so that it would slip easily over his ears: do not forget to take it up again and to fit the snaffle correctly before you let him stand with the bridle on. If the snaffle is left hanging too low it tends to start the tongue over the bit habit (see Figure 41 with the snaffle drawn well up into the corners of the lips so that they appear to smile).

Head difficulties vary enormously, but most of them can be dealt with quite easily. Observation and intelligent application is the real answer — and no force.

How Your Activities May Appear to the Horse

Only too often we tend to think of a lesson as being only those things we want our horse to learn. It is much more than that. Everything he learns is a lesson — horses learn by their every experience.

I once had a very difficult mare to correct. When I attempted to put a bridle on her, she threw her head from side to side with such violence that she would have smashed my face in if she had hit it (and it was extremely difficult to avoid her). She became terribly excited and upset: it was just as though she didn't care how much she hurt herself as long as she knocked me out.

It took several days before I realised that she thought I *wanted her to hit me with her head.*

It hurt her, too, of course; and that is what upset her. Her experience had proved to her that she had to hurt herself badly before you 'rewarded' her by "ending the lesson." What actually caused her handler to stop or "end the lesson" then was that she had usually knocked him out when that great mass of bone, her head, did connect.

The lesson she had learned, the lesson she had unwittingly been taught, was: "Hit my head really hard against him (her handler) and he will stop worrying me." It was perfectly clear to her what she had to do, not so much hit the handler with her head, but to *bash* her head against him. She had learned, someone had taught her, that she had to hurt her head badly before she was given rest and peace.

I thought up a plan of action to correct the mare, and when her owners came for her a week later they were amazed to see her take the bit in her mouth when it was presented to her, and she positively pushed her ears into the bridle.

She showed every sign of being really grateful *that we had learned to behave decently.* (I won't go on and say how this was done as the mare's condition was so unusual as not to warrant the quite long story!).

DIFFICULTY IN REMOVING THE BRIDLE

A few years ago a prominent rider and exhibitor of horses asked if I knew how to deal with a horse with this fault.

The horse, not a large one, was not particularly bad about the head. Putting the bridle on was not difficult. But the horse became quite a problem when the time came to take it off. As soon as his owner's hand grasped the bridle near the ears to slip it off, the horse would wrench his head away, ripping the bridle over his ears as he did so. He would then throw his head up and to one side — and the bit would be pulled down on to his jaw in a most painful way by his action. It would tear down the bars of the mouth and strike the tushes, where it would sometimes become trapped. The horse would then wrench and fight with his head until he tore his head and teeth free of the bit. A very painful business.

How the Horse Sees It. You and I know that he causes the trouble himself, but he is not capable of seeing the matter that way. He will only know that his mouth is badly hurt when the bridle is being taken off. Once it has happened he will look for the same thing to happen next time the bridle is removed. It is easy to see that if it does recur, grasping the bridle near his ears seems to him to be a preliminary to a most painful incident.

Horses observe and reflect, and look back over what has happened. An older horse speaking to another might well say: "When his hand grabs the top of the bridle, you are "in for it" until you can get that thing out of your mouth. Do anything; but get it out of your mouth."

I did not know what to advise then, but I have successfully treated two such horses recently. It is not the hand taking the bridle over the ears that hurts the horse, but that this precedes or forms part of a process of having the bit *torn out of his mouth*. As long as the two things are linked, the horse will continue to behave in the same way.

To correct the trouble, I decided to separate the taking of the bridle over the ears from the removal of the bit from the mouth. I found a way to do this and it worked like a charm. The first horse took a fortnight before the bridle could be taken off in the normal manner, the second took a week. We learn as we go: notice, think, plan. The horse can only notice and reflect — think back.

What to Do in Such a Case.

First, get a piece of string some five or six feet (2 metres) long. I used twine from around a bale of hay; a piece without knots is best.

Tie one end of the twine to the ring of the bit on the off side and pass the twine over the horse's neck from the off to the near side, where you will be standing. If he is *very* touchy about the head or ears, let the twine lie well back from the ears, a foot or even more if necessary.

Next, tie the twine to the ring of the bit on the near side, with some two feet to spare at the end. It should be tight enough to keep the bit a little higher in the mouth than the bridle ordinarily keeps it. Tie it with a slip knot on the near side — for you will want to untie it soon.

The twine will continue to keep the bit up in the horse's mouth after the bridle is slipped off over his ears. Remember, the aim is to separate the removal of the bridle from the removal of the bit.

Now slip the bridle off. The horse will put on his usual 'turn.' Let him. Let the bridle go completely at first, and don't attempt to hold the horse with the rein, either. Do not interfere with him, or his head in any way; if you do, you may again be instrumental in him hurting himself. The twine will now keep the bit up in his mouth — don't interfere; he can't hurt himself unless you interfere with his head. You will have him in a yard and there is no reason to hurry or worry.

Take your time; allow the horse to take his time. Left calmly to himself he soon notices that this is no longer a painful business although he will, at first, repeatedly toss his head about with the bridle hanging.

When he has calmed down and his head is resting and still, make a fuss of him and untie the slip knot. Again, don't be in a hurry and DO NOT try to keep his head still or hold him, or the bridle. Give him a chance to notice there is nothing to fear now, *and there will not be, if you do not try to hold his head in any way.*

> When you are ready, do you take the bit out?
> No! You do not *take* the bit out.

You loosen the string a fraction at a time. He has to learn to 'spit it out' — he has to learn to allow the bit to drop. Let gravity take it out of his mouth. Keep your hand away from his mouth; if the twine is well back and down his neck, you will not need to undo it at the bit. Just slide it forward along the neck a little at a time. Every time he feels the bit move, he will think he is "in for it" again: he will jerk his head up a few times; but don't try to help him at all. Left alone, he will find it a painless process.

Remember the bridle will be hanging down all this time, and when the bit comes out of his mouth it will fall. If you don't have an old bridle, improvise one; use no noseband, I need hardly say, for this lesson. Let the bridle be as light as possible — and if you have a rein on the bit, take it off the first time or two.

Use Horse-Sense

Talk quietly to your horse. Let your voice 'purr' to him each time he behaves a little better. The calmer you keep him, the more he will notice and ponder on what is happening.

You may have to take it off like this quite a few times, and I found it convenient to tie the twine to a snaphook at one end to save time. How long it takes you to cure the habit will depend upon how strong is your 'way with horses.'

Nothing one can write will tell you everything you may need to know. We continually meet new problems and problem situations. I can give you ideas, methods and principles to guide you, but *you* still have to find the resolution, the observation, the thought and the judgment to do what is necessary with each particular horse.

Weigh the situation with both resolution and confidence. Know you are going to win — although you know, too, that you will almost certainly not have a 'walk over'. Assess *this* horse with *this* situation; *look for the basic trouble and then look for a way to deal with it.* Be sympathetic with the horse even though he may hurt you — and that 30 lb. (15 kilos) odd mass of bone that is a horse's head *can* hurt if it connects. It hurts him, too.

I am sure that although horses know kicking and biting hurt, they do not know that things like striking your leg against a post, stepping on your foot, hitting you with their head etc., also hurt.

They may notice that you stop worrying them (while you nurse your crushed toes) but they have no idea what has happened. If the same thing happened several times, the horse might note: "Every time I do that (hitting the rider's leg against a post or stepping on his toes) he stops worrying me. Obviously, then, *it is a good thing for me to do!*" That is NOT vice.

The Tongue-over-the-Bit Habit

Figure 43 shows Danny Fitzgerald's home-made mouthing bit which he finds effective in stopping the formation of the tongue over the bit habit.

The bit is easily forged from a 17-inch length of rod, with a single link of chain welded on to each side, about ¼-inch in front of its centre line.

The back, being thus slightly heavier, raises the front of the bit which hangs in the mouth, making it more difficult for the horse to get his tongue over it. Hanging as it does more or less horizontally, with its front in the horse's mouth, its length (5¼ inches from front to rear) gives the bit a tendency to push forward off, or away, from the tongue; and this, too, makes getting the tongue over it very difficult. (This is a matter of suspended weight trying to get its centre of gravity under its point of suspension).

As soon as the youngster has learned to keep his tongue under the bit, switch over to the snaffle you favour.

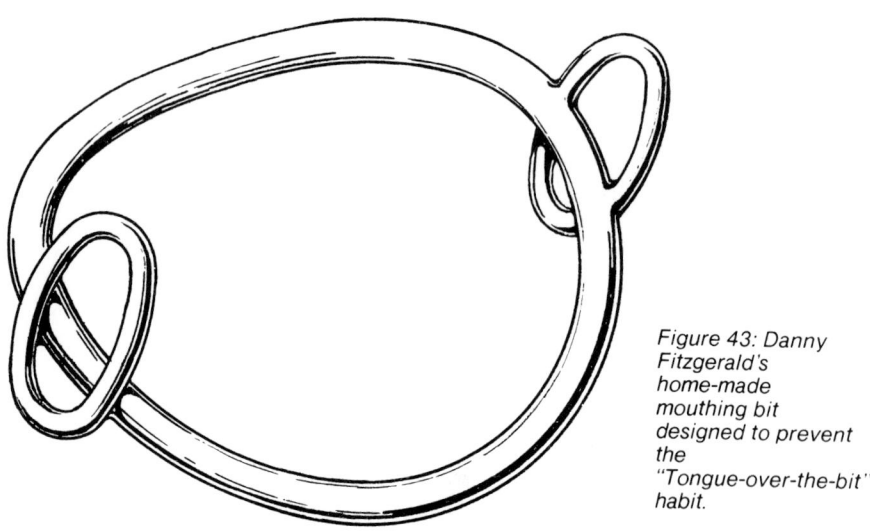

Figure 43: Danny Fitzgerald's home-made mouthing bit designed to prevent the "Tongue-over-the-bit" habit.

TO SUM UP

Never tie the horse down to handle his head.

Plan ahead: handling the horse's head comes into your scheme of training even before handling his feet.

When introducing the bridle to your young horse, see that it is loose fitting; don't increase difficulties by having a bridle even correctly fitted — have it too loose when first putting it on. Adjust it when it is on.

If you have reason to expect trouble, take the browband off; the bridle will then pass over the ears much more easily.

You can teach your youngster to take a bit in his mouth without using a bridle; tie a light bridoon snaffle to the off side of the halter and let him get the idea of taking the bit before you use the bridle. Change back to a thicker one after he has learned to take the small snaffle easily.

CHAPTER 9

CAVESSON HEADSTALL — MOUTHING GEAR — SIDE REINS

The Cavesson: its fitting and use
Mouthing Gear: its fitting and use
Side reins: the Fitzgerald weighted side-rein, its advantages; other types;
Side reins: Adjustment — length and height.

CAVESSON HEADSTALL

We often find the name "Cavesson" these days applied to the ordinary noseband of a bridle. "Cavesson," I understand, is correctly used only in connection with a complete headstall especially made for use in lunging. "Cavesson" is short for "Cavesson Headstall."

Not only is the noseband different, but the whole headstall is different.

A Cavesson Headstall is a convenience, but is certainly not a necessity unless you are to lunge the horse in a very large enclosure, where he might possibly break away from you (see Chapter 5). In a suitably sized yard where you should have little difficulty in holding your horse, you can use an ordinary halter and buckle the lunge rein on to the side dee — unless you have reason to anticipate trouble.

If you are likely to be lunging the horse with mouthing gear on, there is more to be said for the cavesson. Buckled to the cavesson, the effect of the lunge rein is quite separate from the effect of the side reins, which are usually attached to the snaffle. Figure 44 shows a Cavesson Headstall, or "Cavesson."

The strong noseband of a cavesson has a steel centre hinged at its front, the whole being well padded and covered with leather.

The Front Dee — Use not always Recommended

The foremost dee projects up to two inches to the front of the noseband. When the lunge rein is buckled to this dee it has a big leverage effect, which makes holding the young horse from the side much easier. Unfortunately, the same leverage effect also causes the

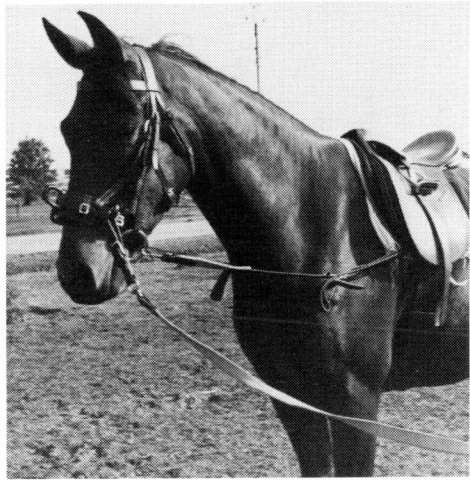

Figure 44: Mrs. Pat Hutchens' "Bey Peter" prepared for lunging. The side reins buckled to the snaffle are quite independent of the lunge rein, which is buckled to the cavesson headstall.

horse's hindquarters to fly outwards if the rein is used too strongly — often resulting in injuries by causing one leg to strike the other.

The same leverage also affects the noseband itself and tends to revolve it around the horse's head — creating a difficulty usually unseen by the man with the rein. As the noseband revolves it draws the headstall on the opposite side forward, where, unless precautions are taken, it will foul the horse's eye.

This will upset even quiet horses and cause them to resist.

To counter the revolving effect, two jowl straps are usually provided and both these and the noseband should be buckled quite closely.

The use of the foremost dee is not recommended for a young horse that will perhaps fight the restraint of the rein.

Later, when they are used, side reins will check the revolving effect of the rein fastened to the front dee and also, to some extent, the tendency of the hindquarters to fly outwards.

For the work we are doing at this stage, I recommend you use the dee at the side — usually. Each horse is different; check from time to time to see which is the more effective with your youngster.

Fitting the Cavesson

Like all the gear we use, the cavesson should be comfortable; and when the foremost dee is not in use, the noseband need not be buckled quite so tightly (be sure you read Chapter 2 of *"Horse Control and the Bit"* and note the disastrous effects of any worrying distraction).

When using a cavesson headstall together with a bridle, the cavesson should be put on first and the bridle on top of it, as the cavesson should normally be buckled closely.

On the other hand, an ordinary halter — if used together with a bridle — can go over the top of the bridle as the halter is loose-fitting and will not interfere and cause discomfort. *Uncomfortable gear distracts the horse's attention — making him more difficult to handle and to teach.* For the same reason, do not leave any gear on a young horse for long. Remove it and, if necessary, replace it after a short spell or after giving the parts it has pressed upon a good hand-rubbing.

Consider your horse all the time.

MOUTHING GEAR AND SIDE REINS

Mouthing gear can comprise just a pair of reins, adjustable for length, that run from snaffle to surcingle or girth each side of the horse, or it can include an especially made 'Mouthing Pad.'

Danny Fitzgerald's Mouthing Pad and Side Reins

Shown in Figure 45 is Mr Danny Fitzgerald of Cummins, South Australia, with his mouthing gear in use. The mouthing pad itself calls for no comment unless you are unfamiliar with the girth without buckles — a long thong runs from girth rings to pad ring, returns several times and, when tightened, is held by friction. Its free end can be hooked up anywhere: it is not necessary to tie the end.

This type of fastening is favoured, too, for saddle girths in the outback as it can be tightened from the saddle while a horse is still bucking. We are not interested here in riding them out like that — but

Figure 45: Mr. Danny Fitzgerald handling a young horse, "Waltzing Matilda" for Mrs. B. Lord, of Kolendo Station, South Australia.

I would like to draw your attention to Danny's most effective, simple, and inexpensive mouthing rein.

A single length of nylon sash cord is all that is used for the side reins. The photograph speaks for itself, but what is not easily seen is that the cord is passed through a small pully previously fastened to the top of the mouthing pad. This permits flexion of the neck to either side. The saddle-cloth is pulled well forward to prevent the ends of the mane catching in the pully.

Look closely — and you will see that the cord is also passed through the end links of a hobble-chain before going through the snaffle rings and back to the crest of the neck, where the ends are tied at the required length. One end of the cord then goes back and is tied to the crupper.

The several horses of Danny's breaking that I have ridden have all had very good mouths — and this might well be due to the *light weight suspended on the side reins when mouthing.*

This weight, about 6 oz. each side — keeps the snaffle in light and constant touch with the mouth without being heavy enough to worry the horse. It prevents the horse getting into the habit of 'dropping' the bit, while at the same time he learns he can not force the bit once the rein is stretched. He learns, before he is ridden or driven, the difference between a light springy hand which permits movements of the head and the same hand when it becomes resistant.

The idea of suspending a light weight on the reins I have found to be most useful with horses that will not "take" the bit. Such horses duck their noses in and refuse to take any pressure on the bars of the mouth. They are said to be 'behind the bit' and they will not permit a rider to keep a rein stretched, no matter how light the contact.

If used during the breaking-in period, the lightly-weighted side rein prevents the formation of this habit. It teaches the horse — before he is ridden — that as long as the rein feels springy he is free to move his head within the limits of that spring. It also teaches him that when the feel of the rein changes and it loses its spring-like feel, he will do best not to try to stretch it further.

I need hardly say that the young horse should first have been accustomed to the feel of a girth before using side reins of any kind — only when he has become relaxed to the saddle or pad should you think of adding anything more. As always, one thing at a time — and first things first.

Other Side Reins

I have shown Danny's reins and their fitting, but many people fasten the reins much lower down — on or near the girth. It is claimed this leads to the horse engaging his hindquarters more. This may well be so, but on the other hand the horse illustrated shows no sign of trying to avoid engagement of his quarters.

The best leather side reins have a short length of elastic sewn into them in such a manner that the rein is shortened an inch of so by the elastic. This warns the horse when he is nearing the limit of the rein. The elastic cushions the shock of a sudden resistance — but the horse can still 'drop the bit' by bringing his nose back and letting the rein hang loose.

Adjusting Side Reins

Whatever type of side-rein you use, always adjust it rather too long than too short at first. Give the horse an opportunity to learn to give to its constraint.

If put on too short at first, it can cause a horse to rear and fall backwards; do not risk letting your horse have such an experience. Horses do not forget these frightening things, and something similar even years later may cause him to repeat the action — perhaps with a rider up.

So adjust the side reins loosely at first, so that the horse has to stretch his neck to find the bit. As he comes to understand how to deal with the constraint, the reins can be gradually shortened. Keep in mind that the task is *not to pull the horse's nose in but to limit the degree to which he can poke his nose out.* It teaches him not to oppose the hand when the feel changes to resistance.

The practice of letting the horse stand for long periods in his yard with the mouthing gear adjusted is not recommended. As with all innovations, the first experience should not be a long one. If you want to leave him standing, it will do no harm but don't let him stand for more than 15-20 minutes at a time. It is better to give several shorter periods rather than one long one. Avoid giving the horse a sore mouth, but if he should get sore, remember there is nothing quite so good for abrasions than the old fashioned and inexpensive Zinc Ointment.

The full benefit of side reins is only obtained when the horse is kept moving forward once the reins are adjusted.

When the horse has started to lunge, it will be sufficient if you use the side reins only when lunging. Getting the horse used to the feel of the side-reins: letting him learn how to deal with them: forms part of the process of 'mouthing.'

TO SUM UP

A Cavesson Headstall gives a definite advantage when lunging the horse with mouthing gear on.

The cavesson should be buckled fairly tightly and is normally underneath other head gear.

Because of its excess leverage and revolving action, avoid using the foremost dee of the noseband.

Let the horse become accustomed to the feel of a surcingle or girth before adjusting side reins.

A light weight suspended on the reins teaches the horse to accept the bit.

Mouthing gear and side reins of any kind should always be adjusted very long at first, and only shortened one hole at a time thereafter.

The primary purpose of mouthing gear is to teach the horse to adjust himself to the reins, not to draw his nose in. It shows him the futility of fighting the rein and the advantage of yielding to it.

CHAPTER 10

FOR THE HORSE: THE "GO-FORWARD" LESSON
FOR HIS TRAINER: A LESSON IN TEACHING

Importance of Going Forward on Demand;
Preparation for the lesson; where to place yourself;
The horse's reaction; kicking at the whip;
This is more than the Go-Forward Lesson;
Teaching teacher to teach;
What the horse sees from a different angle to him is different;
Restraint in use of whip;
Benefits of the Go-Forward lesson are incalculable.

>   Old Chinese Proverb: "A
>   thousand mile journey begins
>   with a single step."

IMPORTANCE OF GOING FORWARD ON DEMAND

In one respect horses resemble most other forms of transport: to be able to do anything useful with them, you first have to be able to get them moving forward. So with our horse. If he will not go forward when required, he will be of little use to anyone.

So one of the first things we have to teach our youngster is to understand the various means used to indicate "Go Forward," i.e. voice, whip, legs and later the spurs and the seat.

Then he has to be brought to respond instantly to these aids. He has to be trained and schooled until ultimately his responses become automatic and compulsive: without trace of delay or reluctance. The response of a trained horse to the leg aids of his rider must be as instant, precise and as predictable as a motor car to its throttle.

It is a great advantage if your horse can be brought to understand and respond as well dismounted as mounted, and this is the lesson I suggest you give him as early as is practicable. You will find it most useful immediately; throughout his breaking in; later in his schooling and especially in difficulties met in his everyday use.

A well-trained cavalry horse, for instance, was required to precede or follow his rider, whichever was decided, through places that would have been inaccessible were he compelled to remain on the horse's back.

To negotiate an obstacle under a low branch or through a space like a doorway, for instance, the rider took his reins over, climbed over or through the obstacle — and the horse jumped and followed him *at the click of the tongue.* This was especially valuable in mountainous or in difficult country.

You may never need to call on your horse to do any such thing today, but you *will* want him to go forward into a horse box or float or other transport, or past something he is frightened of, or even to go forward tomorrow or next week on a lunge rein.

He should be taught this requirement deliberately and in a manner that will make it easy for him to understand what we want. Teach it long before you ride him; you will never regret it.

In Chapter 20 I explain how to use this Go-forward lesson to get the horse to walk quietly into a horse-float without hesitation. *Horses that have defeated every previous effort to load them usually walk quietly in after only one lesson.* The 'Loading Lesson' is a most interesting, instructive and sometimes almost incredible lesson to watch — and it has never failed with me so far.

PREPARATION FOR THE GO-FORWARD LESSON

If the horse to be taught is unbroken, then use the best yard that is available to you, one less than 50 ft. x 50 ft. if possible, and also a lunge rein that you can play out should it become necessary.

Handle the horse and if he is of a nervous disposition, move quietly about him until he calms down. If the surroundings of the yard are strange, let him have a good look around first. The calmer he is, the easier he will learn — ALWAYS remember that.

You can use either an ordinary stable halter or a special cavesson headstall. I also put on an ordinary snaffle bridle, which you will need for a lesson that may come shortly after this, lunging.

Put the bridle on, even if you do not intend to use it immediately; and, as a cavesson headstall has always to be buckled tightly, the bridle will go on over the top of the cavesson.

If you intend to buckle the lunge rein to the snaffle ring, first run a strap from one ring of the snaffle to the other, behind the jaw. String, several strands, will do just as well if a suitable strap is not available (see Figure 46). This prevents the snaffle being pulled through the horse's mouth should there be an attempt on his part to break free. It is also a wise precaution to take with any young horse, whatever you are doing with him (you can read more about this in Chapter 5, "Horse Control and the Bit").

I usually use a light, straight little runner from our plum tree, some 5-6 feet (1½-2 metres) long, for a whip for this task.

WHERE TO PLACE YOURSELF — WHERE TO STAND

When giving a young horse this lesson the first time or two, I like to have him near the rails or fence, which will be on his off side. Not so close that he feels 'penned in,' but about a metre away so that he cannot escape far to that side if he should feel inclined to do so. Thus placed, it makes it easier for him to do what is wanted and harder to do what is not wanted. Make the lesson as easy as possible for him — always.

When ready to begin, stand on his near side facing the same way as the horse, with your toes about in line with his forefeet (see Figure 47). With your right hand you will be holding the lunge rein near the ring of the snaffle. In the left hand will be the coiled end of the lunge rein and also the whip, with its end directed to the rear.

Keep in mind that this is to be a "Go-forward" lesson, "Go" forward, not "Come" forward which has been dealt with in Chapter 4. The horse has to be taught to GO forward; if anything, somewhat in front of you. You stay about in line with his forefeet: try to keep his head and neck in front of you the whole time — at this stage of the lesson.

BEGINNING THE LESSON

When you are ready, softly click your tongue.

One horse will 'jump a mile;' another will barely show interest.

You, on your part, should notice his every reaction. Study your horse all the time; never stop studying your pupil. Don't just dismiss anything you can't understand with the thought: "That's funny." *There's a reason for all strange or unusual conduct,* and it is for you to first note the behaviour, then to find the reason for it. Observe and then think — and think — and *think.* There IS a cause or reason for it.

If the horse does not move, allow a second or two and then 'Click' again. Only once, and then pause. (I am assuming you are dealing with a quiet young horse, remember). By the third click or so, he should be showing some definite interest and he *may* move. Some become excited at the first sound.

If the horse moves forward — or even displaces weight to the front, e.g. leans forward somewhat — make a fuss of him. Stroke him, "End of Lesson." For he has shown a tendency to do what you want of him: to move forward. Every *tendency* to move forward must be encouraged at this stage. *"That* will profit you," you show him.

Should he take a step to the rear, however, you also take a step to the rear; you maintain your relative position. "That will profit you not," you show him; and you keep clicking your tongue so that he will understand that backward movement will not profit him. No "End of Lesson" that way, you gently show him.

If, after a few clicks, he continues to stand still or moves back, or in any case fails to step forward, you begin to give him a very light touch or tap with the whip after each click: click-pause-tap; click-pause-tap.

To use the whip, carry the left hand, which holds it, as far back as possible. You remain in position and still face the front. Tap only very lightly with the whip — barely touch the youngster. He will, perhaps, get excited; but you must not.

THE HORSE'S REACTION

Running Back

Each horse behaves differently. Some get very excited and upset. Others just stand still, ears playing, eyes active, trying to make out what it is all about.

Don't hurry; don't show irritation or annoyance for he does not know what is wanted of him. He is willing, but can't yet understand. On no account get tough with him; nothing is more important at this stage than quiet deliberation, plus observation and thought.

If he runs back quickly and you are compelled to turn about and face him in order to move fast enough to stay with him, do so (see Figure 48); and when he stops (but not before), pause in your click-tap procedure for an instant or two.

To stop running back is an improvement on running back; and as it has to precede forward movement it has to be encouraged. At this moment the lesson he has to learn is: "Running back is wrong, and will get you nowhere. To stop running back is better, and will be encouraged — but, moving forward is *right* and will be rewarded."

Don't hang on tight in an effort to stop him when he runs back like this. Horses oppose force, and he is the stronger. Keep a light hold only, and as far as you are able go back with him rather than try to stop him. Try to keep with him and continue giving very light taps with the whip — not on his hindquarters now as they will be out of reach, but on the shoulder, as that is as far as you are likely to be able to reach.

Use no force and do not tap him harder with the whip than you could with a pencil. "Running back will profit you not," is now the lesson; and even though you are facing different directions, he will catch on — if *you* keep calm and keep him calm.

The Horse that Kicks at the Whip

The type of horse that stands quite still when you get to the whip-tapping stage will quite often kick at the whip before he tries anything else. He may have been standing quite still for several minutes while you have been 'click-tapping,' with only his ears showing he is noticing what is happening. It may seem quite a long time to you, but don't worry; don't put it down to stubbornness or any other 'nasty' trait of character. Just keep quietly on.

Figure 46: Preparations for the Lesson. (Ann Finger's "Ginger" — not a young horse). A length of string is tied from the ring of the snaffle and the riding reins 'put up' around the horse's neck.

Figure 47: The start of the lesson. The horse has moved forward a short step. The whip has stopped and my right hand is moving towards his neck to tell him he is doing well.

Figure 48: "Ginger" is stepping back and I have had to turn around to keep in touch with him. By continuing with the tapping I show him "That will profit you not".

Figure 49: A little later the pupil has grasped the lesson that only by moving forward can he stop the click-tapping. His worried look has gone and my right hand is touching his neck to let him know he is doing well.

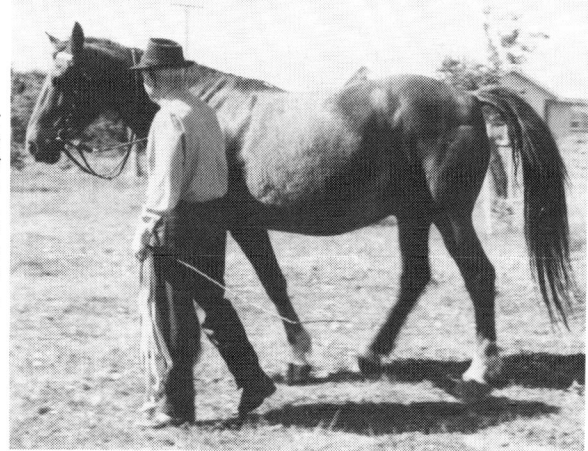

Figure 50: The horse has just made his first step forward with me on what he considers to be the 'wrong' side. My left hand is telling him, "He's clever", and "Ginger's" expression indicates: "Well, now! Evidently that click-tap means go-forward no matter where he stands!"

If he should kick at the whip in these circumstances he must not be punished, as he is only trying to get rid of the irritating whip in the same manner as he has learned he can deal with an irritating fly. It is most important that we try to understand how he sees things and what motivates him.

If, when he kicks, we quietly continue with our click-tapping, we are showing him: "That line will profit you not." He may try a few more kicks perhaps, and the later ones will almost always be harder than the first; but when he finds it does no good, produces no effect, he will eventually stop kicking and try something else. He will have proved that kicking at a whip 'profits him not'; that, itself, is a very worthwhile lesson.

To become tougher or harsher at this stage would be a mistake, because he obviously does not yet know what is the best thing for him to do about this new experience. He is trying to find an effective counter to this new irritation and he *must feel free to try.* How else will he find the correct answer?

Sooner or later, if we quietly persevere, he will move. It may be forward, sideways or backwards; and it is then up to us to encourage or discourage in appropriate degrees, as already pointed out.

> What I want to impress most strongly upon you is that anything the horse does will be an attempt to stop or avoid your click-tap. It will be an attempt to escape from — or cause the discontinuance of — this persistant click-tap: to free himself of it.

We must not show irritation or annoyance when he happens to try the wrong thing. We should welcome his efforts to try this or that until he finds what we do want of him, and *then* really make a fuss of him.

More often than not when we first encourage him, he is not quite sure (cannot quite remember) what he did that pleased us, and sometimes we may have to go through the same process several times before he is certain as to what action on his part 'ends the lesson.'

Be patient; watch and notice and think over all you see. Be sympathetic, too; remember that although millions of horses have been through this or similar experiences, he has not: and he hasn't a clue as to what you want him to do.

WHEN HE GOES FORWARD....

Don't keep him going. Stroke him, 'purr' to him — even if he takes only one step, and then gently stop him again if he does not stop himself. Rest for a moment or two. End of Lesson. And then start again when you are ready.

When he first moves forward, don't try to keep him going — because that means he gets no 'End of lesson' rest period, no encouragement. We want him to learn that this noise (the click of your tongue) means: "Move forward. If you don't go on, the whip will tap and worry you until you do — *then* it stops."

Start to encourage him while he is still moving forward, if possible; not after he has stopped.

Once he has learned the Go-forward lesson thoroughly, there is never any difficulty in keeping a horse going. Any time he goes too slowly or looks like stopping or going backwards, just demand: "Go forward," and that's that.

After three or four starts with progressively shorter rest periods between them, the youngster will have a good idea of what is wanted of him. Then, instead of stopping him as he will expect (because that is what you have been doing) just click your tongue again — which means go-forward or what is nearly the same, "Don't stop." It is the start-and-go-forward lesson we aim to teach him, so we stop fairly frequently so that we can start him frequently (see Figure 49).

Be sure you always stop him *gently* on these occasions: do nothing that will make him afraid to go forward, even if he should jump forward. Certainly you should watch out that you do nothing to lead him to conclude: "Going forward *may* mean a crack on the jaw is coming up."

THIS IS MUCH MORE THAN THE GO-FORWARD LESSON

The Horse Must Obey the Rein, Too

Once the horse is responding to your go-forward demand, you should also require him to answer the reins so that you can control the forward movement. It is clear that the 'forward' lesson is of little use if the horse can decide in which direction 'forward' lies. He has to be brought to check his pace or stop, as well as be kept moving in any particular direction we have in mind.

First, he has to learn to stop when the reins resist his further forward movement. This applies at all times, mounted or, as in this case, dismounted. He must not be *allowed* to acquire the habit of dragging you along by the reins. If he leans hard on the bit, give the reins a light vibration or two. Just enough to make the bit or halter a not-so-comfortable place to rest his head. If he persists with it, you must eventually give the reins a quite sharp vibration and make him learn to respect the bit, halter, or whatever you are using to control him.

Deal with this matter now. From the earliest days of his education he has to learn to keep light on the rein. Sooner or later you will need to load him into a horse float and it will increase your difficulties enormously if he has been allowed to ignore the rein or force your hand. See that from the beginning he is taught to respond to light rein effects — to respect the rein and the bit.

If your young horse is learning quickly and easily (which means your instruction is good), then you may ask for more — but not until the last section of the lesson is well understood and has been practised a few times. Remember, each lesson should prepare the horse for the next.

You might ask him soon now to go from a walk into a trot. Again, don't get sharp if he is a little slow to catch on the first time or two; maybe he was not prepared quite enough. In later lessons, though, you can become sharper if he continues to be slow off the mark.

Importance of "End of Lesson"

Before I go further, I should stress again how important it is in the beginning to call "End of Lesson" when the horse takes only one step forward — or makes *any* progress in *any* matter. On no account ask for more without first telling him: "That's right."

Surely you will see why?

He can try a score of things that are wrong and you will quietly tell him, show him: "Not that," "that will profit you not." How foolish of you then, when he does hit on the ONE thing you want him to do, if you continue tapping as if to say: "Not that," "Not that" — because *you want more.*

This policy applies throughout the horse's training: extending the paces, teaching the halt, the pirouette, the rein-back — everything he has to learn. Here, in this simple 'Go-forward' Lesson I might seem to be wasting my time on so small a matter. But this is not a small thing, this is 'IT.' We have to learn *how* to teach our horse.

If the horse is not learning quickly and easily, it means your instruction is not so good. Take credit to yourself if he learns quickly, but also accept the blame if the opposite is the case. Think over all you have been doing, particularly those things in which you are quite certain you are right. If the horse is not making good progress, you are in error somewhere — make no mistake about it, it is you who are at fault. You, the trainer.

TEACHING TEACHER

Why this detail

My aim in this chapter is to give two lessons, one to the horse, the Go-Forward Lesson, and one to his trainer. The apt man or girl will learn, while teaching the horse to go forward, the *main principles of educating a horse.*

If you first grasp the principles involved and then learn to act quickly on recognition of what should be done, you will have far less difficulty with the many other lessons you will have to give your pupil later on. It will give you confidence.

So not only have I gone into detail — but some details I have repeated, and will continue to do so several times.

The man or girl starting off with horse-schooling will not get results quickly. Allow yourself more time, and if you can, 'unlimited' time. Never commence any lesson without sufficient time to finish it should you run into trouble.

It is also good practice to give this lesson to any broken-in horses that may be about; give yourself a little practice on an older horse. It will be good for him, too.

Encouragement

Encouragement is the most important feature in the scheme of education of the horse; the young horse; and throughout his whole training. We quietly discourage any wrong or unwanted efforts and repeatedly ask him to try some other line of action — until we can convey to him, "That's right," or not quite so enthusiastically, "That's better."

Try and view it as the game children play, "Hunt the Thimble." Any move in the direction of the hidden thimble is encouraged by "You are getting hotter," "Hotter; or if the move is away from the hidden object: "You are getting colder," "Colder."

As long as the horse tries, you can teach him, so do not get annoyed at his wrong moves — make use of them for he has at least tried. How dare you punish him or show annoyance when he has done his best and has hoped to please you? How can he learn but by trying to learn? And he is trying.

When at last he tries to do or tends to do the one thing that you DO want, the important thing is to be able to convey your approval *instantly*. Two seconds later will be too late as he will than have difficulty in knowing what he did that pleased you.

For you, the teacher, the real test is your ability to recognise and immediately encourage the horse's slightest tendency to do right: in this lesson, to move forward. I should remind you again that if at first he as much as displaces weight, leans forward, it should result in your pausing momentarily in your click-tapping routine. Encourage even the slightest tendency to do what you want. He is looking for a way out, can you help him find it?

Working with a young horse brought up more or less in stables and not very frightened of humans, it seldom takes me as long as ten minutes to have him walking or trotting at the click of the tongue and with only an occasional touch with the whip.

I never, now, during this part of the lesson at least, tap harder with the whip than I could tap with a pencil. Later on we can become sharper — indeed, later on we look for things that might cause the horse to refuse to go on, so that we can justly use the whip a little sharper in order to impress the lesson. But not at this stage — not while he is still learning.

Whip Can Become Sharper

If you are doing the job well and he is doing well, the horse will begin to relax and show unmistakable satisfaction at his own cleverness; pleasure at his being so clever as to have worked out so satisfactory an answer.

However, when the first novelty wears off, he may just as clearly show that he does not intend to keep on doing it indefinitely. Any steps he might take to put this last thought into action must meet with instant disillusionment. A sharp flick with the whip and perhaps a somewhat sharper "NO" at the moment he shows any inclination to disobey or slow up in obedience, is usually enough. It is the promptness of your action rather than its severity which will register with the horse.

Here, again, we must be 'nice' to him the instant he behaves again; we must encourage him in doing right *particularly* after he has shown a distinct inclination to do wrong. We should seek co-operation rather than enforce servility.

WHAT THE HORSE SEES FROM A DIFFERENT ANGLE — TO HIM IS DIFFERENT

Changing to the Off-side

From your position on the near side you will eventually feel you 'have him' and you do not expect any difficulty just changing sides.

That, you will almost always find, to be quite wrong. More often than not, you will have to begin with all the care and attention you spent on the near side. With you on the off side, the horse often turns and faces you at first, as if (I sometimes think) to say: "I suppose you realise you *are* on the wrong side?"

Again, be tolerant. Take all the careful steps you took when on the near side. So many horses do not realise what is wanted, at first, that it cannot be just stupidity. I suspect it is we who are stupid, not being able to see things as the horse sees them. Once he gets the idea, however, much faster progress is made this second time (see Figure 50).

What is worth noting about the matter of changing sides is that you thought the horse had learned that the click of the tongue meant "Go Forward." He proves you wrong. He still has to learn that where you stand has nothing to do with what he has to do. Just think over this most important lesson he has given you, as this characteristic of his will show up in many ways, i.e. seen from a different angle, a different position, a thing to him *is* different until he learns otherwise.

Another instance of this characteristic: should you ride around any enclosed space that is strange to him, he will again exhibit this peculiar conduct. The young horse sees things when going around right-handed, say, and settles down after a turn or two; but change direction and move around the other way and he has to inspect and accept everything afresh.

Other Changes

A small jump, for instance: he learns to hop over it when jumping in one direction, but when later you put him at the same obstacle from the opposite direction, he may behave as though he had never seen it before.

We have *knowledge;* we know very much more than we suspect. But not the horse. He *sees* things; he sees things in relation to himself. He knows very little more than that which he learns from experience.

You may find this more difficult to accept than most things I am telling you; but whether you accept my theories or not, you will find with experience that the horse's position in relation to his surroundings and to you, affects him a good deal. Note and allow for this characteristic of his.

RESTRAINT AND THE SHARP USE OF THE WHIP

With some horses it pays to use the whip a little sharper, or even quite sharply, now and again. But we must not do this without good reason.

Start taking him into places where he may show reluctance to go: over poles laid on the ground, over very small jumps, through pools of water, or anything he may want to avoid. Later on you may walk him up to poles 18 inches to 2 ft. high — but instead of you stepping over with him, walk past the end and make him hop over. Gradually and progressively you increase your demands in small things until it becomes clear to him that he has to go forward when it is indicated to him — whether he would or not.

If, for any good reason you feel you should give him a sharp cut with the whip and you do so, do all you can to avoid having to repeat it. It is much better, much more effective, if you leave that sharp cut as an awful memory in his mind.

If you repeat it several times, it loses its effectiveness; it tends to become commonplace and perhaps he will find it quite bearable. The memory of a single sharp cut is much more effective — 'Familiarity breeds contempt.'

The whip is not to be used as a weapon but as an aid. It should have one purpose only — to enforce forward movement, or more prompt forward movement. I stongly advise against its use to produce lateral — — sideways — effects. *The whip plays one role and one role only: to demand and enforce forward movement.*

A horse that moves sideways away from the whip when it is used, mounted, can become a very real problem.

This, too, is why I say do not use the whip as a weapon: don't ever thrash him. The horse must not be brought to suffer the whip patiently. He has first to know that it means "Go Forward" — and be quite confident that he can avoid or escape it by taking that course, pronto!

Do not confuse your horse by giving it two meanings.

BENEFITS OF THE GO-FORWARD LESSON ARE INCALCULABLE . . . AND LAST A LIFETIME

What a lot to say about so small a matter. Or is it so small?

When we can say to our horse, and enforce our demand "Step to the front" —
- that is the end of . . . rearing
- . . . bucking
- . . . running back
- . . . refusing
- . . . shying
- . . . jibbing.

When we can enforce our will we don't have to worry about telling the horse: "DON'T do this," and "DON'T do that." In fact, we don't need to say "don't" at all. We just say: "DO...." whatever we have in mind.

This is a really important lesson and I am not in the least apologetic if I have repeated myself...well...repeatedly.

The late Lynda Colliver of Western Australia often said: "You have to repeat a thing 30 times before it is learnt" — she, too, taught languages.

TO SUM UP

Whether mounted or dismounted you must be able to obtain forward movement at all times and under all conditions.

Use a lunge rein, or other long rein.

Use the "It will profit you" and "It will profit you not" principle throughout.

Once the horse understands, insist on obedience.

Where the trainer is positioned in relation to the horse must not be allowed, eventually, to affect the horse's forward movement.

Only become sharp with the whip when, *knowing* what is wanted of him, he fails to move forward instantly.

The whip must not be used to obtain other than forward movement.

CHAPTER 11

EARLY LUNGING ... AND HANDLING

*Lunging — the beginning of serious preparation
Lunging follows the Go-forward Lesson
To stop or slow down — the voice helps
Keeping the horse 'out' when on the lunge
Don't hurry to canter
General handling — lessons other than lunging
Preparations for Saddling: girthing up usually starts trouble
Preparations for Shoeing.*

LUNGING — THE BEGINNING OF SERIOUS PREPARATION

Lunging marks the start of the serious preparation of the riding horse. During these lunging lessons we give the youngster a great many "End of Lesson" breaks and intervals, and these breaks can be used to accustom him to being handled all over the body and head, to prepare him for shoeing and to get him used to a saddle and bridle. He has also to be prepared for mounting and being ridden.

Mouthing, too, side reins, should begin after the young horse has been accustomed to the feel and constriction of a girth.

I advise you to take more time over this lunging and other preparation than would a professional breaker or station hand. For one thing, you have plenty of time and you would be foolish not to take advantage of it. Danny Fitzgerald has a favourite saying: "Don't hurry; you'll take longer," and I could well quote him on another point: "It you are frightened of the horse, don't start." He speaks with the voice of experience — great experience.

TEACHING YOUR HORSE TO LUNGE BECOMES A MATTER OF MINUTES ONLY — FOR ONE MAN

Teaching the horse to lunge presents little difficulty if the horse has first been given the Go-forward Lesson described in Chapter 10. Lunging itself is little more than an extension of the Go-forward lesson (see Figures 51 to 57) at first.

In the go-forward lesson you have been walking and maybe **running**

Figure 51: The youngster has taken no notice of the 'click' of the tongue and is now a little worried over the touch of the whip, as she does not know what it is or if there is anything she should do about it.

Figure 52: After several hesitations she realises that she can get rid of the light taps by moving forward. I have dropped the rein to touch her neck and 'purr' to her to let her know she is doing well. Her expression shows she is happy and relieved to find out what is wanted.

Figure 53: A little later she walks quietly on at the click of the tongue. "Old Hat" she thinks, as she keeps one ear on me and the other on another horse. I let the rein gradually slip through my fingers and hold it a little longer.

with your horse, and keeping him well ahead of you. To convert this into lunging you need only drive him a little further ahead and gradually play out — lengthen — the rein between you and your pupil. You get him to 'take' a little more rein.

As the rein gets longer, be sure you move out and away from the horse, not just further back. Don't get too far behind the line of his forefeet — not much more than a foot or so. At first, you may move away from him, moving somewhat into the centre as well as driving him forward and away from you. Later, he will be required to move forward and around *you*, with you standing still in the centre of the circle he is making. But that will be a little later.

Always watch that you do not come within range of his hind feet; gay youngsters are very apt to let fly, and you will be well advised to expect

Figure 54: Before long I am able to play out the rein a little more and change the whip into the right hand.

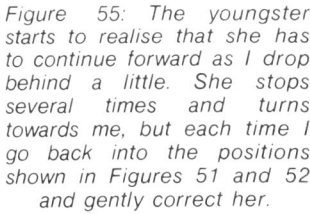

Figure 55: The youngster starts to realise that she has to continue forward as I drop behind a little. She stops several times and turns towards me, but each time I go back into the positions shown in Figures 51 and 52 and gently correct her.

101

and be ready to avoid it. (They often swing their quarters well in when they kick, and you may need all of a 12 ft. clearance). Don't mistake this for vice; it is just fun on the young horse's part — the effect, however, is the same whatever the cause.

End-of-Lesson Encouragements

You are starting off on a series of new lessons — and you must, as always, take every opportunity to encourage the youngster each time he begins to grasp what you want of him. When you can walk around with him a few feet from you, after a few moments stop and encourage him; avoid going too far too soon. "Make haste slowly," particularly if you are a novice yourself at teaching this lesson.

Every now and then he will stop and face you instead of walking on. In the early stages, it is always best and quickest to start again from the beginning when this happens, but see that he does not get a break or rest which would encourage him to stop again. *Immediately* get back alongside his shoulder and forefeet and start him off again. Any pause for any reason will encourage him to stop again, whereas you should be aiming to give him the: "That will profit you no!" discouragement.

TO STOP OR SLOW DOWN — USE OF VOICE

You will find the use of the voice a great help throughout lunging, particularly when you want to stop or change pace.

When you want to stop your horse once he is in the lunging stage, 'sing' rather than say, "W-o-o-o-y." If he does not stop at first, keep the rein lightly stretched and begin to move towards his front, shortening the rein as you do so. By 'move to his front' I mean take such a line that if you and the horse continued you would meet, with you slightly in front of the horse. Let your respective lines converge, with yours a fraction in front of his — this will require your line to be a curved one.

I like to have a few pieces of carrot, apple or a handful of oats in my pocket and give him a morsel occasionally when he has done well. Not big pieces: a 4-inch carrot I might cut into eight or more pieces. The horse learns to come in to you when you call "W-o-o-o-y" — and later on, when he is first ridden — you can cut short any threatening bout of bucking by just calling: "W-o-o-o-y!" I should say, though, that many professional horse-breakers do not approve of this practice of giving out tit-bits.

Not until the horse has been moving around you reasonably well at the walk on either hand, will it be time to think of trotting (see Figures 56-57). Again, use your voice and sing out: "T-r-r-o-t" several times. Say it quite clearly and crisply, and follow the demand with the go-forward click of the tongue. Later, if it is necessary, drive him quietly on with the whip. Take care to stop whatever you are doing the very moment he shows the slightest sign of trotting.

Figure 56: With many "End of Lesson" stops and encouragements whenever she behaves well, I have "Sheba" walking freely on each rein before asking for the trot.

Figure 57: A very short trot the first time. As in all lessons it is better to repeat a short lesson than to wear the horse out with a long one. She is loose and relaxed, and I then take her on the other rein and finish the lesson long before she becomes bored with it. Her first lesson in lunging has been a pleasant one for both of us. (Mrs Gaye Disney's "Sheba").

Before you get to this stage, you will have found it necessary to transfer the whip into your right hand (if you are working on the left rein, anti-clockwise). You will also find it useful now to change to a long lunging whip, if you have one, with a very long lash. Improvise one if necessary: it should be light and long itself, as well as the lash. You only want to reach him, not to thrash him.

KEEPING THE HORSE 'OUT' WHEN ON THE LUNGE

It will not be long before some horses begin to 'cut-in' on the circle and your natural inclination will be to loosen the lunge rein a little, or completely, when this happens. This is not to be recommended, as it results in the horse 'profiting' by doing something we do not want him to do. He soon notices: "If I cut-in, the weight on the reins gets less — so cutting-in is a good thing to do."

When he cuts-in, endeavour to maintain, to keep, the lunge rein stretched. Lightly, of course, but stretched just the same. At the same time lightly drive him forward more with voice or whip. *You* want him to move on a larger circle than *he* wants to. Try to get him to move on a line that is less curved, or (if you can agree) on a straighter line.

Keep the contact on the rein and drive him forward more, making sure the lunging rein does not hinder or oppose his outward movement when he starts to follow that line. Note that I have used and emphasised the word "keep." To 'keep' the rein stretched you must first have it stretched: to *keep* anything, you must *first have it.* Whenever the word 'keep' is used in these pages, it means exactly what it says: continue to 'keep' whatever it might be.

Should your horse persistently cut-in despite your forward drive and continued stretched rein, then you can, with a little practice, 'throw' a ripple of rein up towards his eye. You produce in the rein a ripple or wave along its length which, when it nears the horse's head, seems to move up towards his eye. It is produced in much the same way as the flicking of a towel or lash of a whip. This is quite effective when done well, but takes a little practice.

It may have to be repeated several times — and the horse kept driven forward at all times.

Start Now to Become a Little More Exacting

All these things tend to show the horse that he has to do what he is told once he understands and knows what he is being told. At first we make only small demands and encourage him with peace and quiet or a change of work for a short while as he complies. But as we progress we become more and more exacting.

> *Do nothing to encourage the horse to make decisions for himself; to anticipate. As soon as he shows any sign of anticipating your next move, make a small change. He has to wait for the order, for the aids; then you can think of encouraging and rewarding him. He has to learn to do what he is told — not to go through a routine performance. Aim to establish this relationship long before you are mounted on his back.*

Begin to concentrate now on getting your pupil to change smartly into a trot when you say 'Trot' and back again into a walk when you sing out 'W-o-o-y' or 'Walk.' Make no attempt to enforce instant obedience to the rein; there is no easy way of enforcing obedience to a stop on the lunge. Stopping easily is much more difficult to teach at any time than prompt and easy starting. Try to get easy, calm decreases of pace: quick stops are hard to teach and we should leave this matter to later lessons. Seek easy, light stops and decreases of pace rather than sharp ones. Prompt increases, but light decreases.

Use your voice to help the horse, and make a point of working equally to each hand.

Always go back to the Go-forward position if the horse stops and turns in to face you; don't get worried about it, just see that he does not profit from it in any way. After a few corrections he will know what is wanted as soon as you start to approach him and 'click' 'click,' your tongue. Don't *expect* him to know; *ensure* that he knows — teach him.

THE CANTER ON THE LUNGE

Don't be in a hurry to canter your horse, either now when he is on the lunge or later when you are riding him. In both instances the more schooling he has had before he takes the canter, the easier he will be to control. And that means, among other things, the less you will pull him about and hurt his mouth unnecessarily.

If he takes the canter himself while on the lunge, let him canter on if he is enjoying it. If he is checked each time he takes the canter unasked, we may give him the impression that to canter is wrong. That will only add to our difficulties when we do ask him.

When you decide the time has come for him to start cantering on the lunge, utilise a corner of your ground (you will be working him in an enclosed area) particularly if he seems loath to make the transition. ('Transition' is the word used to indicate the change from one gait to another, including to and from the halt).

If he changes into a fast extended trot at first, he will almost certainly go on to a larger circle, or try to do so. Remember that driving him on is what you have been doing to make him enlarge his circle.

His outward pull will cause the lunge rein to draw his head in towards the centre, forcing his hindquarters outward. Placed at such an angle it will be difficult for the horse to canter on the correct lead, which means it will be difficult for him to canter at all. Read what is said in Chapters 16 and 17 about the paces and then try to get the horse to take the canter as he *enters* a corner of the enclosure. With the corner fence stopping him moving outwards, you can loosen the lunge rein a fraction and he will be better placed to get away on the correct lead.

Except to *know* that it is easier for him to canter on the correct lead don't give a thought as to what lead he is on at this stage. When he makes the transition easily and stays relaxed, he will usually lead with the correct inside leg. It is correct because it is easiest.

Teach him, first, that when you sing out: "Can-ter" it means what it says, just canter. When he has grasped that, then later you can think about checking him back to a trot again with a view to starting on the correct leg. One thing at a time, remember.

Let the circle at the canter be as large as possible, and do *not* keep his head drawn in towards the centre. It often causes the horse to strike himself; it also makes cantering difficult and he will want to break back to a trot. The use of side reins will check this to some extent.

Give him only short periods of cantering, both on the lunge and when first saddled. In this lesson of the canter particularly, attend to all that has been said about End-of-lesson and 'It will profit you — it will profit you not.' Better not to canter at all on the lunge than plough around with the horse fighting you; if you have much trouble, he is not yet ready for the canter and more preparation is needed.

GENERAL HANDLING

Lessons Other than Lunging

In each of the many, many, 'End of Lesson' rewards you give the horse when teaching him to lunge, you should change the lesson rather than rest him. Go from lunging lessons to handling lessons, "a change is as good as a rest." Again, each horse is different. How quiet is he now? Can you already handle his head, his neck, his shoulders, his back, his hind-quarters — and his legs? Is he ready to accept mouthing gear?

Each time you stop the lunging you take your handling a little further. You end a lunging lesson and return to a handling lesson: one lesson yields to another and to some extent it adds interest and variety for both you and the horse.

By handling, I mean gently rubbing or stroking him with your open hand and even with as much of your arm as is possible. Let your contact be firm and over as large an area as you can manage, even letting your body contact him where it is practicable. Touching or stroking lightly with the tips of the fingers, you will find to have a disturbing effect on a nervous young horse. I quote Danny Fitzgerald again: "When you put your hand on your horse, do it as though greeting a friend — not as if you were expecting to put it on a spark plug!"

Don't forget to 'End the lesson' each time the horse permits your handling to go a little further; this encourages him to let you go further still next time. It soon becomes: "Old Hat." Do not end the lesson when he moves away from you or takes evasive action of any kind.

Move lightly and (apparently) casually from lunging to handling, until the horse takes little notice of what you are doing.

PREPARATIONS FOR SADDLING

When your handling has advanced sufficiently, begin to make preparations for putting on the saddle or mouthing gear. "Preparations for" — we should not just slap a saddle on his back and girth it up.

You can start handling him now with a piece of cloth in your hand. *Always let a young horse have a good look at whatever you are going to introduce him.* Generally, once a horse has touched a thing with his nose, he loses much of his fear of it; let him do this with all new gear, the saddle cloth, the surcingle, the mouthing gear and eventually the saddle. The saddle, hard and heavy as it is, comes last.

At first, whatever is put on his back should stay there only for a few seconds. It should then be removed and more lunging follow. Repeat this until eventually you can go up to him and throw the pad or surcingle over his back quite casually and leave it there.

GIRTHING-UP USUALLY STARTS TROUBLE

It is when a young horse feels the girth or anything similar binding his ribs for the first time that you might get a bout of bucking.

As soon as they feel it bind, most horses 'blow out.' That, of course, makes the binding worse and they often bound away and do what they can to get rid of whatever is on their back. Some squeal and put on quite a turn, and you occasionally strike one that for several days repeats the performance each time the girth is tightened.

Try to get the youngster accustomed to the feel of a surcingle or similar strap before you introduce him to the more frightening saddle with its many loose appendages. I usually use a surcingle and nothing but a folded piece of cloth over the spine at first, or, if it is for a foal, a stirrup leather is usually a better fit.

A single strap will not move about so much and so does not frighten the horse to the same extent. As it does not move about so much, you don't need to tighten it to the same degree until he has become used to it. Don't hesitate to take the single strap off a few times until he accepts it as 'Old Hat.'

Once he is accustomed to the feel of the strap, you can take the lunge rein off and let him loose if your yard is a good one. If he tries to buck a surcingle or stirrup leather off his back, what an "It will profit you not" task he faces. Don't try to make him buck, but if he wants to, let him. (The shape of some horses allows a loose strap to work back -- improvise a sort of breast-plate of binder-twine, if it becomes necessary).

When he is used to the girth or other strap you can start to put more under it or substitute the mouthing pad, side reins, and later the saddle. A mouthing pad is little more than a surcingle anyway.

All the lunging now can be done with something on his back.

It is never a good idea to tighten the girth fully when a saddle is first put on a young horse. Avoid giving him that initial fright, for some do not forget it for a long time. Each day when you girth up, just make it tight enough to keep the saddle secure; leave it at that for a minute or two or walk him a few paces, and then tighten it a little more.

With very young things that are really too young to ride, you can just put a folded blanket under the stirrup leather or surcingle, and rest the pup on it for a minute or two. Get him used to all sorts of odd things resting on the protective pad.

Be discreet though; you are not out to upset him but to get him used to things. You may want to carry a lamb or a child on his back later. If what you do frightens him, you have gone too far too soon.

Figure 58 and Figure 59: You can begin to prepare the horse for mounting even before putting a saddle on him. Mrs E. Jarvis is letting her "Narilla Beverley" feel some weight on her back for the first time. A few repeats and the horse will no longer be interested.

Move him with empty bags and such-like soft things on his back and let them drop off. When they drop, stop him and put them on again — until he realises that when something falls off, he is to stop. A handy habit for him to have acquired if you are in the Bush and miles from home.

PREPARATIONS FOR SHOEING

Picking up and holding the foot can be both easy and safe if properly tackled and is one of the several things that should be attended to before or during the lunging lessons.

You have been content to handle first his neck, then his shoulders, back and hindquarters, 'ending the lesson' and going on with your lunging each time he permits you to make progress. So, now, with the legs.

Divide the task into its parts: handling the legs first; then picking up the foot; and then holding the leg up while you examine and perhaps tap the foot. As always, you should not go on to the next task until the horse is quite at home with the lesson being given.

Start from the shoulder or neck, and by a number of short strokes, quietly run your hand down the shoulder towards the leg. Make progress by a succession of strokes or rubs, with each stroke going a little further than the last. Keep one hand on his shoulder (or rump) and go down with the other. Repeatedly stop and go back each time he permits you to go further (see Figure 60). Let your hand contacts be firm and keep as much of your hand and arm in contact with him as you conveniently can. Go a little further each time — and repeatedly go back again; go

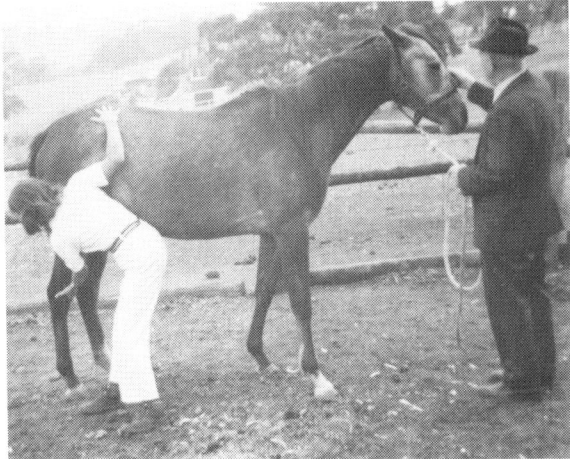

*Figure 60:
This young horse had shown a decided disinclination to having her off-hind leg picked up. Only the one leg proved troublesome and we tried the effect of a 'distraction': as she was still nervous about me I engaged her attention, which allowed Erica to work almost unnoticed. "Distraction" can be used to advantage, once you grasp the fact that it can be either useful or a nuisance.*

back a little less each time — and down a little more. Repeatedly 'end the lesson,' lunge him again and perhaps go on with something else.

Mix this in with all the other things you have to do with him; don't suddenly 'attack' his legs. Handle the near-fore this time, off-fore next. Leave the hinds till later. Let your fingers go well around his leg; get him accustomed to that, as you will shortly have to grasp his leg and try to pick it up. Let one lesson lead to the next.

Treat his legs as just another part of him — which of course they are — but remember, you will now be bending down for the first time and that itself disturbs some horses of the nervous type.

Don't attempt to pick his foot up until you can run your hand from shoulder down to fetlock without the horse showing undue concern. When you can do that, start to 'dwell' down by the fetlock, for until you can spend a minute or two at fetlock level, you won't have much chance of holding his leg when you do come to pick it up.

Picking the Foot Up

Like everything else to do with the horse, the more force you employ the more resistance you will meet. Horses resist force. If you grasp his leg and begin to pull on it, the very least the average horse will do is to put all his weight on to that leg.

To pick his foot up, he must first bend his knee and fetlock joints; so instead of wrestling with the leg — and several hundredweight of horse — try giving suggestive little taps or pushes on the back of the knee to indicate he might bend that joint.

To do this, he has first to take his weight off that leg. Taking the weight off the leg is itself a big advance, something that must precede picking the foot up; so you immediately encourage any such tendency by ending the lesson and back to lunging.

Your task is not so much to pick up the foot as to induce the horse to pick it up: induce him, persuade him, to do it himself. To *pull* the foot up off the ground requires a tight hold of the cannon bone or fetlock, and that itself can alarm a young horse. The tight grip of your hand, the force you may use, the stooping position you have assumed, all these things happening together upset many horses.

It is not that he will not do what you want; it is that he does not yet KNOW what you want. It is for you to take the time and trouble necessary to show him — remember you still have the hinds to tackle and you would like him to view picking up the foot as 'Old Hat' before you get that far.

When eventually you do get the foot off the ground, end the lesson immediately. Let him see: "Picking my foot up makes them happy and they stop worrying me."

Don't keep the foot off the ground until you can run your hand down the leg and get him to pick his foot up without any fuss.

Always run your hand down the leg by short progressive strokes and keep the other hand on his shoulder or rump — never reach down and grab his leg or fetlock without warning — even the most staid horse is likely to kick or strike if you do.

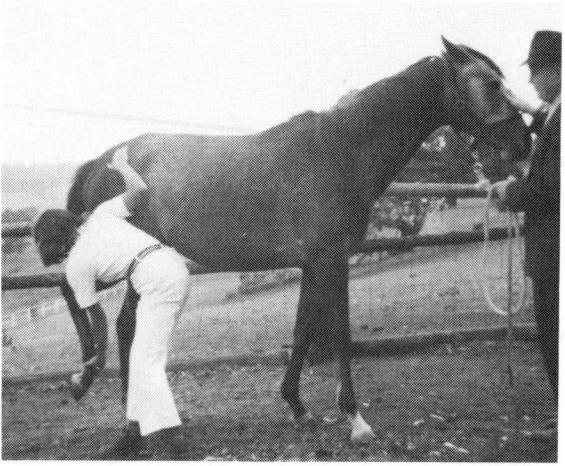

Figure 61: The handler should face the opposite direction to the horse when picking up a fore or hind leg. In each case the leg should be handled and picked up by the hand furthermost from the horse.

The handler should keep as much as possible of his own body and arm (the closest) in contact with the horse so that in the event of trouble he can push the youngster away or push himself away.

Holding the Foot off the Ground

Having now reached your second goal — picking the foot up — let the youngster get the 'Old Hat' feeling about it before attempting to keep the hoof up off the ground. When you do try to keep it up, let it be for a matter of seconds only. You may find it worries him less if at first you hold the hoof, not the leg. The clamp-like hold of the fingers adds to any misgivings he might have.

Let the foot down again before he tries to pull it free if he gives you a chance, but if he struggles and pulls it free, no end of lesson reward. Pick it up again immediately, and when he lets you hold it (by the toe) for a second or two, then let it go and rest him *before* he tries to pull it away. Stay with him if he resists, just quietly persist, for a while at least. Only end the lesson when he gives in.

Again, each horse is different and if he is of a nervous disposition, don't hurry him. Don't be grim about it. Take time, for again you are forming what may be a lifetime habit. What is a day or so at this period in his life? Keep in mind the degree of progress you have made — not the little hold-ups you meet.

Tomorrow, you should be able to go further again if you don't push him too far today. *You* have to prepare him for the blacksmith; it is the breaker's job to have him prepared. This includes getting him accustomed to some hammering of the hoof, and just taps with a piece of wood will do for a start. You have days, weeks or perhaps months. You will expect the farrier to shoe him in an hour.... Fair go!

WHEN THE FARRIER COMES

I need hardly say that when your Farrier comes to put shoes on, you should try to be present. The horse will appreciate having you, a friend there, when this stranger tackles him — the Farrier, too, will appreciate it.

When being shod for the first time or two, the horse should be held by hand rather than tied up. If you are holding him while the Farrier handles his hind legs, be sure that you stand on the same side of the horse as the Farrier, not in front and not on the other side. By pulling the horse's head towards you, you can throw the hindquarters away from the man working on the hind leg, if it should be necessary.

Think of your horse and think for him, too. If, for instance you see he is standing awkwardly when he has one foot off the ground, let the foot down again and next time you pick it up he will probably be better balanced. If flies are bad while he is being shod, throw a sheet of some sort over him for protection, and get a green twig from a branch to keep them away.

Keep him entertained — distracted — if you can, while the shoeing is going on; get his attention away from the Farrier. Children playing — not too closely — will hold his attention, or tie the pup where he can watch its antics: any 'distraction' that is not frightening.

Handling the legs and preparing for shoeing, like getting him used to a girth strap, is something that can be taught a foal in his earliest months. But whatever his age when you start on his legs, don't hurry — and don't resort to force. Don't leave the Farrier to do in one hour something that should be spread over many.

TO SUM UP

Teach the Go-forward lesson first; it merges into lunging and is easier on horse and trainer.

Work in an enclosed area.

Be alert to avoid the heels of a young horse on the lunge.

If difficulties appear, go back and repeat the last lessons; use the voice to help the horse understand.

Keep the circle on the lunge fairly large and the rein lightly stretched.

Demand instant starts and increases of pace as training progresses, but try to get easy, light *stops,* rather than fast ones.

Don't be in a hurry to canter; but if he takes the canter himself, let him bowl on for a while before checking him.

When you do decide to canter him, make use of the corners of your arena or enclosure. Try to teach him to canter on command; it simplifies matters a great deal later on when you want him to canter with the rider up.

Whatever handling has not been done should be completed during the breaks in lunging.

Let the horse have a good look at anything you want to put on his back.

Accustom the horse to the feel of a surcingle or strap before introducing the saddle and tight girth.

Complete one lesson before you start the next of that series.

Commence with the front legs and continue with the hinds only after he treats handling the fronts as 'Old Hat.'

Be present when the Farrier comes the first time.

Hold the horse by hand while he is being shod at first; see that he is standing comfortably and not worried by flies.

When holding the horse, stand on the same side as the Farrier so that, if necessary, you can move the hindquarters away from him.

CHAPTER 12

LUNGING ... AND MOUNTING

*Preparations for mounting; Check that all gear is strong;
Driving from over the saddle;
'He shall stand still while mounting and dismounting.'*

CHECK THAT ALL GEAR IS STRONG

Whatever saddle you are to use, be sure the girth, girth straps, surcingle and stirrup leathers are strong. I have had a girth strap break and very annoying it is — and bad for the horse, too. Make a point of using a surcingle over the saddle when eventually you do mount. A surcingle tends to keep the back of the saddle down when the horse puts his back up. The saddle is much less likely to work forward over his shoulders, too.

If you have been lunging with mouthing pad and side reins, you can continue to do so with the pad on over the top of the saddle. It has to be removed, however, when you start making preparations for mounting.

Stirrup Irons

When first lunging with the saddle on, run the stirrup irons up; but once the horse settles down they can be left hanging down. Don't leave the irons down, however, if you leave the youngster loose in the yard with the saddle on — or if you are to lead him through gates etc. They can easily get caught on the catches. I have even known a small pony kick at a fly and catch his hoof in a low-hanging stirrup iron.

Avoid small and light stirrup irons as they are dangerous. They tend to cling to the foot if rider and horse part company. Use plain *heavy* stirrups of steel or stainless steel (see Figure 11). Some non-rusting stirrup irons are of soft metal and can bend and wrap around a foot if the horse falls on his rider's leg.

LONG REIN DRIVING

Unless you have some special qualifications, such as being a trotting reinsman, I do not recommend you to attempt long rein driving. You can get into some nasty spots of bother with both reins running back to the saddle and the horse facing you.

Remember, I am writing, primarily, for the man or girl without experience in horse-breaking. Long rein driving can be a great help if done by an experienced person — but can be disastrous to the inexperienced. Don't try it. Try the following instead.

DRIVING FROM OVER THE SADDLE

I find it helps the horse understand the reins almost as much as a course of long rein driving to "drive him from over the saddle," as I call it, for a few periods before he is ridden (see Figures 62 and 63 and back cover).

It is easy, safe, and certainly helps the horse to understand what will be required of him when he is first mounted. Try it first in your yard.

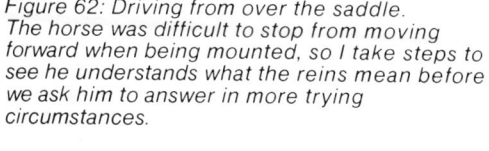

Figure 62: Driving from over the saddle. The horse was difficult to stop from moving forward when being mounted, so I take steps to see he understands what the reins mean before we ask him to answer in more trying circumstances.

Figure 63: In Figure 62 he is worried and not at all sure what is wanted of him. A few minutes later he has an idea of what we want and is more relaxed.

Place yourself alongside the saddle on the near side, facing the same way as the horse — as for the start of the Go-forward Lesson. Put your right arm over the saddle and take a rein in each hand, as if you were mounted. I carry an ordinary riding whip in my right hand so that I can tap him on the off shoulder if he fails to move when I click my tongue as in the Go-forward lesson.

I also keep the coiled up lunging rein in my left hand — for all these lessons go on in the breaks from lunging. In any case, the long rein might be useful if anything should go wrong. Why burn your bridges?

Now, from this position, I drive him about the yard. I don't move out of a walk, but I start, turn and stop him, and take him everywhere I will be likely to take him when he is first mounted. The only difference will be that he will then be carrying the rider. Everything else he will have experienced before — "Old Hat."

You will find this driving from over the saddle most useful. For the first time the horse will be required to turn away from the side you are on — and you will find he is quite reluctant to do so.

If you are on the near side, you may find it difficult to turn him to his right when first you require him to do this. You should quietly persist: just keep the right rein lightly stretched until he yields to it. Maintain the forward movement by clicks of the tongue and light taps on the shoulder if that is needed. On no account get rough with the bit.

If he hesitates too long, give the rein an 'Open' effect (see Chapter 18) by taking the right hand well out to the right. Maintain the light tension on the rein until he yields to it — whereupon you immediately cease your demands (see 'Yielding to the rein,' Chapter 4).

Practise this — and the Go-forward Lesson and lunging — on an older broken-in horse first if you have an opportunity.

Figure 64: When later his owner, Mrs. Lesley Thonemann, makes a similar demand, he understands and stands still when asked.

"HE SHALL STAND STILL WHILE MOUNTING AND DISMOUNTING"

The above is the first requirement of a well-schooled riding horse and we should keep this in mind throughout these pre-mounting days.

Note the words: "He shall *stand* still"... not "He shall be held still." HE must stand still (see Figure 64).

PREPARATIONS FOR MOUNTING

These include:

    ... gathering up the reins as for mounting;
    ... taking hold of the stirrup iron as for mounting;
    ... placing the foot in the stirrup and hopping close to the saddle, as if about to spring up.

Make each of these a separate lesson — and, as with every lesson, do not go on until your horse stands quite still throughout that particular lesson.

The first step is gathering up the reins preparatory to mounting.

Keep the coiled up lunge rein in your left hand, free the riding rein from wherever you have had it fastened (usually tucked under the stirrup leathers), and go about gathering the reins up and shortening them as if you were then and there going to step up into the saddle.

Gather the reins carefully, and see that you have an equal length each side of the neck when you lower your hand on to his crest or mane.

The reins should be slightly loose when your hand is resting on his neck.

If he moves forward, tighten them by moving your hand back a little: stop his forward movement and then loosen the reins again. Show your approval by loosening the reins again when he stops — you want him to know that to remain still throughout the mounting process is what is required.

If he moves backward, don't try to stop him but move back with him. Maintain your relative position as I advised in the Go-forward Lesson of Chapter 10; show him "That will profit you not." When he stops moving back, gently and quietly go on with your rein gathering and hand placing as if you had not noticed his movement.

I recommend taking this course with *any* horse that will not stand still for mounting. Gently stop his movement by use of the reins if it is to his front; and just quietly move back with him if he should move backwards. Do not hurry; quietly persist. "End of lesson" for a moment when he stands. I have never known this procedure fail; and it is quiet, gentle and easy on both horse and man.

Make use of the opportunity to give the horse a lesson in obedience to the reins if he moves forward un-asked. Stop him with the lightest possible stretching of the reins. Do not hasten to get heavier, even though your light contact seems ineffective at first. Give him an opportunity to notice what is happening — and immediately loosen the reins again when he stops.

Treat it as a misunderstanding if he does not stop immediately you stretch the reins. Be patient with him. Do all you can to guard against his associating your gathering up the reins for mounting with his mouth being hurt: when he is hurt, the horse worries rather than studies our actions.

You usually have to go through the gathering up of the reins routine several times — repeat it as often as is necessary in the breaks between lunging. He has to learn to stand still throughout the whole of the mounting process.

Keep in mind all the rules for teaching: "End of Lesson;" "It will profit you" and "It will profit you not." Gather the reins, shorten them, throw the end to the off side; and keep working at it until he takes absolutely no notice of what you are doing. From the very start, he has to learn to stand still.

> These things I am writing take much longer to write than they will take you to do, but a moment or so now may save you no end of trouble later on. "Don't hurry: you'll take longer."

When your horse stands still while you gather up your reins as if to mount, then and not before, start to take hold of the stirrup iron as if about to put your foot into it.

If he stands and takes no notice, repeat it a few times and then start to raise your foot towards the stirrup. Should he move when you lift your foot, then repeat this, too, until he takes no notice; and, of course, you continue to do all this between bouts of lunging.

Occasionally put your arm over the saddle. Prepare him for your leg suddenly appearing on the off side, although driving from over the saddle prepares him for this too.

Don't think to attempt to mount until you can gather up your reins quickly and correctly, take the stirrup iron in your right hand, put your foot in the stirrup and hop around and grasp the saddle without any movement or great interest on the part of the horse.

Repeat everything to both sides between sessions of lunging, before you think of going further — laying across the saddle. Indeed, when you have a youngster at home, all this can be done months before you think of actually riding him. Run through it any odd time that is convenient to you.

AN ASSISTANT WILL BE USEFUL NOW

You have prepared the horse as if you were about to mount in the usual way, which, of course, you will do eventually. However, unless you are young and agile, the saddle gets quite a pull mounting in this way and the horse may find it upsetting. If you are working alone, you will have to mount using stirrups; but the people I have in mind to help should have an assistant now.

It is best if the man doing the lunging remains in charge, on the ground, and the assistant be put up. The assistant, after the horse has become familiar with him, stands facing the saddle, holding the pommel and cantle. He can jump up and down a few inches to prepare the horse for what is to come, and eventually the man with the lunge 'lifts' him up a foot or so — and immediately lowers him again. "End of Lesson" (see Figures 65 and 66).

Lunge, repeat, until the assistant can be left leaning across the saddle, most definitely 'feet heavy': ready to drop down on to his feet at any moment. Repeat .... repeat .... until, if you like, you can move the horse a pace or two with the rider leaning over the saddle.

Again, don't be in a hurry. Repeat the lifting both sides until the horse thinks nothing of it. Then, all being calm and quiet after moving the horse a few times with the rider lying across the saddle, he puts his leg over it. He sits there *for a moment only,* and then dismounts quietly — and lessons are ended for the day.

If the horse is uneasy, immediately dismount, but no rest yet. A short run on the lunge and repeat. When he stands relaxed and quiet for a moment, dismount and finish for the day.

Tomorrow he will come out and it will be "Old Hat."

Dismount carefully. See that your right foot is well clear of the stirrup iron before you attempt to take your leg over his back to the near side; and see, too, that your left foot is placed so that it can easily leave the iron. Many knowledgeable people recommend dismounting with both feet out of the irons.

 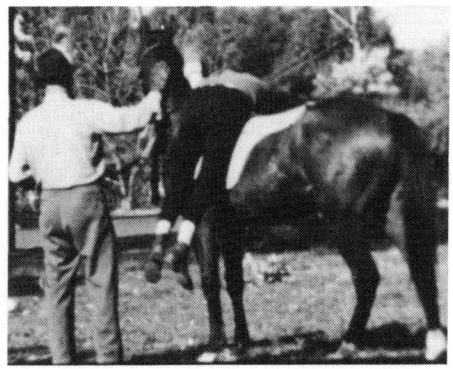

Figure 65 and Figure 66: Using my knee as a step, the owner Mrs Christine Black, rests across the back of her youngster "Reo" before quietly dropping down. These steps can be taken at any convenient time, in this case with only a felt saddle-cloth under the mouthing pad. This is all part of the horse's lunging prior to mounting.
Notice the disturbed look of the horse in Figure 65, and a little later on, in Figure 66, when he is more interested in other things. It is becoming "Old Hat."
(taken from 8mm demo. film by Prestige Studio).

Make no sudden movement which may cause the horse to jump. Now and again we meet a horse from which it is difficult to dismount and it is both a nuisance and dangerous. Be deliberate in all your movements, and take precautions not to upset the young horse during dismounting.

Many coltbreakers draw the horse's head around short to the left and spring up into the saddle to sit out whatever follows. To take this course you need either a well-built stockyard or a wide open space, and it is hardly suited to the amateur. You will do best to follow my recommendations and see that your horse *"Stands still while mounting and dismounting."* Have your reins of equal length so that you can use them should you want to.

* * *

We have gone to some trouble to prepare the horse for his rider. Maybe it is not always necessary, but better take too much trouble than too little.

A horse's good habits, once acquired, often pass unnoticed. But a bad habit, once acquired, can be a real nuisance and is continually forcing itself upon our notice. Almost all bad habits *can be rectified* and we should never accept them as being incurable —but correction is much more difficult than preventing the habit forming.

If you are fond of a horse and wish to do him a real favor — train him well. Teach him good manners, good habits, both in the stable and under the saddle. You need never worry about the future of such a horse if for any reason you may have to part with him. *You assure him of friends wherever he goes.*

Perhaps the greatest kindness you can do any horse is to educate him well.

Figure 67: Danny Fitzgerald — who works alone — sitting on Mrs. B. Lord's "Waltzing Matilda" for the first time in the yards at Kalendo Station.

TO SUM UP

Let the horse see and touch everything that is to be put on his back, and let him become accustomed to the binding of a surcingle or girth before the saddle is fitted. One thing at a time.

Do not attach the mouthing (or side) reins until the horse is quite at home with the saddle or mouthing pad.

Use a strong saddle and a surcingle, too, for the latter tends to stop the saddle working forward on to the horse's shoulders.

Avoid long rein driving unless you are a reinsman or have other experience.

Insist on the horse standing still through all the preliminaries leading up to mounting. Repeatedly correct him and don't go on until he stands.

Inexperienced handlers should obtain the help of another person for the first mounting. Don't change the person in charge of the lunging at the last moment.

Lift the rider up and down a few times and let him lay across the saddle before putting a leg over the saddle.

Finish work for the day as soon as the horse has stood quiet for a moment or two under the rider.

DO NOT HURRY. Hurried, nervous mounting upsets the horse and may put progress back several days.

CHAPTER 13

THE FIRST FEW DAYS UNDER THE RIDER

We go back to the lunging: the man with the lunge rein stays in control at first;
Taking control from the saddle; the first trot;
Repeat rather than prolong a lesson;
Vary the paces; avoid possible causes of shying;
Don't 'hang on.'

> "His horse who never in that sort
> Had handled been before,
> What thing upon his back had got
> Did wonder more and more —"
> (John Gilpin)

THE SECOND DAY UNDER THE SADDLE AND ON

Yesterday we mounted, sat in the saddle for a moment only, and dismounted. We then not only ended the lesson but also terminated the day's work, having deliberately timed it for the mounting to occur at the end of the lesson.

Today we do almost exactly the same as we did yesterday; lunge, handle, go through the preliminaries of mounting without actually doing so, and then — all being satisfactory — we again mount with all the care and preparation of the first occasion. Sit there for a moment only, and dismount.

Keep in mind that this is still a lunging lesson and the mounting preparation or practice goes on between periods of lunging. So, having mounted and dismounted, return your pupil to lunging.

Stop repeatedly. Again go through all the preparation for mounting, and notice all your youngster's reactions. Does he show dislike, nervousness or unrest, when you get to any particular part of the routine: picking up or shortening the reins, putting your foot in the stirrup, passing your leg over the saddle — or anything else?

If he moves or shows unrest, go back. Not to the start but a stage or so; and keep going back and coming up again until he remains quite still. When he does remain still *then* you may stop and 'end of lesson' and go back again to lunging if you like.

Include also more of the driving from over the saddle. Get him at home in that practice.

After you have mounted (or your assistant) and sat in the saddle a few times, the horse can, if he appears to be quite relaxed, be led forward a step or two. Lead him rather than drive him at first.

Continue to mount and dismount, mount and sit for a moment, lead forward, halt again and dismount. Move a little further each time. Halt and dismount and give him a little more work on the lunge — until he starts to look upon the work under the rider as a pleasant break in the more demanding lunging.

THE RIDER STARTS TO TAKE CONTROL

The rider should not be in a hurry to take control. *Let the man with the lunge stay in control,* and he should now be lunging the youngster with the rider up — at a walk.

Little by little the man in the saddle begins to take control: should anything go wrong, however, it is for the man with the lunge rein to take charge again and he must keep in mind all the rules for holding a horse from the ground (Chapter 6).

Gradually the use of the rider's legs takes the place of the click of the tongue, and the use of the reins to stop is only helped occasionally by the voice of the man on the ground. Don't hesitate to dismount and give the horse a little faster work on the lunge, but don't excite him.

He will learn much quicker if you don't hurry him. You have two things to teach him:
   1) to tolerate the rider on his back; and
   2) to understand the rein and leg aids.

At first the rider should sit reasonably still in the saddle, but as the horse starts to become more relaxed, the rider, too, can relax and begin making small movements. Remember, you will start bumping about in the saddle when he trots — gently prepare him for that.

The rider should on no account hang on to the horse's head with the mistaken idea that it will prevent him bucking. It hurts and worries the horse and often provokes the very action you wish to prevent. Better you hang on to the saddle than on to the reins — and leave control to the man on the ground. It is a good idea to have a 'monkey strap' on the saddle — you probably will not need it, but it will make you feel more confident and relaxed to know it is there.

If, during the early stages of lunging you have made a practice of giving the young horse a titbit when he comes up to you after your call of "W-o-o-y" — and the man with the lunge sees him becoming upset or uneasy with the rider up — a call of "W-o-o-y" will distract the youngster (Where's my piece of carrot?) and so stop whatever he might

Figure 68: Miss Robin Wilson and her "Diana", who was gradually accustomed to a rider rather than broken-in. Robin is about to take a rein in each hand after mounting. Notice "Diana's" ears, showing her relaxed but close attention to her rider.

have been thinking of doing. Next time the same condition applies, he will view it as 'Old Hat.' This is better than trying to 'sit out' whatever he might have intended to do.

Teach the horse as much as you can first on the lunge, and then with the lunge rein removed, the work continuing as though the lunge rein were still connected. Stop, start; stop, start, stop, dismount, mount; and so on as if he were still being lunged.

Do everything at the walk with the rider up at first. If you need to do a certain amount of faster work to let out some of the young fellow's surplus energy, work him on the lunge at the trot and perhaps the canter, first with an empty saddle and later (and steadier) under the rider.

Go Back to Lunging

Don't hesitate to put him back on the lunge if you have any reason to do so. Be ready at all times to go back a stage or so, particularly if he is inclined to 'play up' under the rider.

Whatever you do, don't get off him when he is inclined to play up. It is very easy to cook-up a good excuse to do so, but don't do it. Stay with him until he quietens — and then give him some harder duller work on the lunge again.

THE FIRST TROT

There is no need for the horse to be trotted with a rider up the first day or two; and when you do trot, only cover a few paces the first time you do so each day.

Nervous young horses tend to get upset when first they get trotting and cantering, so why rush it? Let the trot be short, very short the first time each day until you get to know how he reacts; trot a few paces and then walk again before anything goes wrong. This checks many a little spree by the horse.

When I am instructing a group of riders, several of whom are on young horses ready to skip about when first moved on at a faster pace, I counter this tendency by using the 'Old Hat' technique.

First I prepare the riders. I say: "We are going to trot in a moment. Get ready to trot. We are going to trot only a few paces and then drop back quietly into the walk again. Are you ready to trot? Quietly: trot now. Quietly."

I may only allow them to trot some dozen paces or so and then I say: "Trot no further. Walk now. Trot no further. Walk. Relax and make your horse walk out. Walk on; walk out."

This is a trait with horses, a characteristic that we do well to keep in mind for it can save much trouble. A horse put into a strange place the first time will settle down much more quickly if he is taken out after a few minutes and then put in again. When a thing has happened before and no harm has come from the experience, it somehow seems to reassure a horse.

REPEAT RATHER THAN PROLONG ANYTHING NEW

Follow this practice with your young horse. Only trot (or canter, when you get to that stage) a short distance the first time each day if he is in any way inclined to be nervous or gay. Then go back to a walk, and get him calm again before you repeat your demand. Watch and feel what his inclinations are — and act accordingly. Repeat the trots rather than prolong their length if the horse is in any way unsettled; the bumping and other movements of the rider when trotting are new and alarm some horses at first.

The second time, he will be much calmer if things went well the first time, no matter how short the first experience was: 'Old Hat.'

With a class such as I mentioned just now, a few minutes later I may ask them to trot on again and perhaps go a little further. It depends upon how the horses behave. Again I watch them closely and if I see even one of them not settling down, I take them back to a walk again. 'End of lesson' *before* things go wrong. In any case, what's wrong with a few starts and stops? Treat your young horse this way, too.

By the end of the third day after mounting, you should be walking and trotting around your yard without incident. Remember, you don't have to ride him every day, particularly if he is very young. Put him back on the lunge and the mouthing gear without hesitation. It will do more good than harm.

Not very long ago I had to do the first re-ride on a youngster (she had been broken in and then spelled) around the streets here in

Richmond. Wishing not to upset her with a rider up for the first time in months and in such strange circumstances, I first drove her from the 'over the saddle' position as shown in Figure 63 and on back dust cover, around the streets where I proposed to ride her.

I need hardly say she was a quiet gentle little thing, but nevertheless she found a lot of strange and weird things to stop and stare at. Next day I rode her around the same course, and we made only an occasional stop for a second look at something.

On later rides we went around the opposite way and then each day I introduced a variation of the course of one kind or another.

Don't fight their weaknesses — take advantage of them. A little slower perhaps the first day or so, but much more satisfactory for horse and rider in the long run.

AVOID LONG PERIODS IN A MANEGE

How long will you work your young horse in your yard or other enclosure? This will depend upon how big your piece of ground is and what other ground is available — and within easy reach. Going round and round in a small arena becomes extremely boring: if there is another area or paddock at hand, start to use both of them. Go from one to the other and then back again.

Walk around the other paddock at first and with as loose a rein as is practical. Dismount and drive him from over the saddle if you prefer, but in such a case put the lunge rein on again as you had it at first. Just walk around the new paddock once and back again to the old one — next time you go there, he will be much more assured: 'Old Hat' again.

These days, when everyone wants to do dressage, there seems to be an idea abroad that you should school your horse in a small arena; I advise you not to stay there for **more than half an** hour on any one occasion, unless you are in a class. Introduce variety when you can.

Alternating between lunging and riding makes the time pass a little quicker for the youngster and breaks the period somewhat, but once you have reached the stage where you **can** mount and ride without lunging, twenty minutes in the manege is long enough; half an hour a possible limit: then a walk around the paddock.

Very young horses, particularly, should not be kept going round and round for long. **They are not mature** enough to stand long periods of work without damage to their legs. In addition, horses of three years or less should have at least two days a week without work and, to their advantage, can also spend six months or more turned out in a field or paddock.

AVOID FRIGHTENING SIGHTS AND SOUNDS

Keep the young horse away from strange sights and sounds as long as you can. Away from things that may cause him to shy and where you, particularly if you are not sure of yourself, are likely to treat his mouth roughly. Not only will he have difficulty in understanding the demands of the bit which will be new to him, but whatever he is shying at will be more important than the bit (I have more to say about shying a few pages later on).

The ideal condition for early schooling is to work the youngster on his home ground, where he knows and is accustomed to the surrounds and where distractions are minimised. When you do take him further afield, the company of a staid, stolid, well-behaved companion horse is invaluable.

DON'T "HANG ON"

If at any time you feel a spot of trouble coming up, don't hang on to the reins and hope for the best. Don't wait for the 'explosion'. Instead, gently start asking your youngster to *do* something. Making him do what YOU want stops him from doing what he wants to do, and this is the best way to deal with this sort of situation.

The continuing pain to his mouth caused by your hanging on to the reins causes the horse to try something — anything — that might bring him relief. Your usual demand *should* be: "Move forward and with long steps." ("Long steps?" I could imagine him moaning if he could talk, "Long steps will ruin my bucking technique — I want 'fun and games' not long forward-striding steps"). Make clear and easily-met demands on him and avoid being rough handed.

Nothing provokes a horse more than continually hanging on to his head. Only too often he learns that getting rid of his rider brings relief to his mouth — and so, "That is a good thing to do," you have taught him!

LOOSE REIN WORK

Do a fair percentage of work on a loose rein each day as soon as you can (see Figure 69), first at the walk and later at the trot and canter.

He has to learn, as time goes on, to maintain both the pace and direction he has been set before the reins were loosened. At first you will have to pick up the reins repeatedly and correct him: do so, and as soon as he is corrected, loosen them again. He will quite quickly learn that a loose rein does not give him freedom except to stretch his neck and relax.

Figure 69: Mrs. Pat Hutchens at a later stage with schooling still reverts repeatedly to a loose rein. She is taking a walk outside the dressage arena after "Bey Peter" has done a task well.

VARY THE PACES

After a few days or weeks — for there is no hurry — occasionally practise walking and trotting a little faster or slower. Walk out and walk slow, at different times. The same with the trot: trot out, and trot slow; trot out, trot slow; for short periods.

It is important your horse learns to vary the paces.

One very good reason for doing this is to prepare him for the time when you ask him to canter. The first time or two he canters under a rider is almost always at a faster rate than is required, and unless we have accustomed him to variations of pace at the walk and trot, we will have trouble getting the message through to him at the more difficult canter.

You will remember I advised you, in the chapters on lunging, to allow the youngster to canter on for a while if he takes that pace on his own initiative. This applies, too, when you are mounted, unless the circumstances are unfavourable. If he quietly takes the canter, let him roll on for a while and then return him to a trot or walk.

Teach everything quietly and calmly. Prepare the youngster for the next lesson as far as you know how, but when he does understand and knows what is wanted, then you can and should become progressively more demanding in that particular matter.

You should certainly not be looking for perfection, but you must expect and demand progress and improvement. This will mean that in the same half-hour or session, you can go to the extreme of patience and tolerance when leading off into a new lesson and either a short time earlier or later, be quite demanding if asking for something the horse now understands. He has to respect your demands as well as understand them.

LET HIM HAVE A RUN LOOSE, DAILY, IF POSSIBLE

The more boxed-up or yarded the youngster is kept during his breaking and early riding days, the more likely he is to 'let off steam' when you take him out for his ride. Give a young horse the run of a paddock some part of every day if you possibly can. Even a short spell outside before you ride him will help. His tricks when loose may frighten you out of your wits if you watch him, but when he comes in again he will be feeling: "Ah! That's better!"

This is another advantage of being out of town with a horse to be broken in. Allow at least ten minutes, though, for him to calm down again after his frolicking.

Too Much Grain Feed

If he comes out 'too full of himself' regularly: in addition to putting him on the lunge for a while, consider increasing his bulk food, hay, etc., and cutting down on his concentrates — oats, grains of all kinds and other high protein foods. Not only is he a nuisance when he is over fresh, but he can do damage to his limbs. Good feeding does not damage a horse. A young horse should not be doing enough work to utilise grain foods — concentrates.

WHEN IN DOUBT

When in doubt as to how to deal with a difficulty I have not foreseen, go back to Chapters 1 and 2 and read again the general rules governing training processes.

'Introduce only one new thing at a time' is a cardinal rule and where a lesson (anything new) can be broken into several parts, do that — and teach each part separately. You can run them together later.

Our Aims: At this stage of his training, we should aim to get *light easy responses to the rein* rather than quick stops and turns. On the other hand, we should aim at getting prompt and *immediate* attention to the legs:

    ... light responses to the reins plus

    ... light and immediate responses to the legs.

TO SUM UP

Always go back over the last day's lessons before going on.

Treat the early work under the rider as just another part of his lunging work.

Don't 'hang on' to the reins in the mistaken idea that it will prevent the horse playing up. It hurts and worries him and he may find putting you down to be the only way to get relief. DON'T HANG ON TO THE REINS.

Stay on the lunge; let the man on the lunge maintain control at first — and if trouble comes up, leave it to him to deal with it. Better you hang on to the saddle than to the reins.

When the lunge rein is taken off, there is no need to hurry. Continue with the same work and in the same place, for a while at least.

Don't keep working the young horse in an enclosed area until he gets fed up — and when you do leave his breaking yard, don't take him near strange and frightening sights. If you are compelled to, then get the company and example of a staid old horse.

If your youngster is very fresh in the early days, work some if his energy off on the lunge.

Encourage every sign of progress; when he does anything well *do let him know it.*

Aim at getting instant obedience to the legs as time goes on; but aim at light, rather than speedy, responses to the reins. *Remember he cannot be light if you are heavy handed.*

Read what is said in "Horse Control and the Bit" (Chapter 2) on the *correct fitting* of the saddle amongst other tack — you are certain to run into trouble if the gear, the saddle particularly, is hurting — even if it is only occasionally. Borrow the book if you haven't one and read Chapter 2.

CHAPTER 14

GETTING AND KEEPING A LIGHT MOUTH AND HAND

Control from the saddle;
A good rider is essential to the training of a young horse;
Don't think 'Pull up': think 'Go no further',
A simple trial 'Just for fun';
'Limited resistance; With how little force can we control our horse?
Changes in pace.

CONTROL FROM THE SADDLE

Legs Without Hands : Hands Without Legs

Much depends upon how you act in these early days, particularly during these first short rides. Don't worry the young horse into fighting the reins, which should be held lightly and long in the hands. Whatever you do, do NOT use your hands and legs together — at the same time — either in these early days or for a good many months yet.

The guiding rule of the dressage experts for all the early work is: 'Legs without hands; hands without legs'. This does not necessarily mean that you loosen the reins when you use your legs; it means that your hands should not *act*, i.e. get stronger, at the same time as you use your legs — or vice versa. So, when you use your legs, when the legs become active, you must see that the hands are passive — not active, resistant or pulling. Better, much better at this stage, to loosen the reins completely when the legs are active than to hang on to them.

A good Rider is Essential to the
Training of a Young Horse

It is the failure to get easy and light responses to the hands that seems to plague the inexperienced rider most.

Riders who have had the benefit of beginning their riding on well trained horses will have a great advantage in this matter. A well-schooled horse will respond correctly to light pressures of bit, rein or leg, and this gives the rider an opportunity to learn that being rough or heavy-handed is not only unnecessary but that it usually provokes resistance from the horse.

The dressage experts say: "A trained horse is essential to the training of the rider," and: "A well-trained rider is essential to the training of a young horse."

Another apt quotation is: "The best instructor a rider can have is a well-trained horse".

Only too often the rider who has not had the advantage of riding a well-schooled horse starts off with an idea something like this: "If you pull on one rein, the horse should turn that way, right or left; if you pull on both reins he should stop. If he does not turn, or stop, as the case may be — *pull harder."*

Although it is in schooling the horse — not the rider — that I have set out to help you with in this book, I feel that in the matter of using the reins, the most simple use of the reins, I must give any who need it something better than the above idea.

Why does a Horse Go Slower or Stop When the Reins are Tightened?

He stops, if he stops, *in the hope that any inconvenience, irritation, or pain the bit might be causing him, will be discontinued.*

Bear in mind that the whole principle of horse training is for the rider to do something, with hand or leg, and then for him to cease or decrease that something when the horse responds as required.

We want *not* to hurt the horse; indeed we go to a great deal of trouble to show him what to do to avoid even the slight irritation a very lightly used leg or bit might occasion. And of course, the horse has to be given *the opportunity* to avoid it. What is the use of his knowing how to avoid it if you fail to give him the opportunity to do so?

You must, by using the **reins VERY** lightly at first, give him the opportunity to avoid a more painful use of the bit. The young uneducated horse *has first to be taught what to do* to avoid a slightly more painful effect.

Even when he does understand, if you use your reins sharply and quickly without **warning**, how can the horse avoid its punishing effect? You will have done the damage; he will have suffered the hurt. Whatever you may do eventually, your first rein effect must be a light one. How can the horse become — or remain — light-mouthed if *you* are heavy on the reins?

You must not only give the horse warning, but he must also be allowed a fraction of time to change his balance in order to carry out the task you set him — any task. I cannot stress this point too strongly: if you suddenly and roughly use the reins, there is nothing your horse can do about it. Nothing.

DON'T THINK "PULL UP": THINK "GO NO FURTHER"

When you want your horse to stop or reduce his pace, I would like you to try putting your requirements into these thought-words: "Trot (or canter) no further" — or "Go no further" — whichever it is that you want of him. Discipline yourself into never thinking the words "Pull up".

Just thinking in these words: "Go no further" when they want their horses to check, produces a wonderful improvement in many riders.

When you ask the horse to "Go no further", your hands will be inclined to resist his continued forward movement. When you think "Pull up", your hands will tend to pull backward rather than to say exactly what you want. You will be demanding too much: more than you want and more than the horse can give.

"Go no further" is what a ship's hawser says as the ship draws into a wharf. The hawser is thrown ashore and a loop is dropped over a bollard, or post. The hawser then says to the ship, in effect: "Go no further". Nobody does anything more. The bollard doesn't pull. Nobody, and nothing on the wharf, pulls. Any pulling or tightening of the hawser is done by the moving ship.

The post merely keeps still; resists.

To riders with trouble stopping their horses, the point I want to stress is that the bollard also stays still when the ship stops pulling. By staying still, it permits the hawser to get light, even loose, as the ship stops.

The post never pulls. Pulling is movement.

The post never gives. Giving is movement.

The post only resists, and resistance is stillness in the face of applied force.

A resistant hand and the **resistant** post both remain still when force is applied to them, and again I stress it, they *continue to remain still when the force applied lessens or discontinues.* As long as they are resistant, they do not move either way; they neither give nor take.

A still hand, a resistant hand, encourages a horse to stop pulling, to discontinue his forward movement. If your hand moves back when the horse makes any move to lessen the hold he has on the bit, you have ceased to be resistant — you are pulling, using a contra force.

It means that not only are you not encouraging him — teaching him — to yield his jaw and decrease his pace and remain light, but you are actually preventing him from doing so. YOU are a puller. You are heavy-handed. You won't allow him to become light. You are showing him: "That will profit you *not*" even when he tries doing what you want.

'Just for Fun': A Simple trial that May Help

Buckle a pair of reins onto a snaffle bit and then place the rider's end of the reins over a post. Get someone to tighten the reins from the snaffle-end while you place the fingers of both hands between the post and the reins. Let the backs of your fingers rest against the post. Don't hold the reins at all; just let the back of the fingers rest against the post so that they don't move.

I want you to notice what changes you *feel* when the reins are tightened or lightened from the bit end.

If your friend pulls, you will immediately feel the increase of pressure on your fingers. But most important of all, if the tension is lightened to the slightest degree, you will detect it immediately if your hands, fingers, maintain their same contact with the post.

Get your partner to make some very tiny changes in the weight on the reins and see how easily you can detect them: lighter, heavier, lighter, heavier. You will detect them instantly, no matter how tiny the changes, if your fingers remain still and against the post.

Now reverse the reins and bit, and try putting the back of your head against the post, resting the snaffle bit on the bridge of your nose. Instead of having soft pliable leather against your well-padded fingers, you now have what the horse always has — steel, resting on bone covered only by sensitive skin.

Before you get your friend to repeat the test, do warn him not to use the reins with the freedom you use on your horse's mouth. I wish I could mean it when I say, "Try it just for fun"; but you won't find it fun if he uses anything like the force some riders are so prone to use on their horses' mouths. If you would sooner try this while alone, put the end of the reins around a post and the bit on your nose, and then notice how *small* a change of pressure you can detect.

Do try it; you'll never talk about "hard-mouthed" horses again. Notice, most of all, the relief of pressure on your nose the instant you lighten up. *The post does not move.*

Can you see how hopeless the horse's position is if you suddenly pull on the reins and also if you allow your hands to move back towards your body every time he gives and tries to lighten the pressure? What he eventually does in these circumstances is to set and fix his head in the least painful position he can find, and he then just 'hangs on'. He finds a still bit hurts less than a moving one.

Of course, we do not deliberately take our hands back when the horse yields a fraction — the tiny fraction you could feel so easily when you had the bit resting on your nose. Why, then, do we do it when we are mounted?

It is because the muscles that stop the hands being pulled forward when the horse leans on the bit are the same muscles that draw the hands back. We are either too slow to detect the horse giving, too inattentive, or what is more likely we lack the skill necessary to *relax our muscles instantly.*

In this little test it is the lessening of the resistance that I have asked you to note. It tells the horse so clearly: "You yield, and the reins get lighter — instantly."

Show him, clearly prove to him, "That will profit you."

"LIMITED" RESISTANCE

The reins will be much more effective if you only lightly *resist* his unwanted movements and follow the 'It will profit you' or 'It will profit you not' principle. So far, I have written of the resistance of the post or of your hand; its stillness. I have said nothing of what happens when the horse gets excessively heavy on the bit, when we find we are not strong enough to resist his head movements.

Were we strong enough to keep our hands absolutely still, the horse could put a tremendous weight on them. But our hands are not strong enough to resist him fully. We can only resist to the limit of our strength and then, as in all tests of strength with him, the horse wins.

We should not let this situation develop. Long before we have used our full strength to resist him, the horse is being terribly hurt — and if it is repeated often enough, he learns to do something desperate. (If you cannot understand what drives the horse to desperation, I feel sure you have not tried the snaffle bit on your own nose. Try it and get someone to give the reins a good hard pull for a few moments. To get the full benefit of this experiment, have the man on the reins draw first on one rein and then on the other, dragging the joint of the snaffle over the bridge of your nose from one side to the other).

We should, instead, revert to what I call "LIMITED" or "reduced" resistance. Our hands should only resist to a certain degree and then follow the 'It will profit you not' technique. The resistance of the hands might be increased until the pressure on the bit is, say, twice that normally used. We then maintain that contact — waiting for, feeling for, the slightest sign of the horse reducing pace or reducing pressure so that we can then reward him, or let him reward himself, by our hands reducing their resistance.

We follow the same policy as an angler with a big fish on his line. He resists only to a certain point — knowing that beyond that point his line will break. He holds the fish, but by *partial* resistance and not total or complete resistance.

This, then, is what I mean by 'limited' or 'reduced' resistance. Our objective is to prevent the horse hurting himself beyond a certain degree: the angler aims to prevent the fish breaking his line; we aim to keep the horse calm and observant and co-operative.

It is here we reap the benefit of having used side-reins for mouthing prior to riding him. The side reins, at first fitted very long and progressively shortened as in Chapter 9, will have taught the horse not to fight a resistant rein.

WITH HOW LITTLE FORCE CAN WE CONTROL OUR HORSE?

Note the question is "How little?", not "How much?"

I don't think I can do better than to reprint here what I said in the second paragraph on the last page of "Horse Control and the Bit" (which you should have read before this):

> "It is the tiny, minute changes of pressure at the exact moment that are so effective. When feeling for his mouth, while being conscious of how much more sensitive his mouth is than your fingers, you must nevertheless concentrate on what you feel at your fingers. FEEL at your end what is happening at his, and you do this at the finger where the rein first touches your hand on its way from the horse's mouth.
>
> Don't *think* of his end of the reins, FEEL your end. *Feel.* Concentrate on 'feel'."

The horse has to be taught how to deal with the slightly increased pressures on his mouth. Read again what has been said about "It will profit you not" in Chapters 2 and 4; you should not punish him by continuing to *increase* the pressure.

Just maintain the *slightly* increased pressure until you can feel the horse try the right thing — you then show him: "THAT will profit you" and you do that by instantly reverting to a light normal contact.

Figure 70: "Havildar" strides freely forward under his owner Mrs. Christine Black, who at the moment is introducing him to a Controlled Walk.

CHANGES IN PACE

Teach changes in pace at the slower gaits first. *Teach almost everything at the slower gaits first,* as it is then easier for you to control your aids.

For instance, it is quite unreal to expect a young horse to canter slowly *before* you have taught him to walk and trot slowly — and with a light rein.

Each time he decreases his pace by the slightest degree in response to **your demands,** you must encourage him with a lighter rein immediately. The rein says in effect, "That's it; that's it"; and coming instantly on his check of pace, the horse should have no difficulty in recognising what caused the encouragement.

If the horse fails to understand that he is required to decrease pace, it will almost certainly be because he has been — or is still being — hurt and worried too much. Don't punish him more by letting your resistance continue to increase. Take the "It will profit you not" course, and quietly maintain the increased tension you already have on his mouth. Let your hands remain *relatively still* (see Chapter 4). If he continues to fail to act on the first pressure, seconds later, perhaps, you might think to increase the pressure a little.

The increased pressure in this case might be compared to shortening the reins a 'short hole', not to pulling — a trifle shorter, a fraction shorter — and then resist again. All the time, you are waiting and feeling for the slightest *tendency* the horse may show of slowing down so that you can instantly encourage that tendency.

If the horse consistently leans on the bit, try to break the support he **gets** from it by several very short slackenings of the rein, and not more **than** a ¼-inch and about two a second. Just break the support of the **reins.** Vibrate the reins, and see if you can get him to accept the lighter **feel** — the slackened rein.

*   *   *

Should you find all this theory too complicated or too boring, then **revert** to the advice I gave earlier in the chapter:

"When you want your horse to stop or reduce pace, put your thoughts into these words: 'Go no further' or 'Trot no further'."

This works like a charm with a great many riders. Just try it.

TO SUM UP

Take every opportunity you can to ride a well-schooled horse. Riding such horses will raise your aim as a horseman.

Never give up in your efforts to get the horse to respond to lighter aids; and you must give him the opportunity to answer light aids. He cannot have a light mouth if you are heavy-handed. YOU try to be lighter.

Concentrate on what you can feel at your fingers rather than trying to imagine what the horse feels at his mouth — develop *feel* and encourage lightness of mouth rather than punish the horse for being heavy.

Throughout the early training of the horse, ask the horse to discontinue his forward movement rather than try to stop him: get him to 'cut his motor' as a first step, rather than trying to force him to a stop through the reins.

Think: "Go no further", rather than demand: "Pull up". Avoid the use of force on his mouth; horses resist force but yield much more readily to persuasion.

Work at improving yourself (if this were easy we would ALL be good horsemen with good hands). Work at improving yourself first: work at it as you need to do at anything that demands skill.

CHAPTER 15

TRAFFIC, SHYING AND GENERAL 'SPOOKINESS'

*Avoid traffic and frightening objects until your control is satisfactory;
Do not become sharp with a frightened young horse;
"Spookiness" and things to avoid.*

> "Sometimes he scuds far off
> And then he stares:
> Anon he starts at stirring of a
> feather...
> Shakespeare

"THE YOUNG HORSE AND TRAFFIC

What should be our policy with a youngster? Should we take him into traffic as soon as we possibly can or should we leave it until as late as possible?

Whatever motivates the horse when he shies, our first concern will be to maintain control of him. If we are able to do that, we are in little danger. It is obvious that the more advanced his training, the easier our horse will be to control; so until he has reached the stage when he understands our aids easily and acts upon them quickly, we will be well advised not to take him into traffic — if we can avoid doing so.

Do not, as so many are inclined to do, take him into traffic early "to get him used to it."

The partly-trained horse has his attention taken away from the rider and what he is doing by the object that frightens him. Later on, he will still be distracted — but he is much more likely to obey instinctively the aids he by then clearly understands.

The younger, greener horse not only is frightened and distracted but does not clearly understand his rider. This usually results in the use of more force — which hurts the horse and excites him more — for pain does not make our meaning clearer, it only draws his attention more forcibly to what we are doing. If this happens several times, he quickly notices that to be frightened is to be hurt, too. He now has two things to fear; the original object and the rider's legs and hands.

The further the horse's education has advanced, the better and quicker he will be able to recognise what is wanted of him; so it is a real advantage if, before we take him into a difficult situation, he has reached a stage where he clearly and quickly understands what our hands and legs mean. Only too often the horse taken into traffic too early starts after a while to dance and prance, not only from fear of some unusual object but from fear of what his rider is going to do when HE sees certain things. By his light, it is the rider who is 'spooky.'

So I recommend you avoid traffic and similar situations until your horse's education has made some progress.

If you have to take the youngster into traffic — well, then, you have to; but obviously the more advanced his training, the better he understands you, the easier he will be to control. The less you hurt him, the calmer he will remain...

The above is an article by author Tom Roberts, published in "The South Australian Rider," the magazine of the Dressage Club of South Australia Inc.

SHYING

When you are riding a young horse and you see something ahead of you that might cause him to shy, allow him to keep as far away from it as you can. Let him give it a wide berth. Where circumstances permit, let him stop and look at it a few times, and if he is inclined to do so, let him go up to it and examine it. Encourage him to do so. *Let* him see and examine it, but *don't force* him up to it.

"Really, Princeton, it isn't that bad!"

Figure 71: Traffic — Keswick Bridge, by Princeton's owner, Miss Jacqui Cotton

DO NOT BE SHARP WITH A FRIGHTENED YOUNG HORSE

When you expect trouble, don't gather him up with tight reins unless you intend him to stop. He is a young horse and I must remind you again the rule for young horses in their early schooling is: "Legs without hands and hands without legs." Use the reins as little and as lightly as you can; face him *past* the object with the lightest rein possible. Apart from anything else, a very short rein proves you are nervous — and as soon as a rider becomes nervous or frightened he becomes stiff and harsh.

See that your hands remain light and springy when you do have to use them, and check that your *arms and elbows* remain light and springy.

If, under some circumstances you do have to force your horse past something, try to make him look *forward and past* the object, not at and into it. Do not force him by pulling his head towards the thing he is frightened of. To him it will appear that you are forcing him into the very thing which is frightening him — remember we have been trying to get him to understand that "forward" means where he is facing. Do all you can to get him to face past the object and let him take as wide a berth as you can.

HOW THE HORSE SEES THINGS

Horses do not see things as we do; what they see from the front of their eyes they seem to think IS in front of them. Later, when your youngster understands the aids better and particularly when he understands the 'opposing' rein (see Chapter 18), you will have more control and you will be able to make him look away from the object he fears. Then, as he passes, he will see it from the back of his eye and he will think it is behind him. He will think he has passed it.

If you find this difficult to believe, notice the behaviour of a horse with winkers on. As soon as he cannot see an object — as soon as it is blotted out of his view by the winkers — as far as he is concerned it isn't there.

It is almost inconceivable the things we know that he hasn't a clue about.

"SPOOKINESS"

A 'spooky' horse is one that sees 'spooks' or ghosts in the most unlikely things, or apparently in nothing at all. He suddenly and without warning jumps forward or to one side or swings about.

'Spookiness' is something that you cannot do much about except to do all you can NOT to make it worse. Some horses remain spooky all their lives; others get over it quite early. The best treatment is the company and example of a staid, steady older horse.

The worst thing you can do with such a horse is to snatch suddenly at his mouth as he jumps. Your action will be too late to stop him jumping and the jab on the mouth you give him only upsets him further. Holding him tightly by the bit does no good whatsoever. As his training progresses, you will find *riding him forward is more effective.*

When we hold a horse 'tight by the head' we are more or less trying to say to him: "Don't do anything" — "Don't shy" — "Don't jump" — "Don't" do anything.

It is best, when control improves, to give definite orders on *what to DO,* such as "Walk forward (or trot forward) with regular steps." If he does what you ask, it prevents him following his own inclinations.

Whatever you do, do not pet or stroke such a horse when he shies. Maybe you are aiming to reassure him; whereas to him it will appear you are encouraging him in what he is doing. Quietly to ride him forward is the best plan: gently try to convey to him what you want him to DO.

AVOID RIDING NEAR FENCES, HEDGES, WALLS, ETC.

He cannot see what is happening on the other side — or if there *is* anything there — and even a steady horse may shy badly if something unexpectedly appears.

AFTER RAIN

Most young horses get jumpy when ridden after rain and pools of water lie on the ground. It isn't the water itself that frightens them but the reflections they see in the pools. You and I know exactly what reflections are, and we don't usually notice them when they appear to move about in the water as we move forward. The horse knows nothing of reflections.

Be tolerant with him. Give him all the rein you can when first you take him on a wet road; let him get his head down and examine what he sees. Almost every horse behaves better if we let them feel free, or part free, when they are frightened.

With a Loose Rein. I like to think of the horse thinking to himself as he passes a pool (or anything else in which reflections appear) — "You are alive, that's certain; I can see you moving. Maybe you are harmless and not going to jump out at me — but I'll keep an eye on you. The reins are loose — and one move my way, I'll be off."

On the other hand, when we have the reins tight, the horse feels he couldn't get away if the "thing" did jump at him. It is not his own reflections he sees in the pool or shiny motor car. Have a good look yourself and see what he sees, and notice how it moves as you move. You know all about reflections; he does not.

You may find the following little experiment with a loose rein interesting and thought provoking — as it was to me.

BULLOCK CARTS AT KIRKEE

It occurred in Kirkee, India, about 1920. Each day I rode a young horse from stables to the Riding School and we passed a spot which, on the return journey, was occupied by a number of bullock carts in which children had been brought to a nearby school. The young horse would shy badly as he passed them, but although I was able to keep him straight and moving along the road, at the end of a fortnight or so his attitude had not improved in the least. "How silly can you be?" I used to think — of him.

So I made this experiment.

The road that led past the bullock carts was the shortest way back to stables and he always *hurried* back to his stable. I wondered how far he would deviate — how far out of his way would he go — to avoid those carts if I didn't interfere with him — and he wanting to get home quickly.

There was a big open space in front of a gunpark on the right side of the road. How far across that parade ground would he circle if I didn't interfere?

So, next day I loosened the reins to see. He began to move away to the right long before he reached the carts — and he went right across the square, watching the bullock carts all the time. He went the full 200 yards or so, and as soon as he was past the carts, he gradually returned to the road again.

How long, I wondered, would he continue to make that big deviation — and he in a hurry to get back to stables?

The next day he repeated the performance exactly. Made the circle as large as the gun sheds would allow and again ran on a little as he passed the line of carts. I didn't interfere in any way; he was free, it would appear to him.

But after the second day he progressively cut the distance he moved out across the square — and in a very short time did not leave the road. Within a fortnight he hardly glanced at the bullocks and carts.

How can one explain such conduct except that the horse felt free to escape if it became necessary to do so?

To understand his view, we would do well to place ourselves in a somewhat similar situation. Imagine you have a friend, a lion tamer, who assures you that his pet "Leo" is absolutely harmless. "Well, he ought to know," you think; but how would you feel if you found yourself alone in the cage with Leo and the cage door locked behind you? "He's quite reliable," your friend shouts as he goes away ...

I feel confident that you would feel much more relaxed had he left the cage door ajar.

That, I think, is how your horse feels when he is frightened and held so that he cannot escape. There may be another and truer explanation for his going better with a loose rein, but this is a certainty — he *will go better* with the reins held loosely or lightly when he is shying.

If you don't feel inclined to loosen the reins (and it does try your nerve), feel his mouth as lightly as you possibly can and gently but firmly ride him forward.

MOVING SHADOWS

You may find your young horse shies violently very early or very late in the day. When the sun is low, as it is at these times, the shadow of an approaching car can reach right across from one side of the road to the other. You, of course, know exactly what shadows are and perhaps you are not even conscious of them; but even quite steady youngsters can show an extraordinary activity when they see this "thing" about to strike them. They often try to jump over it.

Once you know about these shadows, you can act to avoid them.

WINDY DAYS

"Take not your 'ounds out on a werry windy day," advised the famous Jorrocks; and I often think he might well have included young horses with " 'is 'ounds." Like kittens, nothing brings out the fun in a horse as much as a windy day — and one does well to avoid taking a youngster out on such a day during his early schooling.

If you feel he should be worked, then do it at home in the breaking in yard, on the lunge if you like, or under the rider — or a little of both. A very windy day is a lost day with a young horse, as you will find it very difficult to hold his attention.

Work him if you feel you should, but you will be well advised to forget all about new lessons.

* * *

The young horse will frequently shy at such things as:
- a boy bending over a bicycle adjusting a chain;
- a woman bending over a pram;
- a man sitting on a seat — perhaps at a bus stop;
- and — in the show ring — stewards sitting on their heels near a jump.

You may be amazed at his 'silly' conduct: you know exactly what these combinations — apparitions — are. Remember he does not. He sees the two legs, two wheels and a funny sort of body, as one; and the others, too, he cannot recognise.

Be quiet and patient with him.

TO SUM UP

Avoid traffic, strange sights, and sounds — if you can — until a reasonable degree of control is established.

Don't hold him tightly when he is frightened; whatever the reason, it certainly upsets a horse.

If he jumps suddenly, a sudden jab on the mouth with the bit will only upset him further. He has no chance to avoid it. Repeat it a few times and he will start to dance and 'play up', expecting *you to 'play up'*.

His hearing is better than yours — don't ride your youngster close to a hedge or a high fence where he may hear things you can neither see nor hear.

When his training allows it, face him in the direction in which you want him to move — not *into* the object he fears.

Don't start new lessons on a windy day — work him if you feel you should, but limit it to exercise.

CHAPTER 16

MAKING PROGRESS — THE PACES

FOOTFALLS: the Walk;
  the Trot and the Diagonals;
  the Canter and the Leading Leg.

THE WALK: Aids for the walk;
  Attention, understanding, and obedience;
  Lengthening the stride;
  Horses that jig and fret.

THE TROT: Great differences between the trot and the canter;
  Positioning for the trot;
  Aids for the trot;
  Sitting trot.

EACH GAIT HAS ITS OWN AIDS

When the young horse has reached the stage of being easy to mount and quiet to ride at the walk and trot, we might then begin to think of riding him further afield.

Don't ask him to canter yet — as cantering too soon in an enclosed space often upsets a youngster. His rider has to pull him about too much because he is continually turning corners. Don't be in a hurry to start cantering.

So far, it has been emphasised that the leg aids must mean "Go Forward" or "Go Faster." But eventually it will be a great advantage if we can also clearly indicate to the horse at which of the three gaits we require him to go: "At a *walk*, forward," or "At a trot (or canter), forward."

Note the way this is worded: not "Forward at such and such a gait" — but the opposite way around, *"At such and such a gait,* forward."

To convey this, the aids for a trot will need to be different from those for a walk or a canter. It will profit us to study the gaits and to see how one differs from the other. In dressage, the way the horse moves his legs at the different gaits decides what aids the rider will use to indicate the particular one he requires the horse to take — the walk, trot or canter.

First, let us see what differences there are.

THE FOOTFALLS

The Walk

If we listen to the footfalls at the three gaits we find that only at a walk does the horse put each foot down separately: one, two, three, four.

At the walk, the horse leaves each foot on the ground for a comparatively long period as the other three have each to be picked up separately before the first is again moved. If we sit down in the saddle and feel for the movement of the hind legs *only*, we will feel the tempo of the footfalls of these two legs to be fairly slow: o-n-e, t-w-o; o-n-e, t-w-o. We should practise feeling for and be conscious of the action of the *hind limbs*.

The Trot and The Diagonals

The footfalls at the trot are quite different. At the trot we hear only two beats from the four feet as the off-fore and the near-hind come to the ground together and then the other pair, the near-fore and the off-hind.

We find that at the trot the diagonally opposite legs are picked up and put down simultaneously. Each pair is known by the fore-foot it is associated with — the pair with the off-fore coming to the ground being known as the "right diagonal" and the pair with the near-fore coming to the ground as the "left diagonal." One diagonal is coming to the ground as the other is leaving the ground, which means the feet pass each other in the air.

The horse is thus airborne for a fraction of time between each footfall and to allow for this he has to throw himself upwards a little at each step. It is this thrusting action that gives the rider a rougher time in the saddle at the trot, and which he can avoid to some extent by lifting saddle, or 'posting.' (A rider 'lifting saddle' at a trot should not rise and fall constantly on the same diagonal but should change regularly from one diagonal to the other).

We see, then, that the walk and trot in no way resemble each other.

The Canter

The canter is quite different again, for it is a pace of three-time. The three-beat rhythm of the canter is due to two of the four feet coming to the ground separately and the other two coming down simultaneously. The two feet coming down together are placed diagonally opposite each other: sometimes it is the "right diagonal" that moves together and sometimes the "left diagonal."

The "Leading" Leg

When cantering, the legs may move in the sequence: off-hind (one) followed by the right diagonal (two) and finally the near-fore (three); the near-fore, being the last to strike the ground, is in front of the off-fore.

The horse is then said to be 'leading' with the near-fore or to be "on" the near-fore.

When placed down in the sequence near-hind, left diagonal and off-fore, he is said to be 'leading' with his off-fore or cantering 'on' the off-fore.

We find, then, that the canter is a somewhat one-sided gait with either one foreleg 'leading' or the other.

Horses find it easiest to canter when they displace their quarters a little to one side, as this puts one shoulder a little in front of the other. This means that when a horse moves in a more or less straight line, with his hindquarters taken to the left to some degree, the near-fore is a little in front of the off-fore. He finds it very easy when so placed to canter on the near-fore. If his quarters are carried to the right, it is easier for him to canter on the off-fore.

Because of this same 'one-sidedness,' the horse can also canter more comfortably and with less effort if he 'leads' with the inside leg when turning a corner or cantering on a circle: the near-fore when going to the left, and the off-fore when going to the right.

We should note these facts — for we can make use of them.

A loose horse almost invariably leads with the correct (inside) leg when cantering. It is correct because it is easiest for him. When loose, he knows where he wants to go and he goes there in the easiest way, the most natural and relaxed way. It is when the horse doesn't know what his rider wants of him, or he is upset or hurt, or placed in an awkward position, that so often he leads off with the "wrong" leg.

In the next few pages you will see how in some ways we can utilise the characteristics of each different gait to simplify the horse's training.

When we want him to trot, for instance, we ask it of him when he is moving straight and on a straight line. *When we want him to canter,* we ask him to take that gait when he is on a circle or turning a corner.

The easier it is for him to do what we want, the sooner we will be able to indicate to him: "That's it — that's what these signals mean."

CONTROL OF THE GAITS AND PACES

THE WALK

There is nothing truer than the saying:

"THE WALK IS THE MOTHER OF THE PACES"

Attention, Understanding and Obedience

When you want your horse to walk, try by the way you use your legs to suggest to him the gait you have in mind: the walk.

You must first sit well down into your saddle so that you can detect, by "feel" through the saddle, the movement of the horse's hind legs — a comparatively easy thing to do at a walk. Start learning to develop "feel" *at a walk.*

Just as you have to develop your "feel" of the horse, so too does he have to learn to attend to you and the feel of your legs. Horse and rider each have to feel for the other — as do good dancing partners. This is what we have in mind as our goal; not a horse that the rider has to thump and wallop with his legs, but one that eventually will take notice of and act on the slightest, lightest change of pressure of leg or contact with the hand.

First we want his attention, then his understanding, and then his obedience.

Attention First

The best way to get the horse's attention is to give him something to attend to. We ask him to walk fast or slow, as we decide.

During the first weeks we just let him walk more or less at the pace he offers but, after a while, we begin to take charge of his walk. We ask him to vary it. This makes him attend to us and what we are doing.

We should start controlling the walk when the horse is calm; preferably at home. The first goal is to get him to understand: "What I am doing now, means 'Walk.' Fast or slow, it means just 'Walk'."

We teach him that these particular aids or signals mean 'WALK'. Then he will notice when we use other aids — and will more easily recognise them as meaning something different. When we want him to trot, we will use our legs differently.

The Aids for a Controlled Walk

Sit down in the saddle and 'feel,' then, with a longish unhurried "pulsing" of the legs (alternate legs if you like) indicate to the horse: "Walk like this, left, right; keep time with me, stride on — left, right, left, right." Try to convey to him, "Put your hind feet down without haste as my legs suggest — left, right, left, right." It might be a faster walk or a slower walk.

When he does as you want, although only for a stride or two, encourage him: "You clever little horse, that's right... that's right." 'Purr' to him and end-of-lesson. Relax for a while, preferably while he is still doing as you asked. You end the lesson in this case by just returning him to his normal loose-reined walking stride.

Once the youngster has clearly caught on, don't end-of-lesson immediately but just cease urging, for he is now attending and showing signs of understanding. You are making progress. Sit still then and supervise him only: feel for the maintenance of the length of stride and tempo you have set.

Sit quiet and feel. The moment you feel an unasked for change of pace or tempo, faster or slower, instantly correct it — as lightly as you can, but correct it instantly. He has to learn, ultimately, to maintain any pace set, as set. If you sit still but attentive and immediately correct him if he should change the length or tempo of his stride, he will soon learn to maintain the pace without interference.

This "controlled" walk will lead, in its turn, to the controlled trot and canter. A horse seldom walks too fast for us and we rarely have occasion to insist on his walking slowly but without stopping. This lesson should be practised regularly as an exercise which leads to "Canter slowly, but don't stop."

Lengthening the Stride at a Walk

When the young horse understands what is wanted and walks faster or slower as we indicate, we think of teaching him more — to walk faster, cover more ground, by just lengthening his stride.

The horse must not be permitted to quicken the tempo of his steps when we want the strides to be lengthened, as generally the greater the distance the foot has to cover the more time it will take. Quicker steps tend to be shorter steps whereas the longer, the more extended the strides, the slower the tempo, i.e. the fewer steps to the minute.

Again I suggest you think nicely towards your horse when you are teaching this or anything new. Nicely, gently, kindly; for if your horse hurries his strides instead of lengthening them it means he is *trying* to answer, he is doing his best. He has increased his forward movement. He has answered your legs — but not exactly in the way you want. So, as he hurries his steps, by means of the reins say gently to him: "Not that Boy. Not, that way."

To do this, the reins which have kept the bit softly in contact with his mouth, lightly but instantly resist this hurried step. As the tempo drops

Figure 72: Mrs. Pat Hutchens sits down on her young horse and with seat and leg seeks engagement of the hind legs. The hands, light and non-resistant, in no way oppose the demands of the legs.

back again, as he stops hurrying, instantly lighten the reins again to encourage him in that response. As he regains his less-hurried steps, your legs should immediately begin to "pulse" again at the tempo you want him to maintain.

You are asking him for longer strides, not more strides to the minute. This is what you are trying to convey to him; and the slightest lengthening of the stride, as little as one inch, will satisfy you at first.

Such a lot depends on your sense of feel and your ability to act instantly and with apropos; your ability to be able to continue to work on the youngster without upsetting him and your *readiness and ability to show instant approval* the moment you feel the slightest lengthening of the stride.

* * *

If all this seems too difficult, too tiresome, too complicated, then you cannot be very ambitious. If this simple task of learning to teach your horse to walk as directed, with long or short strides, daunts you — you have not the slightest chance of ever attaining flying changes, half-passes and pirouettes, should you be thinking of advanced dressage. You must progress from simple exercises at the slower paces to the more complicated ones at faster paces.

As with *all* new lessons be gentle, be persistent, be encouraging — and be instant. When your pupil tries the wrong thing, as he so often will, or if he is distracted by something he finds interesting, on no account punish him. Gently correct him by the "That will profit you not" technique.

The Horse that Jig-Jogs

Most people teach a horse to go forward and also teach him to stop — but often never give a thought to: "Go slow, but don't stop: walk slow." Even when the youngster is taken out with a group of other horses and he jigs and frets, particularly when the group is headed for home, the rider often fails to recognise the real trouble is that the horse has no idea what the constantly tight rein *means.* He frets and sweats, his mouth becomes tender and sore, and before long both horse and rider are at their wits' end. Each fails to understand the other.

When the horse jig-jogs, an experienced horseman will realise what has been omitted and will go back and school the horse to establish an understanding of what is wanted.

Teach him to walk as you indicate, long and deliberate steps — or slow and relaxed. Praise the youngster each time he does as directed and BEFORE changing the pace again. Remember, too, what was said earlier: "Legs without hands and hands without legs." One must be passive while the other is active. This is applicable in all we are doing at this stage and for much later. And again let me remind you that 'passive' is not necessarily 'loose.' It means "do not demand something with your hands while making other demands with your legs," and vice versa. One follows closely on the other in all the early training — and many great horsemen say: "At all times."

Work on a Loose Rein

The fact that a young horse must work a good deal with a loose rein has not perhaps been sufficiently stressed.

He must repeatedly be allowed to relax and stretch his neck and walk and trot on — with a loose rein.

He must be taught and made to do this as well as being made to maintain an energetic and strong pace. "Taught" first; you cannot 'make' him do anything until he understands what he is required to do.

THE TROT

DIFFERENCES BETWEEN THE TROT AND THE CANTER

The canter. We have seen that at the canter the horse tends to move his quarters to one side, and that he finds it easier to canter than to trot when he is moving even a little sideways. We know too, that he prefers the canter to the trot when he is moving on a curved line such as when on a circle or turning a corner.

The trot. On the other hand, the horse finds it easier to trot than to canter when he is moving on a straight line, and when his own body is straight. He finds trotting on a curved line much more difficult and the more curved the line he has to follow, the more difficult it becomes for him to maintain a trot.

When we are trying to educate the horse to take and maintain any particular gait, it helps if we make use of this knowledge.

POSITIONING FOR THE TROT

When we want to teach the horse to move on at a trot or to change into a longer-striding trot, we should therefore first see that he is moving on a straight line. Likewise when we want him to return to a trot from a canter, he will be more inclined to make the required transition in his early schooling if it is asked of him when he is moving on a straight line.

We make use of these facts when teaching the horse to recognise which gait is required of him, but once he knows what is wanted we start to demand obedience when the circumstances and positioning are less favourable.

It is to take advantage of positioning that in all the less advanced dressage tests, a *strong trot* is asked for only when the horse is moving on the longest straight line available in the test arena — diagonally across the manege. A strong canter, on the other hand, is usually required to include at least one end of the manege with its two corners.

'Positioning' means that we make our demands on the horse when he is in a position where it will be easiest for him to do what we want him to do. We use the correct aids, but as he will not yet understand them, the positioning is much more important. As his training progresses the positioning becomes less important and the aids more and more so, until ultimately we can make our demands and the horse will understand them even when he is most disadvantageously placed. In a contra-canter, for instance, he will be required to strike off at the canter on the "wrong" leg.... but we certainly will not attempt to do this in the early schooling we are dealing with here.

Positioning, then, is a means to an end. It makes the lesson easier for the horse. It is gradually abandoned as the horse's training and his understanding progress.

AIDS FOR THE TROT

Because the gait of the trot is itself square, straight-sided, even and regular, we should use what I call "even aids" when asking for a transition to or maintenance of the trot.

By this I mean that neither leg should be drawn back and neither the left or right hand or leg should be used with more strength than the other. We should keep an even feel on each rein and use each leg with equal strength, particularly when training.

In the early schooling, we should exaggerate the differences between the aids for the trot and canter to make it easier for the horse to notice the differences.

To Start the Trot

First, have the horse walking on a straight line. Check that you yourself are relaxed and then with each leg on or close to the girth, suggest the sharp short steps of the trot.

Your evenly-placed legs, by very light "throbbing" pressures, suggest: "Like this go on: one, two; one, two; one, two," and you should use short, sharp and very brief pressures of the calf of the legs at the tempo you have in mind for the horse to take. Aim to suggest to him: "Let your feet hardly touch the ground before they start leaving it again." Your hands are quiet, passive and the contact is even — equal on both reins — or the reins loose.

The length of each stride at the trot should be regular and even. We only *suggest* "trot" at first. We want the youngster to learn: "These aids mean TROT." When he understands, you can become more demanding.

Keep in mind your ultimate objective might be to be able to signal to your horse: "AT A TROT — go," and have him come to life in an immediate full trot. Maybe you will never want him to do that, but it is sure to be very convenient if you *can* clearly indicate to him the exact gait you want him to use.

Repeatedly and consistently you do one thing when you want your horse to walk, and others when you want him to trot or canter. Each time gently correct him and show him: "That will profit you not," when he tries other than what you want. If he is kept calm he soon comes, first to notice the different aids, and then to understand them.

Of course it is not necessary to use these particular aids to teach the horse to trot or canter — if you just give him a 'kick in the ribs' and he goes off into a canter, it is quite easy to correct him after a couple of paces if you wanted him to trot. But why not aim at better and clearer communications from the beginning?

If a rider is consistent with his aids and gently corrects his horse whenever he misunderstands, the horse will soon learn what to do.

The Head Moves Less at the Trot

This is another way in which the trot differs from the other gaits. Whereas at both the walk and canter there is a marked and distinct movement of the head and neck, at the trot the head moves very little. This makes it easier for the rider to maintain contact with the mouth when the horse is trotting.

As the horse usually shortens his neck slightly when trotting, it is advisable to take a slightly shorter hold of the reins for this gait. Do not increase the pressure or feel on the reins when you shorten them, only take a slightly shorter hold. Check repeatedly that your fingers, wrists and elbows retain their light and elastic springiness. Keep plenty of bend in your elbows — a straight arm tends to lose its elasticity.

THE SITTING TROT

You will find the sitting trot helpful in the matter of using the aids with evenness and regularity. The sitting trot, among its several advantages, permits the rider to use his legs with absolute regularity and evenness at each and every stride.

The rising trot makes for unevenness and irregularity at this gait in which evenness and regularity are the outstanding characteristics. When the rider is lifting saddle, he is for at least one stride, standing with all the weight of his body on his legs and stirrups. While he is so situated (every alternate stride) he finds it difficult to use his legs with delicacy and to the exact degree he has in mind. (A rider of only eight stone has half-a-hundredweight, about 25 kilos, on each leg. Definitely a handicap).

These reasons should influence the rider to use the sitting trot a great deal when schooling. Dressage riders use the sitting trot in preference to the other gaits during earlier training.

(I would like to point out here that I only mention dressage — when I do — to show that the facts I state are recognised and in many cases form the basis of advanced horse control by the expert. These are facts, not opinions or theories and they hold good for all types of horsemanship).

TO SUM UP

The sequence of leg movements is quite different for each gait. Learn the differences and use them to suggest the gait you want.

It is an advantage to be able to vary the length of stride and the tempo of each gait at the walk, the trot and the canter. Start teaching these things at the walk.

Change diagonals regularly when at a rising trot. In most schools you will be required to trot on either the inside or outside diagonal — this permits the instructor to check that all pupils regularly change diagonals.

Use the sitting trot a great deal for schooling — it has many advantages.

Only ask for and maintain a lengthening of the stride at a trot when the horse is moving on a straight line.

These lessons develop FEEL in both horse and rider, and not only give the rider more control but make control easy and light. They start to weld horse and rider into a co-operating team.

Don't be in a hurry to start your horse cantering.

CHAPTER 17

MAKING PROGRESS — THE PACES
THE CANTER

Common causes of trouble at the canter;
Aids for the canter;
Teach restraint before cantering;
"Canter Now" is the lesson — don't give the leading leg a thought at this stage;
About Figures-of-Eight.

COMMON CAUSES OF TROUBLE AT THE CANTER

Some riders have a great deal of trouble with this gait. Almost invariably in cases where the rider meets trouble, he has asked for too much too soon and has not only confused his horse but has given him reason to look upon the canter as a painful experience.

The early canter of an untrained horse is usually faster than is comfortable in an enclosed space such as a dressage arena or anything of similar size. The faster the pace, the more difficulty there is in controlling him and in an enclosed space this may cause the inexperienced rider to use his reins sharply on a youngster, perhaps having his first canter under a rider.

The canter is a succession of leaps, with all four legs off the ground during a part of each stride; and if a horse has any fun in him at all, this is where it will come out — particularly if his mouth is being hurt. Horses kept in small stables or yards and not allowed the run of a paddock where they can have "fun and games" when they feel like it, are most likely to show what they are made of when first asked to canter.

It is for this reason that I have left the canter out of the earliest part of the young horse's schooling. Establish all the understanding you can before you ask for a canter. Then, if you should either intentionally or unintentionally use the reins at all roughly, there will be less chance of a misunderstanding. It is also a good idea to avoid using a very small arena for the early canters.

Should your young horse at any time quietly take the canter of his own accord, however, don't interfere unless you have good reason. Let him go on for a while and later gently ask him to return to a trot. Treat it as you did when he cantered on the lunge unasked, but whatever you do, don't behave in a manner that may cause him to suspect that to canter is wrong.

The head and neck movement at a canter

A page or two ago attention was drawn to the fact that a horse's head moves a good deal at both the walk and the canter. If you do not keep your hands light and springy, or have your reins loose or loose-ish, your young horse's mouth will suffer a great deal if your hands fail to follow his head and so give to his stretching of the neck.

Whether you hit the bit on to his jaw with rough hands, or he strikes his jaw on the bit due to your stiff immovable hands, will matter little to him. He suffers, finds the canter an unpleasant experience, and then shows his resentment.

Check the springiness of your hands when you canter, and remember that the mobility of the elbows is absolutely essential if you are to follow the movements of the horse's head. The somewhat shorter rein you will have been using at a trot will need to be lengthened again for these early canters.

THE AIDS TO START THE CANTER

First, position him by making use of a corner if you are in an enclosed area. Ask for the canter as he begins the turn, as he will most likely trot on a few paces before he canters and he then could be on a straight line again.

As you near the corner at a trot, stop lifting saddle and SIT DOWN. Then draw your outside leg back about four inches and squeeze lightly with *both* legs. The drawing back of your outside leg should precede the 'squeeze' by a fraction.

I said 'squeeze' with both legs — but don't let this be a vice-like grip or of long duration. Lightly squeeze, for a moment only, and repeat it should it be necessary. Think back to the terms I have used to indicate to you how you should use your legs to get the horse to walk out and to trot: "pulse" for a walk, and "throb" for a trot. This "squeeze", too, should have a certain amount of timing about it until the horse has learned to respond by cantering.

The main difference in the aids will be that your legs will be unevenly placed to canter and the pressures somewhat longer, but still intermittent. The pace you want will be timed: "One, two-three". Substitute in your mind — "Squeeze, two-three; lightly squeeze, two-three".

On no account try to force the horse to respond to your drawn-back leg by moving his quarters inwards. Later on, perhaps — but not yet.

How foolish it would be to try to teach him to yield his quarters at the same time as you try to teach him, *"This means canter."*

What you want the youngster to understand at present is: "When I sit down and use uneven leg aids (the outside leg drawn back) and with light pressures more like 'puffs' than throbs or pulses — and I do it while changing direction — THIS I want you to learn, means canter: just canter-on."

Don't worry him about leading with the correct leg at this stage — one thing at a time, remember.

One reason for starting in a corner rather than on a circle is that in the corner you will not need to use the reins to turn the horse. The fence will do it. We want to focus his attention on our legs — not our hands. Roughness of the hands or the use of any force will upset the horse and make him stiffen. As a result, as often as not you will find him on the wrong leg when eventually he does canter.

DON'T LET HIM 'RUN AWAY'

Most horses take the canter immediately but some just blunder on at the trot for a time or two. If your youngster fails to take the canter at the first corner, gently check him and try again at another corner, not necessarily the next. But try, too, not to upset the horse or get upset or stiff yourself. Don't let him run on into an awkwardly fast trot, because when he does take the canter from such a pace it is usually at a very fast and out-of-hand semi-gallop.

If he hurries on into a very fast trot, lightly check him; don't let him blunder on. Try to tell him through the reins, and gently as always: "Not that, Boy; try again." But if and when you feel him tend to change from the even-stepping one-two, one-two, of the trot to the uneven 'one-two-three' of the canter, lighten up with your legs for a moment. Try and let him understand, "Follow that line and I will stop worrying you with my legs" — and 'End of lesson.' Then, after you have done something else for a few minutes, try it again if he is still calm.

The more difficult he is to get to canter at first, the more important it is not to insist on his maintaining the gait for long when eventually he does try it. Only a few strides, then stroke his neck and 'End-of lesson'. Either take him home or go for a pleasant walk where life will be interesting and your demands less **pressing. Let him reflect on the new** experience.

Use the reins with great caution

Every horse is different, and you must study the one you have. The mistake you are most likely to make is to use your hands too strongly. You may be worrying too much about all the things you don't want him to do: "Don't buck;" "Don't run away;" "Don't cut the corner," and so on — whereas you should be thinking in positives, "DO this," or "DO that" — or "Keep up what you are doing."

Generally, we use our hands to say: "Don't." We should be using our legs to say "DO".

Do not keep the young horse going too long at anything new. What you are trying to teach him first, is: "When I do this, I mean 'Canter'." Once you get the message through to him, keeping him going will present little difficulty.

As always, 'cut out' with a new lesson *as soon as you can detect any improvement.* Improvement is progress. Reward progress; let progress terminate the lesson while he is still in the early 'learning' stage.

If you have any real difficulty with the canter, leave it for later on, and in the meantime go back and work on your variations of pace.

Trot out, trot slow. Trot out, trot slow. Drive him on, on the straight runs; and check him before the corners. Practise a lot at very slow walks and trots eventually — real 'drover's walk'; and insist in the end that he does it on a loose rein. Praise him for each quiet change of pace, up and down. Let him know you want *each in its turn..*

This is certain. If you cannot control and regulate the young horse's pace at the walk, and trot, you will have real difficulty at the canter.

Teach Him Restraint

Horses that jig and fret when in company and pull and reef at the bit on some occasions — when hunting for instance — are proof positive that variation of the pace with relaxed restraint has been overlooked in the young horse's preparation. This shows up most when we begin cantering: the young horse goes too fast for our peace of mind and we start to hang on to the reins. He, not having had preparatory training, does not understand what is wanted and becomes excited — fretting at the pain caused by the bit which he doesn't know how to deal with.

Recognise the cause and go back and teach the horse both restraint and energetic paces at the slower gaits of walk and trot. Make it easy for him, simplify it.

We should recognise that the canter and the gallop are the horse's real working paces, be it for polo, hunting, jumping, games, or even hacking when the going is suitable. His real schooling consists of *preparing* him for the faster work. If his canter is faulty, it is almost always because his preparation has been faulty — insufficient.

DO NOT GIVE THE LEADING LEG A THOUGHT AT THIS STAGE

Whatever you do, do not try at this stage to make your young horse lead with the correct leg.

If, when he canters, you stop him and then immediately try to start him off again because he is on the 'wrong leg,' it will hopelessly confuse him. The lesson is not, "On the near (or off) fore, Canter"; the early lesson is: "CANTER". That, and that alone. Encourage *that.*

Once the horse understands what is required, he will stay relaxed and break into a canter quite easily. If he is relaxed when asked to canter on a circle or when turning a corner, he will generally start off on the correct leg. It is the normal, natural and easy thing to do.

If the youngster should start on the wrong leg, don't worry about it — and do nothing to discourage him from cantering on, for a while at least. Encourage him and show your approval for starting off when he did. He will find the wrong lead to be awkward and after he has rolled on for a chain or two (20-40 metres) drop to a trot — 'canter no further': end of lesson. Later on you may stop him with the thought of putting him on the correct leg but even then, many lessons later, don't canter again immediately after he breaks back into a trot.

As he trots again, show your approval, "That's right" (for trotting); then, when he knows he was right in trotting and when you are ready — and if the horse is still calm — start again into the canter as you go into another corner.

"CANTER NOW" IS THE LESSON

"Canter now" is what has first to be learned and it is not until the horse responds instantly to this requirement and has done so many times, that you even begin to think of correcting him for leading on the wrong leg. In the meantime, continue with his other schooling and this will start to prepare him for what he has to do later on: to strike off, not necessarily on the natural lead but eventually on whichever lead his rider indicates.

Never look down to see what the horse's legs are doing. You must learn to *feel down*. Feel for his tendencies, as recommended for the walk. With practice you can feel quite clearly, not only when he is about to start to canter but on which leg he is about to lead. *Look up — and feel down.*

CANTER FROM A WALK

When the horse understands the aids for canter, you may find it easier to take the pace from a walk than from a trot. For one thing, most riders have better control of their own balance and limbs at a walk and so can give their aids more clearly. But do not use force. You must give him a chance to 'catch on', for again this is something new. Don't hurry him.

ABOUT "FIGURES OF EIGHT"

DO NOT ATTEMPT A FIGURE-OF-EIGHT YET

Your horse is certainly not yet ready for a Figure-of-8 at the canter. Should you tackle it too soon and without proper forethought and preparation, you may well set your youngster's schooling back a good many weeks.

In dressage tests the several demands of a Figure-of-8 are each asked for separately. Each transition is judged separately and each is given separate marks. The competitor is never asked just to "Canter a Figure-of-8 with a Simple Change of Leg."

It is not until you reach the Elementary standard of Dressage that the tests include striking off into a canter on a nominated lead, then later changing down to a walk for some two paces and then quietly striking off into a canter again, this time leading with the opposite foreleg. Later in the same test the horse will be asked to repeat this in the opposite direction, with the opposite lead.

The object of the test is to demonstrate that the horse has been prepared for and understands his rider when asked to canter on the required lead.

Only too often a young horse is completely spoilt by his being entered in a hack class at a show where he might be required to canter a Figure-of-8 with changes of leg.

The young horse should have been taught each of these requirements separately before being taken into any showring. Only too often his inexperienced rider hopes that by repeatedly riding the figure, the horse will learn what is wanted. The result is that the youngster has hardly started into a canter when he is pulled — often quite roughly — back into a walk. Then, sometimes before he has walked a single pace, he is driven on into a canter again (perhaps with many kicks and pulls to get him to lead with the opposite leg.)

These demands are too confusing for him to follow if he has not been suitably prepared. It appears to him that he must have made a mistake dropping back into a walk, and that he is being punished for it. If he strikes off with the wrong leg leading, he is pulled about even more by the rider in his efforts to correct him. Whether he puts himself right or not the horse is hardly cantering again before he is once more roughly pulled down into a walk. He hardly walks a pace before he is pushed into a canter again.

The rider usually keeps at him. He repeats the figure and the mistakes several times, and the pain and bewilderment of the horse grows and grows. The gentler horses sometimes put up with the pain, but others become desperate and learn to rebel.

If they find it less painful to 'play up' and intimidate the rider, we may have another 'bad' horse on our hands.

I warn against tackling the Figure-of-8 without proper preparation because so often it is the cause of a young horse becoming difficult in the showring. The better the quality of the horse, the more spirit he has, the greater the chances of his finishing up a 'bad' horse.

Having let you "perceive the wrong" — now to "pursue the right."

THE SIMPLE CHANGE OF LEG PREPARES FOR THE FIGURE-OF-EIGHT

Teach one part at a time. When in any exercise or lesson one demand follows closely upon another (as in a Figure-of-8) we must, when introducing the sequence, make it clear beyond the possibility of error that *each requirement is wanted in its turn:* that one is wanted to follow upon the other.

First, ask the horse to canter on a circle; and when he is cantering smoothly and on the correct lead, quietly suggest: "Canter no further." As he drops to the gait you want, show your approval. Murmur to him and walk on, not merely for one or two paces but for several. Then commence a circle to the other side and if he remains calm, gently ask him to strike off into a canter on the other lead.

Reassure him, as he complies with each of your demands, that he has done right. Compliment him first — and then gently show him that you want him to canter again.

After you have done this a few times, progressively shorten the number of steps at the walk and in a remarkably short space of time your horse "wakes up": "It's a new idea — walk a couple of paces and then off we go on the opposite lead in the opposite direction!"

He has made a "Simple change of leg." Don't think of Figures-of-8 until you can make a single simple change of leg easily and calmly.

If, however, you find he has favoured the outside lead, let him reach a corner where he will find it difficult to follow the curved line on the wrong lead. If he doesn't then change, gently check him back into a trot or walk, let him move on a few paces and ask again for the canter. Don't hurry. Don't let him become upset.

Do not attempt to practise this while there is the slightest doubt in the horse's mind that he was required to canter in the first place. Otherwise, to check him so soon after you asked him to canter will raise the question in his mind as to whether he misunderstood your first demand.

The same with the trot or walk. Each time you ask for it and he obliges, let him know immediately, "That's right" — as you are going to ask him to take the canter again after only a few paces.

Do you see how necessary it is to reassure your young horse when you ask "Canter" — and then make him trot or walk — and then almost immediately ask him again to canter?

Try to see the horse's point of view.

YIELDING THE QUARTERS

You should realise that my point in dealing with the Figure-of-Eight in this book is to point out the difficulties and dangers that can result from its being attempted too soon.

Many of you will know that the horse canters most easily with the near fore leading when his quarters are displaced to the left — then if you can displace his hindquarters to the left the moment he takes the canter, he will lead off accordingly. Hindquarters left : near fore leading; and hindquarters to the right: off-fore leading.

This is so — but very few experienced horsemen recommend this practice during the early months of schooling, and many never recommend it. To explain how the correct aids for canter on a nominated lead should influence a trained horse would need at least a full chapter — and is quite out of place in this book.

Later on and only AFTER we have taught our pupil to yield his hindquarters to a drawn back leg — we will use this influence. We use it, not to displace his quarters in the direction of the leg we wish him to lead with, BUT TO STOP HIM DISPLACING THEM IN THE OPPOSITE DIRECTION which he will try to do sometimes and which facilitates his leading with the leg we do NOT want.

We use it, when we do use it, (and only after the horse has been taught its meaning), not to deflect the hindquarters to the 'in' side but to correct him should he attempt to move them to the 'out'side.

All this is linked up with "Impulsion" and "keeping the horse straight". If you should determine to teach your horse to canter a Figure-of-Eight, carefully follow the advice I have already given. Remember Danny Fitzgerald's recommendation: "Don't hurry. It takes longer." It often spoils the horse, too.

Help your horse all you can, for the harder he tries the easier it is to destroy his calmness. The best horses are the most easily spoilt by confusing demands.

Importance of work on a loose rein

Let me remind you again of the importance of work on a loose rein at the walk and trot — and of work on a long rein at all paces.

Your horse must know he is free to relax and stretch his neck when the reins invite him to do so. The horse that cannot be made to lower his head and lengthen his neck is one of the most difficult types to deal with.

Work with a loose rein at the walk and trot — if properly carried out it will lay the foundation for long, easy-riding, ground-covering movement at the canter.

TO SUM UP

When you think your horse is ready, start him cantering in a corner — and make no attempt to compel him to lead with the correct leg. Be content if he just learns to canter when you apply the aids.

If he 'runs away' into a fast trot instead of taking the canter as required, gently steady his pace, calm him and try again. The young horse usually canters too fast at first and he should be familiar with fast and slow paces at the walk and trot before being asked for them at the more difficult canter.

Do not stop him if you find he is on the wrong lead when you do get him cantering: canter on. When he understands 'Canter' he will usually take the correct lead if you start him off in a corner.

Not until he has learned to take the canter easily should you think to correct him should he canter on a wrong lead. To correct him, gently check him back into a trot when on a straight line and quietly ask him to try again approaching another corner.

Do not neglect work on a loose rein at all gaits.

Use encouragements and rewards whenever you can. Never fail to let the horse know when what he is doing pleases you — when what he is doing is right.

CHAPTER 18

REIN EFFECTS

Names given the several rein effects
The "Open" Rein and the "Direct" Rein
The "Neck" Rein and the "Indirect" Rein
The "Indirect Rein of Opposition"

NAMES GIVEN THE SEVERAL REIN EFFECTS

I am continually faced with the questions: "How much does my reader know? How experienced is he? Do I *need* to tell him this — or that?

Do you know what is meant by:

        1) an open rein?
        2) a direct rein?
        3) a neck rein?
        4) an indirect rein?
        5) an indirect rein of opposition?

Many riders not only know nothing of these names but are also unaware of the reins having the effects defined. They often use the reins in the way described — but without being conscious of the exact effects produced.

The terms refer principally to the direction in which a rein is drawn and to a lesser extent, to the degree to which the rein is tensioned or drawn in that direction. It is well to know the meaning of the terms. It saves a lot of talk when these expressions are understood by all.

THE "OPEN" REIN AND THE "DIRECT" REIN

The right "open" rein means that the right rein is taken away from the horse's neck to the right, and a light tension then applied to it (see Figure 73).

The right "direct" rein on the other hand, is tensioned, drawn, from front to rear (more or less), with the hand and rein in the normal riding position, quite close to the neck and with the rein occasionally touching the neck (see Figure 74).

The fully 'open' rein has a very strong sideways effect and very little front-to-rear stopping effect. It tends to turn the horse a great deal and stop him hardly at all. The extent of each of these effects, 'open' or 'direct', depends on how far the hand is carried to the side, i.e. on how 'open' it is.

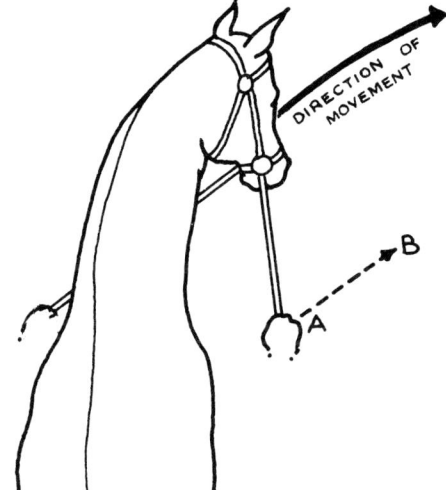

Figure 73:
THE RIGHT OPEN REIN.

The hand is taken to the right and a very light tension placed on it. If the young horse does not turn as required, it is best to make the rein even more 'open' — take it even further from the neck — rather than increase the tension.

Any tension from front to rear tends to oppose the forward movement required of the horse and so the term 'oppose' is often added to the names of rein effects. Thus what I call a "Direct Rein" some may call a "Direct Rein of Opposition". It is not that we disagree — put it down to my desire for simple terms.

We may use the fully open rein a good deal when the horse is first broken-in; hardly ever, if at all, after the first few weeks. The 'open' rein merges eventually into the 'direct' rein as the hand is taken less and less to the side as the youngster's understanding and training progress.

The lunge rein is a very good example of a fully open rein. It has a very marked sideways or turning effect but practically no stopping effect.

The 'direct' rein has a strong stopping effect. There is no clearly marked point at which the open rein starts and the direct rein finishes. As training proceeds, we make the rein effect progressively less and less 'open' and more and more 'direct,' i.e. less to the side and more from front-to-rear. As the horse learns to understand and answer the legs, we can, by use of the legs, counter the slight stopping effect of the more direct rein.

The 'direct' rein is seldom used directly from front to rear except when we want to stop the horse, in which case both reins are used with the direct effect. Ordinarily the hand is taken a little (if only a fraction of an inch) to the side when the direct rein is used to turn the horse; but that fraction of an inch is most important.

We may revert to the open rein on horses that stick-up and also on horses that rear. With each of these resistances the leg effects MUST be brought to predominate over the rein effects. The aim in such cases is to reduce the stopping effect of the rein — with both rearers and jibbers, the great difficulty is to keep them moving forward.

We can more or less sum up: "When the young horse is disinclined to go in the direction required when turning, we may revert to an open rein as it will be less inclined to oppose the forward movement required. As training progresses and we can get predictable results from the leg aids, then the rein becomes progressively more 'direct' and less 'open'."

The open rein should be used only lightly and resistance if it occurs should be met by a relatively still hand (see Chapter 4, p26).

Figure 74:

THE RIGHT DIRECT REIN.

The "direct" rein acts mostly from front to rear and so tends to check or oppose forward movement. In more advanced stages of training the hand is hardly carried to the right at all — sometimes by only as little as a small fraction of an inch.

With the newly broken-in horse, we give the rein a very open effect at first but as his general understanding grows and he comes to understand the meaning of leg aids, we make the effect less and less open and more and more direct; perhaps using the 'open' effect when we meet a strong dis-inclination to go forward in the direction indicated.

The other rein, the left in this case, may remain passive or it may be used as in the 'Indirect Rein' effect, described in the text.

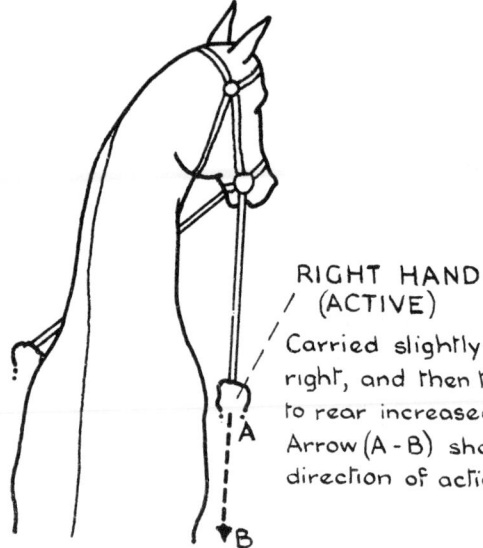

RIGHT HAND (ACTIVE)
Carried slightly to right, and then tension to rear increased. Arrow (A-B) shows direction of action.

THE "NECK REIN" AND THE "INDIRECT REIN"

The neck rein and the indirect rein resemble each other in that each is laid against the side of the horse's neck and he has to be taught to yield to this light sideways pressure of the rein against the side of his neck.

The neck rein is a type of indirect rein, but whereas both the direct and the indirect reins are each almost invariably used with a rein in each hand, the neck rein is usually — if not always — used with both reins held in one hand.

We are dealing only with the schooling of a young horse in this book and we will not be working him with one hand yet — but I feel it necessary to explain the big differences there are between the two rein effects, even though they appear to be similar.

The 'Neck Rein'

The main difference between the neck rein, the indirect rein and the indirect rein of opposition (later described) lies in the amount of weight or pressure used against the neck. The more the rein presses against the neck, the more weight the same rein places on that side of the bit to which it is attached. All three rein effects use the horse's neck as a lever and as with all levers, the further along the lever any given weight or pressure is applied, the greater the effects of that pressure, no matter how little or light that pressure might be.

As the neck rein should place no additional pressure on the bit (mouth) or practically none, it is taken to the extreme end of the neck when the demand is for a fast, quick turn when galloping (see Figure 75). It uses the leverage of the neck to its limit. In almost any copy of the Australian horse magazine "Hoofs & Horns" you will see stockmen and others using the neck rein with the rein actually touching the top of the bridle.

The neck rein seems to have no place in dressage.

Figure 75: The Neck Rein in use. Quite often it is taken even further along the neck to actually touch the bridle. Well-used it is "lightly-used".

The 'Indirect Rein' and its Effects

I have no thought of going on, in this book, into all the effects any rein can or should produce on a trained dressage horse — but I should be sure you know not only that the trained dressage horse is required to yield to rein pressures against the neck, but that he is also required to respond to all pressures of the bit on the bars of the mouth *that the same rein can produce at the same time.*

The left rein pressed against the side of the neck should require the horse to move his forehand to the right, away from the pressure; but any tension on the same rein should at the same time tend to draw his nose to the left, unless the other rein, the right rein, cancels out or limits that effect.

This is the 'Indirect rein' in action. The indirect rein is usually used fairly low down on the neck and it also generally has enough tension on it to draw the nose and head to the side unless the direct rein opposes or cancels out that unwanted effect.

Although on a well-schooled and well-ridden dressage horse it is almost impossible to see the indirect rein in action, most movements, particularly lateral movements, are dependent in some degree on the horse's response to the indirect rein.

We should avoid the use of the indirect rein on a young horse: at least until he responds freely to the open and direct rein effects and also moves freely forward in response to the leg.

Until he understands and obeys the most simple aids, avoid the use of the more complex ones: one thing should lead up to the next.

The First Uses of the 'Indirect Rein'

When the indirect rein is first used, it should be used not so much to get the horse to move his forehand to one side but more to *prevent him making unwanted movements* of the forehand to one side. An instance will help to make the meaning clearer.

You are out riding and intend to go on past a gate on your right. The gate leads back towards the stables, and your youngster tries to turn through it. You try to check his turn to the right with your left rein; but instead of following his nose and continuing on past the gate the

Figure 76: Mr. John Toovey uses the Indirect Rein as the horse 'drops' his right shoulder and tries to move sideways to the right towards home.

horse bends his neck and moves off to the right, shoulder first, with his head, held by the left rein, very much to his left (see Figure 76).

In such a case we say the horse 'drops his shoulder' — his right shoulder in this instance. He is moving more or less shoulder first to his right, the direction in which *he* wants to go.

It is in such a situation as this that the indirect rein (the right in this case) can first be brought into action:

   1) to restrict the excessive bending of the horse's neck; and
   2) to check the sideways movement of the forehand.

The indirect (outside) rein should not resist the bending of the neck until the neck is bent to an un-reasonable degree. But once the bend has reached the limit you think sufficient, that rein ceases to yield and from that point on resists further bending.

The outside rein — the right rein — has come into action as an indirect rein.

We act now as if the horse's shoulder was pushing against the stretched right rein; and of course the more he pushes against it, the more tension there will be on the right hand — and so also on that side of his mouth. The more he pushes against that right rein the more pressure he places on that side of his mouth. It is for his rider then to counter this by adding more weight to the left rein (used more or less as an open rein and somewhat away from his neck).

The position now is that the horse, by pressing his shoulder against the indirect rein, has occasioned increased pressure on to both sides of his mouth; and, as he is still required to go forward in the direction he is facing, both legs have to increase their driving effect considerably.

As always, you must be quite clear in your own mind exactly what you are striving for. You want to show him, "Going forward, in the direction you are facing, will profit you. Going or trying to go sideways, towards home, will profit you not."

Sit down and register all you feel. The instant you can feel his slightest tendency to go more forward (forward lies where his head is facing) he will to some degree press a little less against the indirect rein. This results in the right rein becoming a little lighter on his mouth if you permit it, as you should, and that means the left rein can also be lightened as there is then less to counter (see Figure 77).

If you have a reasonable degree of skill you will soon show the horse, by appropriate encouragements and discouragements, the meaning of these combined aids. The horse has had his first lesson in the requirement of the indirect rein — and combined aids.

I must stress that the indirect rein should not be used in the early stages of training: not until the horse clearly understands and answers the open rein and the direct rein as well as the forward drive of both legs. The leg aids must predominate over the stopping effect of the reins.

Figure 77: A little later John is getting the message through to the still reluctant horse — but now only the top of the horse's head indicates his resistance.

The example of how the indirect rein operates is given here only so that you can fully understand what is meant by the term. It should also make it clear that the indirect rein necessarily requires the use of both hands.

In the very early days of the horse's schooling, however, we would not use the indirect rein as above — we just quietly persist with the open rein to get the youngster to go forward as directed (see Chapter 4 re the **Relatively Still Hand**).

(Later in his training the indirect rein will play an important part in deflecting the forehand in lateral movements such as the half-pass, pirouette etc.).

*   *   *

All this to explain how the indirect rein differs from the neck rein but you will see how it simplifies instruction if the instructor can say to a pupil: *"Keep* the indirect rein and ride him forward".... eight words instead of pages.

THE "INDIRECT REIN OF OPPOSITION"

For brevity and convenience I will sometimes call this the 'Opposing Rein.' It is an indirect rein, the third of the three: neck rein, indirect rein and the indirect rein of opposition.

The 'opposing rein,' unlike the indirect rein, has tension placed on it by the rider who draws his hand back slightly, very slightly, towards the horse's wither — *somewhat* in the direction of the horse's opposite hip.

This causes the rein to press against the base of the neck and has the effect of inducing the horse to move his shoulder (forehand) to the side away from the rein, while at the same time his nose (head) is drawn in the opposite direction.

The hand using the Indirect Rein of Opposition should not cross the line of the horse's wither; the rein should be lightly drawn somewhat in the direction of the horse's opposite hip — in that direction and only lightly touching the base of the neck. On no account should the hand be taken in the direction of the rider's opposite knee or thigh.

The other hand first yields to permit the bending of the neck and then, when the desired bend is obtained, limits its further bending.

The Indirect Rein of Opposition has a decided stopping effect. It will be quite clear that the drawing back of the hand using the opposing rein and then the limiting of the bending of the neck by the other rein, will have a decided tendency to stop a moving horse — and in the case of a standing horse, should cause him to step backwards with the forehand moving away from the opposing rein.

So before using the opposing rein, it is *necessary that the rider be able to counter the stopping effect by creating more impulsion with the legs.*

For reasons we are not concerned with in this book dealing with the horse's early training only, I will mention here that the opposing rein is seldom if ever used in advanced dressage.

We often see the indirect rein of opposition *quite wrongly used* in less advanced grades of dressage competition where the rider uses it to keep the horse's shoulder out (and bring his nose in) when riding through a corner. The rider's inside hand can be seen pushing the inside rein against the base of the neck or shoulder, trying (and quite effectively, as it works!) to keep the shoulder outward in order to maintain the correct bend — inward — in the direction of movement.

Most horses will answer to the opposing rein without special preparation and it often proves to be useful with a shying horse, as we see shortly. The objection to the opposing rein is that it has a 'pull-back' effect. It acts against impulsion and so most judges rightly penalise its use in any dressage competition.

The 'Opposing' Rein in Action

It is likely that you have never heard of such a thing as the 'Indirect rein of Opposition.' Yet, if you are a good practical horseman, it is more than likely that you use its effects regularly.

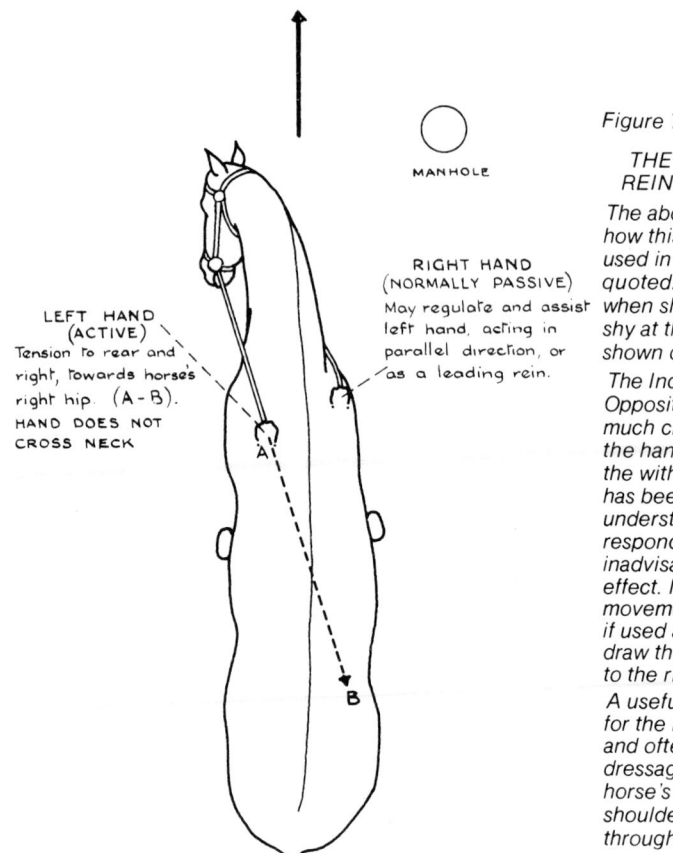

Figure 78:

THE LEFT INDIRECT REIN OF OPPOSITION

The above drawing shows how this rein effect was used in the instance quoted: on "Quintilla" when she was inclined to shy at the manhole cover shown on her right front.

The Indirect Rein of Opposition can be used much closer to the neck but the hand must never cross the withers. Until the horse has been brought to understand the legs and respond freely, it is inadvisable to use this rein effect. It opposes forward movement too stongly and if used at a standstill would draw the forehand back and to the right.

A useful rein effect, easy for the horse to understand and often wrongly used in dressage tests to keep the horse's head IN and his shoulder OUT when riding through a corner.

Years ago I was an Instructor with the South Australian Mounted Police. When conditioning young horses to street work in the City of Adelaide, I rode one day behind a very good 'natural' horseman and I had opportunity to watch him successfully and repeatedly use this opposing rein effect.

Every manhole cover in the road caused his mare, "Quintilla," to try to shy away to the left. Her rider would draw his left hand back slightly — and lightly — somewhat in the direction of the horse's right hip, while quite firmly riding her forward (see Figure 78).

This is the 'opposing' rein in action.

The pressure on the bit had the effect of drawing the mare's head to the left, away from the manhole cover; and at the same time the pressure of the rein against the base of her neck pushed her shoulders towards the right — or at least stopped her forehand moving off to the left away from the manhole. (She was sufficiently schooled to maintain obedience to the legs).

"Quintilla" was thus constrained to continue forward in a more-or-less straight line, with her head bent away from the object she feared.

I found this most interesting to watch for the rider, although a natural horseman rather than a taught one at that time, used both hands and legs with so much tact and was so encouraging to his mount whenever she did what was required of her, that I was filled with admiration.

"Sounds Nonsense"

Inspired by what I had seen I took "Rein Effects" as the subject for a talk a few days later. This Trooper was in the class, listening with a most sceptical look on his face. On my 'prodding,' he described the opposing rein idea as "nonsense" — or words to that effect.

Later, when I suggested it, he saddled "Quintilla" and rode her past a manhole cover in the Barracks Square — and I must say joined in our laugh when we all saw him use the rein as I had described.

Good horsemen have a great deal of inborn ability and skill, but quite often they do not know exactly how they produce the effects they do. When we have to teach or be taught, however, it helps enormously if these descriptive terms and expressions can be used. Every trade, profession, art or skill has its own terms — and these save a great amount of talking when they are generally understood.

The Police Mare "Quintilla" had reached the stage when she could weigh one aid against the other and get the correct answer. It is essential that a horse should have reached the stage when the demands of the legs are understood and answered without hesitation. Once the forward effect of the legs is properly established, almost any horse will respond to the opposing rein when it is used with tact.

Right throughout the early training of the horse the guiding rule is: "Hands without legs; and legs without hands" — so *don't* use the opposing rein too soon, and NEVER in dressage competitions.

To Sum Up the Indirect Rein Effects

The neck rein, the indirect rein and the opposing rein are all indirect in their action; that is, they all contact the neck and require the horse to yield to the sideways touch or pressure of that part of the neck that is contacted.

If anything I have said in this chapter on rein effects has seemed to you to suggest the use of force, let me hasten to correct that impression. We should not think of using force or strength; it will only upset the horse.

Use the rein only slightly and lightly and then watch and, most of all, *feel* for the horse's response. If he does or tends to do other than what you have in mind, show him: "That will profit you not." Quietly maintain your demand, your rein effect.

If, however, the horse shows the *slightest tendency* to move as he is wanted, immediately indicate to him by the reduction of any additional weight you might have previously placed on the reins: "THAT will profit you."

The reins should be used lightly, always, and not forcibly. They should be used as indicators — not like tow-ropes.

Eventually horse and rider learn to feel for each other, with the horse much more sensitive than the rider. He has a piece of steel resting on a thin ridge of bone at his end of the reins; you have leather, flat and wide, resting on flesh-covered and well-padded fingers at your end. To you the extra weight means but little; to him, it means pain — sometimes great pain. How can we expect bright cheerful co-operation if every suggestion from you is accompanied by a sharp pain: or *may* be?

* * *

What a lot of words and explanations to say what one old instructor of fifty years ago described as: "Sniggle them round (with the reins), and boost them up (with the legs)."

Be soft and gentle with the hands, but much more demanding with the legs if it becomes necessary.

Riders with really clever hands make many very small differences of pressure with the reins; often the changes follow very quickly one after the other, encouraging or discouraging, sometimes several changes to the second.

Feel for the horse's tendencies and encourage or discourage them at that stage. First *feel* — and then *act*, lightly and instantly.

CHAPTER 19

IMPULSION

*Impulsion defined — not necessarily action;
Ready obedience to the leg;
The whip should mean, and only mean, "Go Forward,"
About whips;
Lateral movements tend to destroy impulsion;
All lateral movements should be terminated by forward movement;
Impulsion when turning and circling.*

The inclination to move forward is most important. In dressage, the willingness, inclination or readiness of the horse for forward movement, is called "Impulsion."

IMPULSION IS NOT NECESSARILY ACTION

Impulsion refers to an impulse. An impulse is more a matter of mind than of motion.

And so it should be with the horse. A well-educated horse has the inclination or 'impulse' to move forward at all times. It is a readiness to go forward that is not transformed into action until the moment the rider requires it. Like a well-tuned engine in a motorcar, the power, the strength, the readiness to go forward is there under you, waiting to be called upon.

Impulsion in the horse does not have to be held back or subdued by the rider. It, too, waits there — quiet and alert for the rider's call for action. When the call is made, the response from the horse should be as instant and as predictable as that of a fine car to its accelerator.

Pulling is not 'Impulsion'

A pulling horse does not necessarily show impulsion. Impulsion is the inclination and readiness to go forward, waiting the call for action by the rider's leg — not a determination to go forward "Come what may."

A pulling horse is a badly schooled horse, and often proves to be just as difficult *to keep going forward* when — for any reason — *he* wants to stop.

If the rider attempts to lighten the pressure on the reins, such a horse immediately increases his pace. He will not let you take a loose or slack rein when for any reason you want to ride that way. Loosen the reins and away he goes.

The horse with true impulsion accepts the loose rein as permission to relax, not as a signal for more speed. He should feel free to stretch his neck if he wants to, but he should maintain precisely the same pace and direction.

The late Capt. J. J. Pearce astounded his listeners one morning in Adelaide, by saying — on calling for a loose rein — "When a horse is on a loose rein, he is free to do anything...anything! Anything he pleases."

He repeated this but concluded: "As long as it is *exactly* what he has been told to do." That brought a good laugh from us all.

A horse with impulsion, although keen, willing and even anxious to "go," will only increase pace when requested to do so by his rider. He will respond to the 'forward' demand just as promptly when for any reason he *does not want* to go forward — when, for instance, he is frightened.

OBEDIENCE TO THE LEG

Forward response to the leg is the most important lesson the young horse has to learn.

We should use every endeavor to get an easy, quick forward response to the leg. If the response is not immediate or sufficient, *then we take disciplinary action with the whip provided we are sure the horse has understood what was asked of him.*

The use of the whip must stop the instant he starts to behave as we want. He must know what to do to avoid or stop the whip, just as he should know what will provoke its use.

Use of the Whip — Mounted

Your young horse will have learned the meaning of the whip in the "Go-Forward" Lesson before lunging and the lunging will have confirmed it; and the next — last — chapter (Loading) will prove his obedience to it. He will have learned since that a tap with the whip will follow a squeeze or pulsing of the leg if he does not immediately go forward, particularly if we let a click of the tongue slightly precede the tap with the whip. We will also show him that a still sharper rap with the whip will follow 'pronto' if he does not act immediately on the lighter tap.

It is in this way that we teach the horse to act on a light leg aid.

Most riders are loath to use the whip a little sharper, even when it proves to be necessary. But if you do not do it when you should, you will find you will be compelled to do so later on — and sharper still. However, do notice that the words used are 'tap' or 'rap' — not "cut."

Show indignation rather than anger if your horse does not take the notice he should. You must not just keep repeating the lighter aids. You must be *determined* that you are going to have him answer the squeeze or pulsing of the leg only — not a continually-hammering heel which is so useless, so ugly, and so unnecessary.

Make up your mind not to tolerate his inattention. At first, give him several chances (this is his right), then get heavier with your leg — and then the tap of the whip. But as he gets further along in his training, give him an occasional quite sharp smack with the whip if his attitude is too casual. Instant obedience to the leg aids is a "must" — no matter what the horse is intended for, dressage, showjumping, hunting, polo or just plain 'riding for pleasure.'

If, eventually, he shows signs of accepting each increased leg aid without answering it, occasionally follow the first light pressure with an immediate *smart* rap with the whip. Keep him guessing: don't lead him to think that several light taps will always precede a sharp one. Don't be over-sorry for him, either, in these instances. He knows now how to avoid it, and you have given him every opportunity to do so. What sympathy would you expect if you 'dared' the fire and sat on a hot stove?...well!

THE WHIP SHOULD MEAN, AND ONLY MEAN, "GO FORWARD"

This is important. So many horses that have become difficult and brought to me for correction, I find have been taught (or permitted) to move sideways and away from the whip. They move to the left when the whip is used on the off-side, and to the right when it is used on the nearside.

Never use the whip to teach these complications or permit the horse to learn them. The special role of the whip is: *it clearly and decisively spells out "GO FORWARD" and nothing else.*

Introduce nothing, particularly in these early days, that may tend to lead the horse to think that moving sideways is as important as moving forward. Do not use the whip to get the horse to move any part of his body sideways. Do not use it at any time other than to demand or enforce forward movement.

Never use the whip merely to thrash a horse. He has to be taught to DO something about the whip when it is used: to go forward, not just to bear the punishment. He must be both MADE to go forward and ALLOWED to go forward.

The whip should mean, and only mean, "Go Forward."

RESPONSE TO THE LEG AIDS

At first, the legs like the whip must mean one thing and one thing only, "Go forward." Later on — but not in the period covered by this book — a sideways (lateral) effect may be added to the drawn-back leg.

In this important aspect, the whip and the leg differ; the whip means 'go forward' and only 'go forward'; the leg, however, contains a latent lateral effect that we should not develop until much later in the horse's education. It is something additional to the forward response we have insisted upon from the very beginning — and still insist upon.

The lateral effect will never take the place of the forward effect, although eventually a drawn-back leg will mean "Go forward *and* to one side." In this matter perhaps more than in any other, the precept of "Teach only one thing at a time," must be followed. First: "Go forward."

The horse full of impulsion always accepts the order to go forward; if, later on, lateral effects are required, then it is for the rider to deflect the forward impulse into a 'forward and sideways' movement, much the same as the sails of a boat can be utilised to send the vessel in an easterly direction, say, when the wind is blowing to the north.

Be perpetually on your guard for anything that may impair impulsion. Lateral movements asked for too soon, and working a young horse too long on circles, both tend to destroy impulsion.

The importance of impulsion cannot be overstressed. *Lateral effects are properly produced from the forward impulse* — without the impulsion, or the breeze, your horse and the ship stand useless.

Forward, Forward, Forward

Even when you have progressed to the point of carrying out lateral exercises, the forward demands of the leg should always be re-established after lateral movements of any kind. *All lateral exercises should be followed immediately by a "Forward only" demand.*

You may have already noticed that a forward movement is always required immediately after any lateral movement in a dressage test. A halt, for instance, never follows a forehand turn, shoulder-in, rein-back or half-pass.

Whenever other than a straight-forward movement is asked for in a dressage test, that movement is always terminated by the demand "Go forward." Good judges watch closely to see that this response is immediate and free.

ABOUT WHIPS

The riding whip used in this part of the training should be fairly long, although Show-Jumping rules rightly limit its length for jumping. A whip of about 3 ft. 6 inches (just over a metre) is recommended; or even a little longer.

Avoid whips that are too 'whippy': i.e. too flexible. If the horse should throw himself about on any occasion, the end of the very flexible whip can be tapping his flank without you knowing anything about it.

See, too, that there is a quite definite head to the whip you buy. Such a whip will not drop through your fingers when you are holding it lightly — as you normally should. Make a practice of holding the whip lightly in your fingers and not in a closed fist, which tends to make you heavy-handed. It is nearly impossible to use your hand lightly if it is grasping the whip like a Knight-of-Old holding a battle-axe.

The recommended place to use the whip is near the girth and whether you use it just in front or just behind the girth seems to be a matter of opinion. In any case, don't use it a long way back or anywhere near the flank; most young horses resent it and fillies, particularly, often show resentment in no uncertain manner.

You should not stop tapping with the whip if the horse in his early days shows resentment by kicking. If he kicks, tap him again, but lightly, until he goes forward. If the whip discontinues when he kicks, he will note: "Kicking stops that irritation, so kicking at the whip is a good thing to do." Show him rather, "Kicking at the whip will *profit you not. Only going forward stops the whip.*"

IMPULSION WHEN TURNING AND CIRCLING.

When changing direction on the move it is important that we insist on the maintenance of impulsion.

In all circles and corners, the horse's outside legs have to cover more ground than the inside legs. In the early stages of his training, we should aim to get him to step longer with the outside legs rather than to step shorter with the inside legs.

The Inside Rein when Turning.

The horse that has impulsion and is on the bit will always attempt to answer the call from the legs to increase pace. As he attempts to do so he will meet (when the rider intends to turn) a slight resistance from the inside rein — at first. Neither rein is 'pulled back' or 'shortened'; that would be "action" by the hands. Instead, the inner rein will lightly and slightly resist the forward drive created by the rider's legs, until the horse is bent towards and moves in the desired direction. Then both reins resume equal contact and condition.

The Outside Rein when Turning.

The horse, when he goes up to the bit, finds one side, one rein, gives slightly. It is the horse's task to keep an equal contact with each side of the bit. To 'go up to the bit' when the resistance of one rein is less than the other, he has to bend his body slightly, stretch the muscles of the side meeting least resistance. His legs on that side will then step a fraction longer than those on the side that meets resistance. The difference in length of stride — the horse's inside and outside legs — results in a change of direction.

Is this important? Perhaps not for ordinary riding — hacking, hunting, jumping etc. But it is most important for those who, later, would like their horses to go on to the more difficult and showy airs and exercises of advanced dressage.

In another chapter I have said something about rein effects, but I have said nothing about how we induce the horse to stretch the outer side of his body when changing direction. That has to wait until the *next* book — HORSE CONTROL — DRESSAGE SIMPLIFIED (or something like that!).

I'll just say here that the horse has to stretch the rein on the less-resistant side, lightly stretch it. Not the rider loosen or lengthen it. The aids you use should try to convey to the horse: "Go to the left (or right)," not "Come to the left (or right)."

TO SUM UP

The horse with true impulsion gives his rider a most enjoyable ride. The rider has beneath him a horse not only ready, willing, keen and eager to go forward on demand, but one that is also, at all times, ready to drop back instantly into the restraint suggested to him by the reins.

THIS IS IMPULSION. It is this we should be seeking at all times. This is the goal we set our sights upon when we begin the schooling, even before the young horse is mounted. It is this I want to draw your attention to, to get you to recognise, and to get you to strive for at all times.

> *Impulsion is a readiness and keeness to move forward at the rider's request, and includes a similar readiness to follow any other direction given by the rider.*

Develop impulsion in the earliest days of your young horse's training: the willingness, the eagerness, to "DO" what the rider indicates. Loading on to transport (next chapter) gives us an opportunity to impress upon the horse that he MUST go forward on demand.

CHAPTER 20

LOADING A HORSE ON TO TRANSPORT

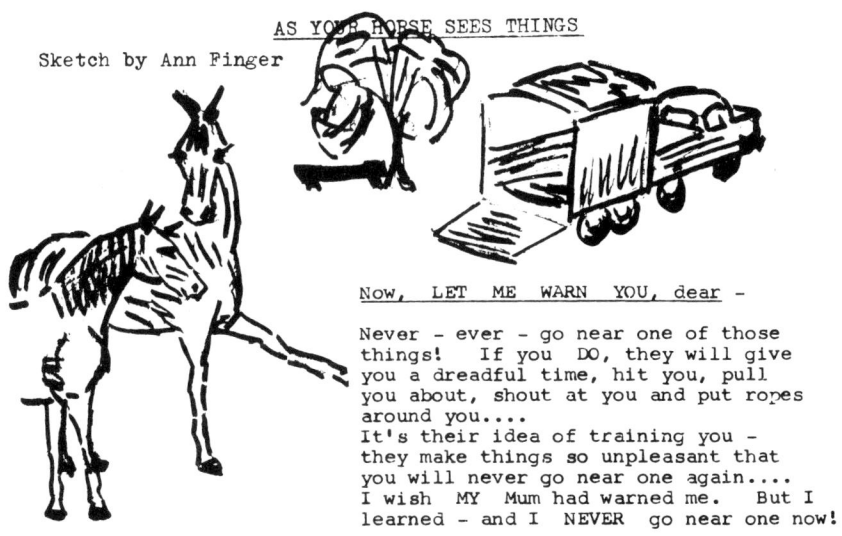

AS YOUR HORSE SEES THINGS

Sketch by Ann Finger

Now, LET ME WARN YOU, dear -

Never - ever - go near one of those things! If you DO, they will give you a dreadful time, hit you, pull you about, shout at you and put ropes around you....
It's their idea of training you - they make things so unpleasant that you will never go near one again....
I wish MY Mum had warned me. But I learned - and I NEVER go near one now!

From "THE SOUTH AUSTRALIAN RIDER"
— the magazine of the Dressage Club of South Australia, March 1970

A 20th Century problem;
Preparations for loading: the Float;
Preparations for loading: the Horse;
Preceded by Go-forward lesson;
Common Evasions — running back
     — forcing the hand
     — turning the hindquarters away;
     — standing stock-still;
Stepping into the float;
When the horse is in: never tie up until tailboard raised;
Off-loading; subsequent loadings; travelling;
Difficult horses.

181

A TWENTIETH CENTURY PROBLEM

Although military horses and mules were moved very long distances by ship and train in the past, loading a horse on to transport is more or less a problem of the Twentieth Century. Today, a horse that will not walk quietly into a horse-float is of very limited value, and teaching him to do so has to be faced as being an essential part of his education. It is a 'must'.

Over the past fifteen years I have been called on to deal with scores of horses: some that could be loaded only by force — ropes, whips, brooms and sometimes as many as five people all being used; some that no-one had ever been successful loading; and others again that could be loaded but couldn't be kept in the float long enough for the helpers to raise the tailboard. All, *without any exception,* learned to walk calmly and easily into the float and stay there without being tied.

Avoid the use of any force. In recent years, arthritis in both knees has not only prevented me making any quick movements when handling troublesome horses from the ground, but the pain stops me using any strength when they resist the restraint of rein or rope. I mention this to show that the use of force and strength is not necessary and will not be recommended to teach this lesson. We teach it by the "It will profit you" — "It will profit you not" technique and other rules we have been observing throughout the schooling of our youngster.

The method I detail leaves the horse calm and confident when loaded. He walks in ahead of his handler and stays there in his compartment, unheld and untied, while the tailboard is raised and secured behind him. This happens notwithstanding that he has been impossible to load before.

Do not hurry. Horses with long bad histories do not take less than an hour to load the first time, and some very difficult ones have taken much longer. DO NOT ATTEMPT THIS LOADING LESSON UNLESS YOU HAVE UNLIMITED TIME. "THE MORE YOU HURRY THE LONGER IT TAKES". Allow time — and take all the time you need.

Usually the one lesson is sufficient, even though it might be several weeks before the horse is loaded again. You will be most unlucky to meet ALL the difficulties dealt with here if there has been no previous attempt to load your young horse, but again, better I say too much than too little.

Don't look upon this as just a matter of getting a horse on to a horse-float. It is much more than that, and when well handled it has a marked effect on the relationship of horse to man. He comes to recognise our indomitability and the futility of his opposition. At the same time he learns that we are kind and gentle when he *tries* to do what we want, and tolerant when he makes mistakes.

PREPARATIONS FOR LOADING — THE FLOAT

Follow as always the policy of making everything as easy and safe as possible.

For the first loadings use a two-horse float if one is available, preferably one without a roof. Have it placed on the best surface available to you, off the road if possible and on flat non-slippery ground. If there is a suitable fence nearby, take advantage of it and place the float as close to it as possible.

Make it as firm under the horse's feet as you can, and have it fastened to a vehicle to minimise rocking when he steps on the tailboard. If the tailboard still moves under the weight, support it with bricks or a piece of timber, etc.

As the smell of horse manure seems to reassure some horses, do not clean the float out too thoroughly — and if it is a new float, scatter some manure on the floor.

Where it is possible to do so, move the centre partition over to one side for the first few loadings; and where there are hinged rails attached to the rear of the partition, I remove them too.

Deal with — neutralise — all projections and slots into which the rein could drop or catch upon and so accidentally cause trouble: it is most important that the rope or rein does not become trapped anywhere when you are loading. Cover projections and stuff pieces of cloth into slits or slots to keep the rein from being caught. If there are projections of any kind on which the horse could hurt himself — sooner or later a horse *will* be hurt on them and be frightened to go on again. Deal with these items before you start.

Always open the front door of the float and have it secured in the open position before you begin loading. It lets in light and although the horse cannot get out through it, most load more easily with the door open. Secure it open, as later you will have the owner or someone the horse knows well standing in the front to give him confidence as he comes in. It is important that whoever is there can get out quickly if ever the circumstances require it.

As some float doors at the front cannot be opened from the inside, take positive steps to see such doors cannot close and lock anyone inside.

PREPARATIONS FOR LOADING — THE HORSE

Put a bridle on over the top of the halter. Tie up the reins of the bridle and the halter rope, and buckle a lunge rein to the snaffle ring. You must not risk the horse breaking away from you. Run a strap from one ring of the snaffle to the other behind the jaw, as for the Go-forward lesson (see Figures 46-50, Chapter 10).

Bandages and any other protective gear available should be used on the legs for this loading lesson and for travelling. On some horses the tail also needs to be bandaged to prevent rubbing.

If the youngster has a history of unsuccessful attempts to load him, he will become upset the moment he recognises the float: "I'm 'in for it again' ", he'll tell himself. Let him have a good look around before you begin work. Do not hurry or fuss — and do not start on the task if your time is limited. This is a most important lesson.

ALWAYS PRECEDED BY THE "GO-FORWARD LESSON"

This lesson of loading is really an extension of the Go-forward lesson. Give your horse the Go-forward lesson or if he is a horse you have handled before, give him a refresher.

When you have him satisfactorily answering your go-forward demands eventually take him on a course that will walk him straight on to the float if he continues forward. Most horses will stop several feet from the edge of the tailboard.

Expect this as normal and very quietly continue with your "go-forward" click-taps. He may have stopped as much as two or three paces from the tailboard — or more — but it is usually not difficult to get him to take a very short pace or so closer.

When he does so, immediately "End of lesson"; stroke him a few times and murmur nice things to him.

After this momentary encouragement, resume your forward demand. Each time he makes the slightest move forward towards the float, encourage him. It is the same "Go-forward" lesson, but now the horse is uncertain of what is wanted of him and perhaps frightened, too.

COMMON EVASIONS

RUNNING BACK

Sooner or later he will try moving back, for it may not yet occur to him that he could possibly be expected to step on to that tailboard. Treat his moving back as you did in the go-forward lesson; go back with him, just keeping the rein stretched — *do not try to stop him by hanging on to the reins.* Your strength and weight cannot stop him, anyway, and you should not try. Read the instructions in the "Go-Forward" Chapter (10).

When he does stop moving back, make a very short encouraging pause and then continue with your go-forward demand. No irritation on your part. Keep calm yourself, and keep the horse calm. You clearly show him, by quietly persisting: "Anything other than going forward will 'profit you not'". Tell yourself repeatedly (and quietly show him, too) that you are prepared to spend hours on him and this lesson.

It isn't just a matter of getting the horse on the float on this one occasion. When properly done, this one lesson will make him easy to load for the remainder of his life.

It is really important that you do not hurry or excite him — the calmer you keep him, the sooner it will dawn on him that he has to go into that float.

Sooner or later the horse will put his head down and touch the tailboard with his nose to examine it. The first time or two he does this, pause; for his examining it means that he is thinking about stepping closer to it or on it. But when he steps back after his examination, as he almost always does, immediately start again with your click-tap go-forward demands.

It may take as long as 15 minutes to get him with both front feet close to the tailboard.

FORCING THE HAND

Quiet horses often turn towards you, and very often push against you with their near shoulder as they do so. They push against you, will not answer your efforts to stop them, and keep moving on to the left.

In Chapter 4, "Handling the Very Young Horse", I have already stressed the need to demand respect for the hand and rein. If you have not done so, you will need to correct the horse now. You *must* deal with this matter of pushing against you or "crowding" you, before you go any further.

By his pushing, the horse upsets your balance and you are then unable to get enough purchase on the ground to stop him when he pulls forward. If he crowds against you repeatedly, push against the side of his face with your hand. You may have to push his head quite sharply eventually, but do not hit the head or the face. Keep at him until he keeps away from you. As long as he can push you off your feet, you will be too unstable to stop him.

Does the horse drag you about? If you cannot stop the horse pushing you off to the left in this way, you may find it advisable to attach another rope or rein to the off-side and get someone to assist you from that side. Whoever takes that rein should not intervene until the person doing the loading is clearly in difficulties. He then takes over from the off side *for a moment or so* and drops out again as soon as he sees the difficulty eased. The horse must not be permitted to profit from this or any other trick. (See the series of photographs at the end of this chapter).

Don't go on with the loading until this matter is settled. You must get obedience to the hand in stopping, just as you must get obedience to the forward demands of the voice and whip.

You must *never* let the horse drag you around by the reins or rope (see Figures 79 to 83). When you indicate 'check' or 'stop', then check or stop he must: not only on this occasion but at all times, mounted or dismounted.

Show determination, not bad temper. Horses that have been brought up with an over-indulgent family are usually the worst offenders in this respect, but you only have to be sharp two or perhaps three times and the matter is settled.

But settled it must be; the horse must respect the hand. He must learn to keep light — and so must you. *Your* only excuse for getting sharp is it permits you to be light and gentle afterwards: you must BE light and gentle as soon as he is ready to be so. You must repeatedly return to lightness.

If the horse forces your hand, make him turn back. It often happens that in the first struggle he has turned completely around to the left before you are able

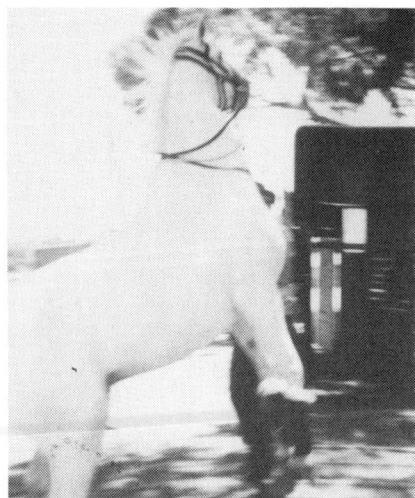

Figures 79-83.
This young gelding had, by deliberately playing rough and forcing the hand, won many a fight. He had to be taught to answer the steering as well as the throttle. He was not a "bad" horse, but one that thought: "They can't make me go on — and so I'm NOT going on".

Notice the stone under the corner of the tailboard to ensure it felt safe when the horse put weight on it. (Lyn Scholfield's "Silver").

to stop him turning. In such a case it is much easier to continue turning left until you again face the float. BUT YOU MUST NOT DO THIS.

This is not only a lesson in loading; it includes a series of essential lessons in control: go, turn, stop. At this moment you have set out to stop the horse turning left, and also to stop him moving around you.

If you allow him to complete the circle left he will have disobeyed you in both matters. Before you permit him to do anything else, first insist on his stopping, and then turn him back to his right — back the way he came.

If you take what you may think is the easy way out and complete the circle, the horse will repeat the performance time after time.

This is a fixed rule for you to follow whether you are mounted or on foot: if the horse turns left or right against your hand, then he has disobeyed you and you must not yield to him. You quietly persist, "That will profit you not" you show him. Do not get annoyed — or at least do not let it show. After all his resistances, just quietly say to him again with your hands: "Now, about this matter of turning to the side I indicated — in the direction I want!"

If you indicated 'to the right', the horse must *yield to* the right. At all times, he must answer your hand and the bit as well as go forward in the direction you indicate. A similar situation frequently occurs during the horse's early lessons when mounted; but mounted or dismounted, there must be no exceptions to the rule: the horse must yield to the rein he has opposed or ignored.

When he does this, you face him back to the open float and again continue with the go-forward demand.

Turning his Hindquarters from Side to Side

The trick most favoured by a young horse trying to avoid being loaded, is to move his quarters to one side when he reaches the tailboard (see Figures 84 to 86).

It is as if he says: "Go forward? Certainly I'll go forward — but in this direction!" This move completely non-plusses some people. Having no control of the hindquarters when leading, they don't know what to do; their usual course is to take the horse back and bring him up again. Only to find that he does the same thing again and again for as long as they like to keep it up.

The horse finds it the answer to his problem. He takes one or two steps to the right or left with his hind legs, which faces him in the wrong direction — and you take him back.

Do not take the horse back. Just show him, "Taking your hindquarters to one side will profit you not".

If he takes his quarters to the right (which will result in him facing left), with one hand I push against his head to keep his head facing the open float, and just quietly continue the go-forward click-taps.

Usually the horse's next move is then to try taking his quarters to the other side — and quite often you have him switching his hindquarters from one side to the other.

Quietly keep his head facing the open float and keep on with your click-tap 'forward' demand.

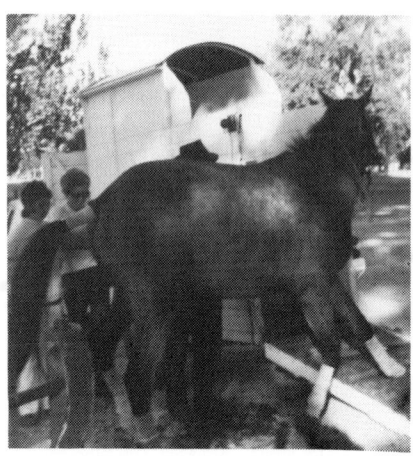 

Figures 84, 85, and 86.

Hindquarters to the left — and to the right of the tailboard. This mare had been given the "Quiet Persistence" loading lesson some months earlier but when confronted with this very narrow single horse float, she tried out each of the usual defences. Wherever she placed herself I quietly insisted "Forward and into that float".

Note the playing ears which tell us she is not excited but calm and observant. She has an idea it is "Old Hat" — but this narrow board and opening . . . ?

Many horses sit back against the tailboard when travelling, as had this filly. A little extra push back and her hind feet had broken the rubber matting loose from under her and it began to slide forward, eventually rolling up her front legs and pressing against her belly.

To calm her in this frightening situation, we had to reach inside from the front of the float, roll the rubber, and let it lay in a roll between her front and back feet: quite a dangerous proceeding. See that any rubber matting is well fastened to the floor by a strip of especially selected tough timber. It is when you have to place yourself at such a disadvantage that you will be pleased you have done nothing to make the horse fear and suspect you.

The horse with a few wins behind him due to his being repeatedly taken back and brought up again, will be puzzled. He will note: "This has always worked before", and he may then move completely around to the other side of the tailboard. It is just as though he is thinking: "I must have gone the wrong side" — or — "I haven't gone around far enough".

You remain quietly determined. He has to step on to the tailboard from whatever angle he places himself; even though the tailboard might be quite high in front of where he chances to be standing at that moment. Show him that turning sideways will in no way profit him; do not alter your demands.

Usually it is quite a task to keep him headed into the float when he places himself like this at right-angles to the opening, but quietly persist: "Step on to that tailboard".

It is not easy for him to step into the float from the side, and he quite often steps on to the tailboard and tries to go right across. Gently check him if he tries to do this and continue with the lesson. At least you have him stepping on to the tailboard — which is considerable progress.

He Now Tries Standing Stock-Still

At some stage of the loading your horse may stand quite still for many minutes and appear to be taking absolutely no notice of your light click-taps. He is usually quite close to the tailboard when this happens.

Only the ears and eyes may move as he stands there, looking and behaving as if he is prepared to let you go on with your click-tapping for as long as you like to keep it up. It is hard to know what goes on in a horse's mind as he stands there apparently stubborn and prepared to stand there all day.

I don't pretend to know *what* goes on in his mind during these long periods of stillness, but whatever else it might be, it is not stubbornness. He could be thinking: "I'll try ignoring him for a while — and perhaps he will go away". It seems his immobility is more to see what will happen than stubbornness.

If you have the tenacity and patience to see it through without upsetting or hurting the horse, you will find it well worth the trouble. Do not lose sight of your real objective: to convince the horse that he cannot withstand you or your demands. You aim to convince him that he is outmatched. Quietly persist with your demands.

Do not get rough. Maybe you can tap a little more quickly, but very little harder. Begin moving the whip from one part of the body to another and lightly tap him there: on top, more to the rear, on the shoulder: but do not get sharper (or if you do, do not lose your temper).

I have had a horse stand like this for as long as seven minutes before he moved.

He will be most observant throughout this period and so too, should you be. Study his face, his eyes, his ears, his mouth — and you will see what is going on in his head. As always, watch, too, for any movement that will give you a chance to encourage or reward him. The slightest *lean* forward should be met with at least a momentary pause in your click-taps.

Eventually he will break the stalemate in one way or another, and it is then for you to show him instantly *"That* will profit you" or "That will profit you not" depending on which way he tends to move.

Each horse Behaves a Little Differently

Some do not seem to have the faintest idea that you want them to put their foot on the tailboard. That just does not seem to occur to them (see Figures 87 to 90).

With such a horse, it sometimes saves a lot of time and it helps him to understand if you pick his front foot up and carry it forward to rest it on the tailboard. He will pull it straight back off again. Gently repeat your action until he leaves it there for a moment or two. When he does, encourage him immediately; rest a moment. Show him, "That will profit you".

Sooner or later he will pick his foot up himself and put it on the tailboard — and leave it there for a second or two. "Purr" to him when he does so, although he is almost sure to take it off again before you can get the second foot up.

Deal with all backward steps by using the Go-forward demand; give the click-taps *the very instant* he shows signs of stepping back. NEVER use the reins to try, by force, to stop his backward movement; keep the same contact on the reins, 'Relative stillness' (see Chapter 4).

Eventually you will get the horse standing with both front feet on the tailboard — a major step — which you will meet with a correspondingly encouraging End-of-lesson pause. You will be lucky if all this has not eaten well into half an hour; perhaps an hour if the horse has a history of unsuccessful loadings.

ENTERING THE FLOAT

The next 'lesson' is to get him to move further forward and to get him to put his hind feet on the tailboard. Some horses will repeatedly run back, and once more I stress that you must not try to stop them by means of rein or rope. It only gives them something definite to resist.

Meet backward movement by the Go-forward order; and let your hands retain their stillness relative to the horse's head.

You might now become a little more demanding: start to show a slight tendency to become a little less tolerant in one or two ways. Not only will you become more urgent with your Go-forward demands when he runs back, but you should not be satisfied until he goes right up to where he was before he began to run back. You demand he recovers *all* lost ground before he gets full encouragement after a run-back.

(What a lot there is to say . . . !)

When the horse does recover the lost ground be very rewarding to him again. You still show how pleased you are with his every progress, but you have to convey to him by your general attitude 'that it is about

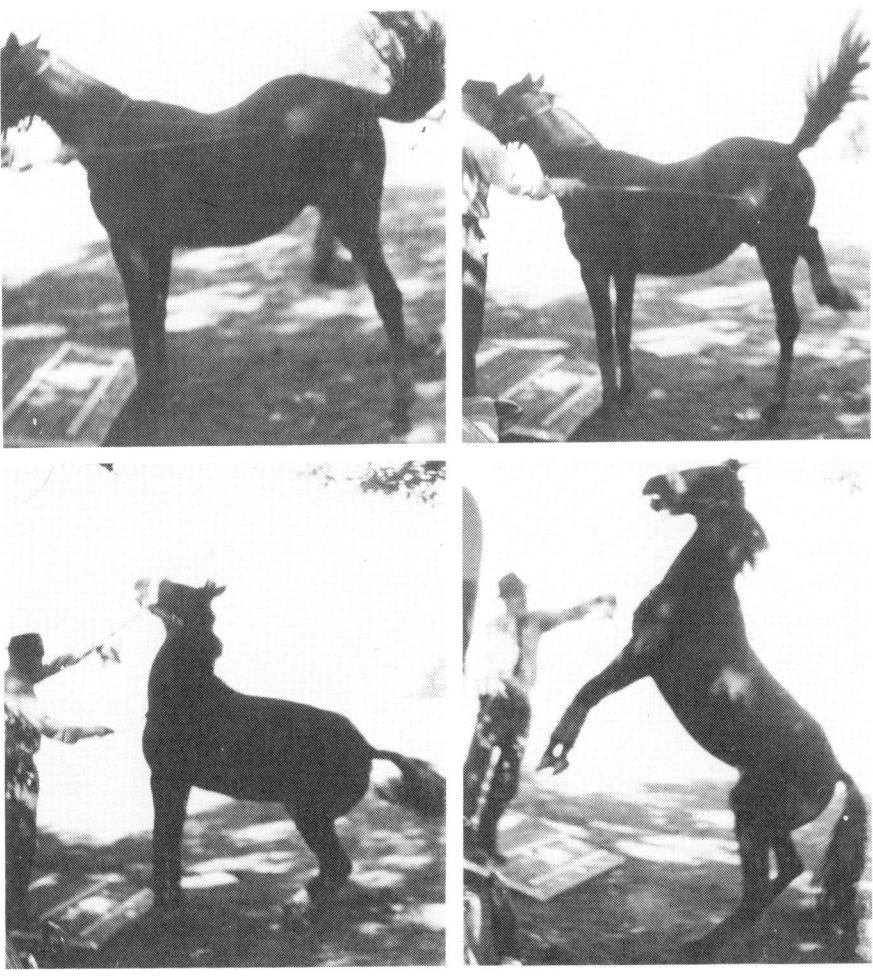

Figures 87, 88, 89 and 90: This 2-3 yr. old filly (Miss Sharon Slater's 'Gypsy') I eventually realised, had no idea whatsoever that she was required to step on to the tailboard. She went forward as far as she thought she could possibly be wanted to go and then, not knowing what else she could do, first kicked and then tried to break free. Once I realised her difficulty and placed her foot on the tailboard, she quickly understood what she was required to do. She looks vicious. She wasn't; she just didn't understand what was wanted of her.

time he learned that moving back will not be viewed as lightly as in the past'. The light taps will come much more quickly until he moves forward again; perhaps a little harder, too.

You will, before now, have someone the horse knows well stationed inside the front of the float with something the horse finds tasty to give to him when he does come right in.

On no account should this person try to help by giving a hand with the rein. The horse has to step in on the instruction of the person loading him. Interference with his head in any way will almost certainly cause him to run back again. It is most important, too, to see that no parts of the rein, rope or bridle can get caught up on projections or around any fittings; if this should happen he will get hurt or frightened, or both, and so put the lesson back a long way.

Worry no longer about his running back. It now gives just another opportunity to repeat the Go-forward lesson — another opportunity to load him, for we will be loading him repeatedly until he not only goes in without stopping on the way but learns to stay in position, unheld, while we perhaps gossip about something or other.

On no account should anyone try to hold the horse in position once he is loaded. If he starts to come back, order "Go forward". Do nothing to stop him other than order him forward. At first he may ignore your go-forward demand and run right back out of the float and off the tailboard, too; but eventually he will take notice of your click-taps, stop before he gets right out, and move forward again. When this happens, the battle is as good as won.

No! I must get out of the habit of thinking in the terms "battle" or "fight". Correction: the lesson is well under way to being learned. I have still to learn to "practise what I preach"!

Now The Horse Is In

And you will feel like putting the tailboard up immediately and keeping him there. Don't do it!

He has to learn to go in and stay in. Feed him with anything available that he likes. "Purr" to him and stroke him while he is in but let him stand there for at least a full minute or two before you put the back up.

If he moves back in the meantime, immediately click your tongue and put him back in position again. Never try to prevent his going back but do insist on his going forward again *immediately.* There must be no pause for any reason (or excuse). Neither is there any reason for you to get annoyed.

Where conditions are favourable, i.e. off the road or where there is no traffic, I off-load and load several times, always giving at least five minutes relaxation after each smooth load and unload. Let the whole thing become 'Old Hat' and casual. See if you can do without the whip and eventually only tap with your fingers — and don't get irritable.

TYING-IN

NEVER TIE-IN UNTIL THE TAILBOARD HAS BEEN RAISED AND FASTENED IN POSITION

Most floats, but not all, have a breeching bar, rail or strap at the back to keep the horse in while the tailboard is lifted. This is a convenience but not essential. If you do not have such a bar, *before* you lift the tailboard see that the *catches are ready for immediate engagement* so that there will be no undue delay in securing it.

If you have a loose-pin type fastener, see that the pins are ready and within reach. I have known a horse panic at the last moment and push the door down before it had been fastened. Stand to one side of the door and not directly behind it — ALWAYS stand to one side of the tailboard when either raising or lowering it. Make safety a habit.

I stress again and again that the person in the float must not attempt to hold the horse in. The rein or rope must not even be allowed to become stretched at this time. *On no account should the horse be tied in before the tailboard is raised and fastened.*

If the rope is tied before the back is up, the horse will almost always pull back, often striking his head against the roof as he does so. He will 'blame' you for that crack on the head: "That's what happens when you get in there" he will rightly notice.

After the tailboard is up and you do eventually tie the head rope, don't tie it so short as to interfere with the horse's normal head movements. Some people never tie the horse in at all; certainly there is no need to do so in a single horse float with a roof. But a single horse in a two-horse trailer should be tied to prevent him turning around in the trailer, or if there are two horses, to prevent biting.

Where there is no roof on the trailer, let the rope be long enough to allow the noseband to become almost level with the top — but not long enough to allow the horse to get his muzzle over the top. Better a little short than too long with an open float until he learns to travel.

WHERE TO TIE THE ROPE

In a two-horse vehicle there are usually two tie-up dees, one on each side at the front. I always recommend *not* to tie to the one on the off side of the float unless there is a door on that side. If things go wrong when travelling, it may be a slow and dangerous task to untie a knot tied on that side.

Instead, pass the rope through that dee, bring the end to the door side, and tie to the dee there. Then you can reach in and untie both horses quickly, easily and safely from outside the door should anything go wrong. (If at any time, you have a horse in real trouble and cannot untie the knot, do not hesitate to cut the rope. The horse is more important than the rope.) *Always tie with a bowline (see Figure 37, Chapter 7).*

Check that the float is fitted with a lock on the front door that can be opened from the inside. If you have one of the dangerous ones that has no handle on the inside, drop a piece of rope, bag or hay on the floor to prevent its closing and locking on whoever is inside. Do not allow anyone to be locked inside a transport with a horse whose actions are not yet predictable.

Take these precautions before you start the loading: certainly before you move the float with a person inside.

MOVING THE FLOAT

Make only a very short move with the float the first time. Just move it slowly forward a yard or two, then stop. This tends to reassure a nervous horse. The 'Old Hat' technique again.

Let someone stay in front with the horse the first short move or two — with the door secured open — but they must not stop in the float if travelling more than a few yards.

OFF-LOADING

At first we do all we can to stop the horse moving back out of the float. Now we have to show him that at times he is invited, asked, to back out.

With all horses, and particularly with difficult ones, I insist that they are not to move back until they are told to do so. Even though I may be ready for them to come out, I will not permit them to do so until I give them the signal. If they back out before being told, I put them back in again — very quietly and gently, but immediately.

You are forming the habits of a lifetime. Do not let the horse learn to "Beat the pistol" for it can lead to ugly situations.

NORMAL OFF-LOADING

The vehicle is stopped and one person gets in with the horse at the front and unties him. If there are two horses on board, it is usually advisable to off-load the more difficult one first.

Whoever is at the tailboard should not attempt to lower it until he has first made sure that the horse has been untied.

Do everything slowly and deliberately with an inexperienced horse. After the tailboard is down, walk up to him from the back — but not in a line that might allow you to be kicked. I usually speak to the horse and place my hand on his rump before removing any bar, etc., but don't remove any breeching bar or strap from behind him until the person at his head *tells* you that he is ready and the horse untied.

Stand clear when the rail or strap at the horse's rear is removed; then whoever is inside calls out loudly and clearly: "Back!", "Back!", and pushes against the horse's shoulder.

Why push against the shoulder?

Because horses resist force, and if you try to force them back they often tend to resist and so move back slowly. So push *hard* with your hand against the point of the shoulder.

If he does run back too fast for the person in front to keep up with him, the rope or rein should be dropped so that it hangs down. It is then quite easy for whoever is at the back to grasp it as the horse passes him.

In this load and unload lesson, the horse has to learn he is to go back when asked but that he is not to move back until he is clearly told to do so. Once good habits are established you do not need to be so particular — *except to untie first and never try to stop his rushing back by hanging on to his head.*

FULL CYCLE — "END OF LESSON"

The horse has now completed his first full cycle of load, lock in, tie up, move off, stop, untie and off-load. He has now earned a long "End of Lesson" break.

Let him relax and graze or nibble at something if he wants to; we want him to associate loading, etc., with "Good things to follow". If it is your own youngster you are dealing with, you might finish for the day.

SECOND LOADING

Take all the care you used the first time. Much of the horse's fear and other objections have now gone but he may still hesitate or stop. Gently give him the Go-forward order again — and don't get angry whatever he does. Just gently and immediately correct him. You want to leave him with pleasant recollections of this loading.

Again have a helper up at the front with a carrot or something tasty. Your assistant may show him this — but must not give him any until he is well into the float. The titbits must be kept the further side of the front rail. Again check that the front door is secured in an *open* position.

Often you will find the horse's hind legs not quite far enough into the float at first and you will want him to take another small step forward with either one or both hind feet. Try clicking your tongue and just tapping his quarters with the back of your fingers instead of the whip. Be casual, but be firm. Let your hand rest on his back or rump once he is in and again be very 'nice' to him. Don't hurry to put up the tailboard; he has to learn to stay there. You want him to be loaded easily by one man or girl.

If he backs out at any time without being told to do so he has to be reloaded immediately — IMMEDIATELY. Not a moment's respite, but do not try to hold him in and remember he has not done wrong, he has only done it at the wrong time — too soon.

In cases where I have to deal with difficult loaders and I don't want to take a second trip to complete his correction, I load and unload the horse many times on this one occasion. It is very difficult for him to understand that, each time, he has to wait until he is told. So do be patient with him.

TRAVELLING

Many horses travel better together if there is no partition between them. They find the contact of another horse more reassuring than the feel of wood and metal.

A horse held bolt upright corners badly compared with one that can lean into any turn of the road the trailer is taking. The more foot room he has, too, the better — he can balance himself much more easily.

If a horse travels badly, try covering any windows the float may have or try covering some of them if there should be more than one. I know one horse that only travels well with blinkers on. Another owner found that moving the tandem wheels of the float a little further back on the chassis made all the difference. A horse-float should be 'front-heavy' — check this point, particularly if your horse travels better down hill than up hill in any particular float.

Many horses also do not travel well in floats that have a dividing partition which reaches within an inch or two of the floor. If your horse is such a one, try him without a partition if he and the other horse do not kick — or try him with a partition that stops some 18" to 2 ft. above floor level.

Do drive with consideration for the horse that is out for the first time.

DIFFICULT HORSES

HORSES THAT HAVE LEARNED TO BREAK BACK

In reporting a successful method of tying up a foal (Chapter 7) I mentioned having tried the same method in a completely different matter — and that it had proved astonishingly successful.

This occurred during a loading lesson and I will tell you about it here, as, although few readers will have occasion to use it in loading, the principle involved is valuable and can be utilised in many different circumstances. The horse concerned had always smashed his way out after loading and eventually would not go near a float.

When I was asked to deal with the problem I found the float itself provided additional difficulties. It was quite new, had never been used, and was extremely narrow. So narrow, in fact, that when I did eventually get the big thoroughbred in, he fitted tight from side to side. Also the roof was galvanised iron and "drummed" when the horse stepped on the floor. Moreover, although I had never failed to get any horse to lead in and stay in quietly, I had not at that time learned the value of not using the whip sharply. (I learned a good deal from this horse.)

We did what we could with the float by muffling the drumming by throwing empty wheat bags over the roof and made the inside more acceptable to the horse by strewing some straw and stable manure on the tailboard and floor.

This horse was really tough and it was not until about the two-hour mark that I was able to get him in and stay in for a while. Even so, the moment he felt anything around his quarters, "crash", he would smash back and out, breaking everything in the process.

What to do? It hurt the horse and damaged the trailer. Moreover — the horse had won.

There is Always a Way

After trying several other schemes I tried the following as a variation of the "It will profit you not", quiet persistence idea: my aim being to cut out the pain to the horse, so 'calm destroying', when he rushed back.

Using a breeching strap about 3 inches wide and fitted with a strong snap-hook, I tried snapping the hook on to a single loop of bindertwine attached to the opposite side of the float.

The horse dashed back and broke the twine instantly. By this time I had him reloading almost as quickly as he rushed out, so again he was put in. He had profited not at all, and for the first time he had not been hurt by his action.

I repeated the procedure a number of times before I began hooking onto a *double* loop of bindertwine. This did not break quite so easily, and although not at all painful it would have been a little unpleasant for the horse to break. This, too, was repeated several times. By then the horse was becoming calmer because he was not hurt, and he was beginning to notice that it was *his* action that caused the discomfort he felt when he went back.

I then tried snapping on to a triple loop of the twine. He had no trouble breaking that either, but as he was calming down and not putting quite such an effort into his backing by this time, it was a little more difficult to break — although far from being painful.

After a few repeats he eventually pushed back against the strap and then went forward again before making the usual effort that broke the twine.

The next time he pushed back, stopped — went forward again — stayed forward. He had discovered that he, himself, caused the trouble and that we were pleased when he stayed forward. He never broke the breeching strap again.

It took two hours to get the horse to walk quietly into that narrow float, and over three before the job was done and we could fasten the breeching strap without him breaking it and rushing frantically back and out. The calmness-maintaining "It will profit you not" technique had been effective. This horse gave me a lesson never to be forgotten.

When helping a teenager recently with her horse that was proving difficult, I heard her remonstrate seriously with it: "Think, you silly horse: think, THINK!"

This is what *we* have to do. Learn the principles of how horses see things and how they learn; and then think, think, THINK how to use these principles in any new problem that might present itself.

HORSES THAT REAR AND STRIKE

I have made little reference to horses that through mishandling or accidents have learned to fight back against their handler when attempts are made to load them. Naturally, it is to horses such as these that I have been most often called.

Occasionally I meet a horse that as a result of previous successes has learned to rear and come at one with his front feet. With such a horse I take action to show him that from now on, that line will 'profit him not'. Always have a helper with a second rein in these cases.

At first I lightly jolt his mouth with the bit and rein each time he rears. I do this *very lightly* at first, but when he comes to realise that a rear results in a light jolt by the bit, I progressively get sharper. If he comes towards me on his hind feet, striking with his fronts, as some do, I step to one side and SHOUT at him as well as really jolt his mouth (I have never forgotten a remount from the Argentine that smashed my nose flat with a forefoot in 1915).

This sharpness should only be used after the horse has been warned, as I have just said, by first lightly jolting his mouth each time he rears. You MUST BE SURE he knows what provokes your action before you resort to punishment, particularly sharp punishment. Remember the previous treatment the horse has received has encouraged this action of his.

Remember, too, that you not only have to show him what is "wrong" but even more important, you have to show the horse what is "right". You must always be looking for any action of his that might indicate that he is thinking of doing what you want him to do — which in this case is to walk forward, first on to the tailboard and later into the float. *You must never fail to encourage him to behave better no matter how badly he has been behaving.*

I am writing primarily for people with little experience. Horses that behave like this almost always have a long history and should be handled by an experienced horseman. Colt-breakers and many horse dealers have methods of using a rope that are quick and effective but need a great deal of experience. The rope has to be used every time the horse has to travel.

We want more than that. We aim to produce a horse that walks into the float ahead of his handler, perhaps a girl; stays there while she puts the back up and is ready to greet her — as if to say, "My word, you're slow!" — when she goes to the front to fasten the rope and see "All's well" before moving off.

The use of force and pain is NOT necessary.

This loading procedure will prove it to you and leave you as it leaves me — realising that there is a "something" we do not yet know of, or at least cannot yet clearly formulate, about the horse.

TO SUM UP: THE LOADING LESSON.
Miss Christine Dehle's "Admiral Nelson"

Figure 91: Vibrating the bit when the horse fails to stay light on the hand when asked to stop during the "Go-forward" lesson.

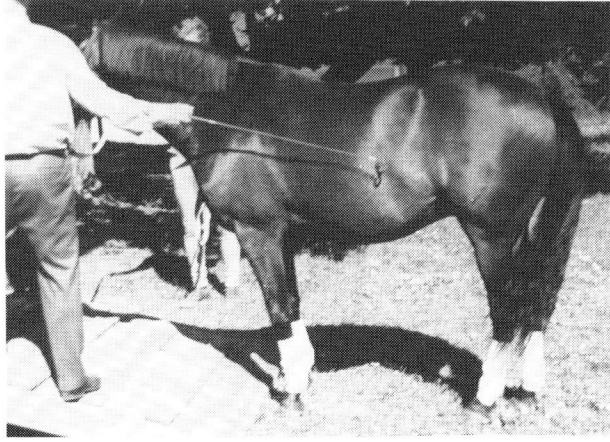

Figure 92: "That is as far as I am going", decides the horse.

Figure 93: He tries turning his hindquarters to one side and also to see if he can stop the irritating tapping by kicking at the whip.

Figure 94: "That did no good, I'll try the other side" — but he finds this, too, has no effect on the tapping or the direction indicated.
I fear he may be too rough for my poor knees, so an additional lunge rein has been attached.

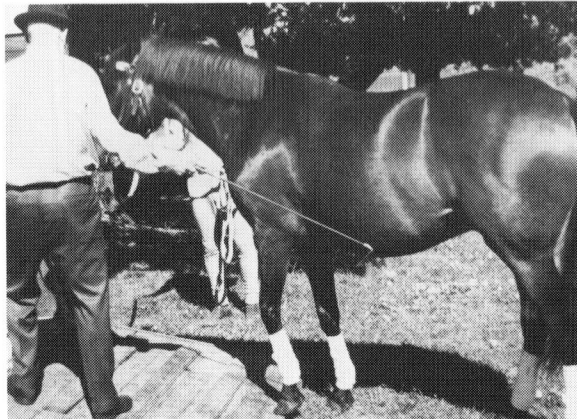

Figure 95: After 15-20 minutes of dithering and fighting on the part of the horse and quiet persistence by the handler, the horse thinks he might see what happens if he puts his toe on the tailboard. The whip stops tapping.

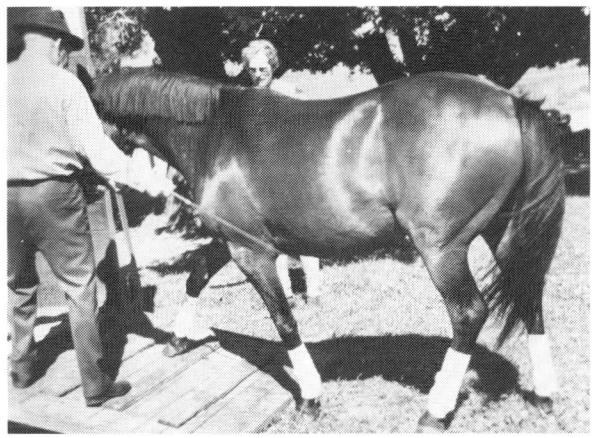

Figure 96: After many more backings away and fights to the side, he again takes a decisive step forward. The tapping again stops: "He's a clever boy", I encourage. But he has not given in — not by any means. He is just making a trial concession — a trial only.

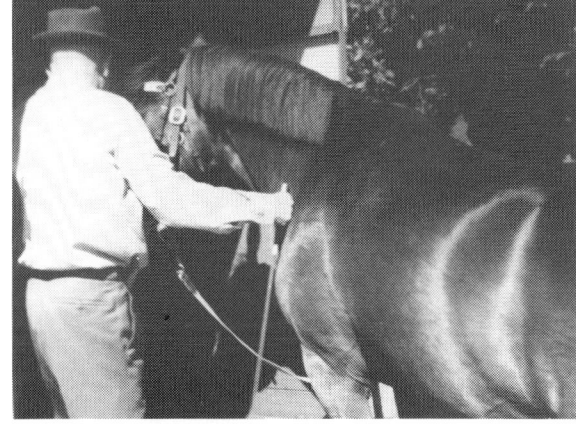

Figure 97: He is now thinking about pushing me away. Michael, with the other lunge rein, rightly does not intervene as yet. Note my right hand letting him know I am aware of what he has in mind — and warning him.

Figure 98: He has knocked me out of the way only to find Michael is alert and ready to intervene when he resorts to roughness, and with the rein at 90° the horse is checked easily. "This is 'crook'", thinks the horse, "that trick has always worked before!"

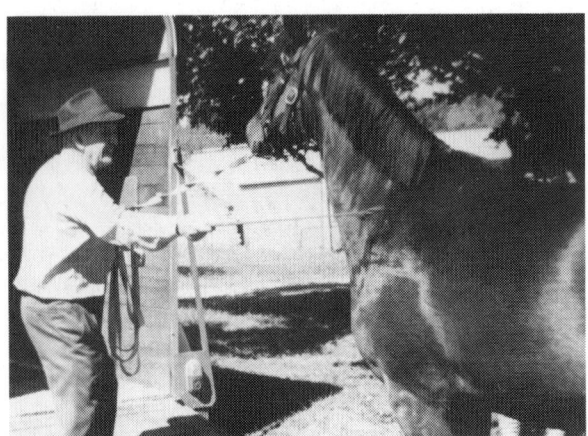

Figure 99: His efforts to push his handler off to one side having failed, the horse runs backwards again and he stands there quite still for a long while, as if checking: "I'll see what will happen if I do nothing. I know what he wants me to do but I'm not going to do it — I'll pretend I don't even notice what he is doing". Michael is quietly watching and not interfering — I might have the rein a little too tight.

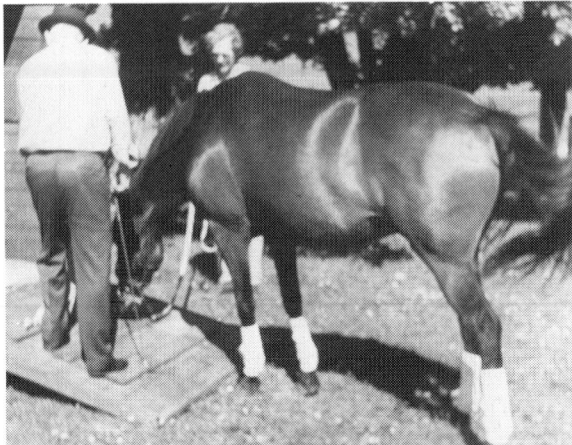

Figure 100: "It's not worth it," he decides, "We could stay here all day. I'll pretend I'm not sure about that tailboard." Maybe this is not what he is thinking, but although he does not know it yet, 'Admiral Nelson' is accepting the situation: "Although they cannot MAKE you go in, they won't let you do anything else until you do".

He is learning a good deal more than just to go into this float.

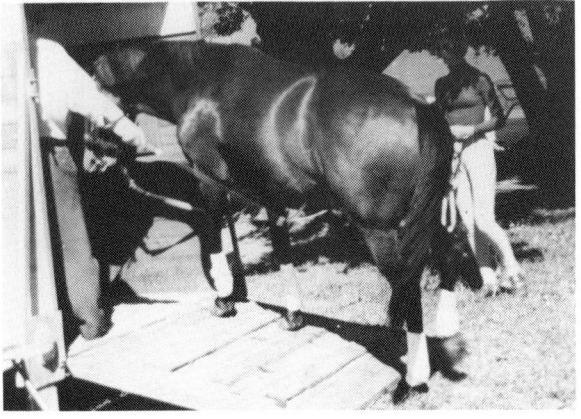

Figure 101: Having tried every trick in his repertoire several times, "Admiral Nelson" decides once more to try making a concession. The whip is ready to tap only if he stops, and Mrs. Kalleske (Michael is answering the phone) watches to see that her lunge rein does not interfere.

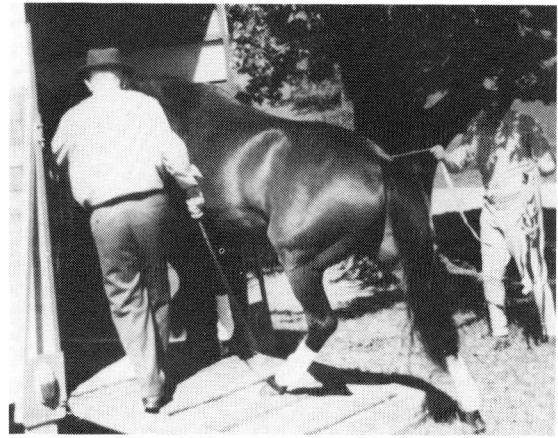

Figure 102: After hesitating and finding that the tapping resumes if he moves backwards, the "Admiral" steps further in. The whip stops tapping for this is a decisive forward movement and Michael (back again) is concerned to see that his rein in no way interferes.

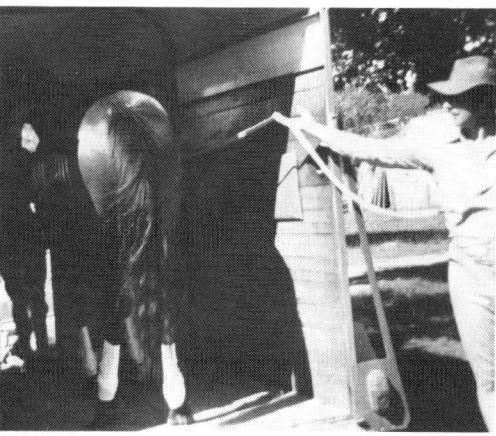

Figure 103: There he is — and we could not be nicer to him. His owner is in the front of the float and giving him a titbit. Every precaution is taken to see that neither rein is likely to be caught up or interfere if he tries to back out. If he starts to back out, his handler tells him to "Go forward". If he continues to go back, we repeat the whole thing until he learns to stay in. No rancour; no reprisals. We KNOW the horse cannot withstand quiet persistence and we have an inexhaustible reservoir of quiet persistence — and time.

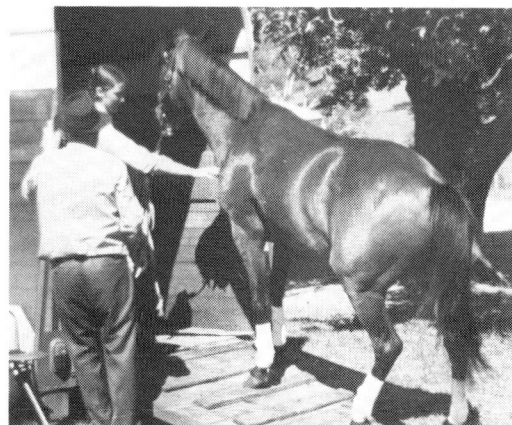

Figure 104: He has stood quietly in the float for two minutes and has been given some titbits he finds tasty. Christine, his owner, then calls clearly and decisively "Back," "Back". She pushes against his shoulder which tends to stop him rushing back, and quietly walks with him out of the float. "End of Lesson" and he gets a rest and a period of real relaxation. We do not box him in as soon as we get him in. We want him to learn that to go in ends his troubles — at first.

203

Figure 105: After a few repeats, the tailboard is raised and a little later we move the float — a few feet only. Then 'Unload', rest. "End of lesson". And after the rest, repeat.

Figure 106: Finally, the position is reversed and "Admiral Nelson" is leading his owner in. Note, too, Christine has her lunge rein correctly coiled — "Be prepared".

"A lot of fuss over nothing", is the Admiral's final conclusion.

This horse was not a bad horse or even a nervous one, but he was tough. The more resistance the horse offers to your quiet persistence, however, the less chance there is of his needing a repeat lesson.

We, too, can learn a lot from the effectiveness of this loading lesson.

CONCLUSION

It is with some reluctance that I bring this book to an end for I know there will be many who will wish I had given more detail on some subjects.

You will surely have noticed that I have not said how long you should take to teach any particular lesson. All horses are different; some learn some things easily and other things with difficulty. All riders are different; one can teach certain lessons quite easily and prove expert in some fields, but other lessons give great difficulty.

Whatever you do, don't 'take it out of' the horse — and if you have prolonged difficulty, see if you can find someone with the knack of teaching that particular thing. This is practised a great deal in big stables and schools. Accept your limitations at the moment, but take steps to correct them under more favourable circumstances. Do not hurry and do not lose your temper.

Not everyone will agree with all I have said, but may I say again what I said in the concluding pages of "HORSE CONTROL AND THE BIT" — *I am still learning.*

The manner in which every horse I have handled has responded to the three quiet principles of "It will profit you — It will profit you not", "Quiet persistence", and "End of Lesson" in the Loading into Transport Lesson, has given me much food for thought.

This success, I think, is due to the fact that the horse remains calm and when he is calm he learns quickly and easily. Once he knows what to do to please us, he seems to take pleasure in pleasing us. He not only becomes our willing servant but he learns to trust us — and once he trusts us he will usually do what we want even when he is frightened to do it.

Do all you possibly can to avoid the use of force except under circumstances you select and under conditions in which your actions or steps taken must prevail. Once your superiority is proved to the horse, do everything possible to establish understanding, so that he can know your requirements and follow them.

If, in the ways we have shown, we quietly prove ourselves superior to him, the horse settles down and transfers to us the submission he is compelled to show to the established leader of his own group of horses when he is free. Once again we are taking advantage of a characteristic of the horse.

We are all inclined to look back at the wonderful and great horsemen of the past and to think of their skills as something that will never be repeated. Now that the universities of the world are starting to recognise the horse and his control as a major field of endeavour, I think it likely that the greatest days of the horse and horsemanship lie ahead of us, not behind us.

As in all art, individual skill will be the paramount requirement to reach the top echelon, but the facts will be set down and from them will stem clear guide-lines that will eventually lead many more people into the fields of first-class horsemanship.

I do hope I have helped you with your young horse.

What next? . . . "HORSE CONTROL — THE RIDER"?

It's easy!

INDEX

Age to start (see Ch. 3), 12
Aids (see Chs. 16 and 17), 145, 155
    aims, 128
    for walk, 148
        trot, 152
        canter, 156
    importance of going forward on demand, 86
Angle, of rein (see Ch. 6), 41
    the horse sees from, 96
Australian Stockman's
    halter-bridle, 72, 73
    home-made bit, 78
    mouthing gear, 82-84
    stirrup iron, 34

Bad habits, how acquired 10-11
    about the head, 69-79
    break back (in transport), 196
    buck, 98
    difficult to stop 130-136
    drag you about, force the hand, 27, 93, 185-7
    drops his shoulder, 169
    jib, 98, 165
    jig-jog, 150, 158
    kick at the whip, 28, 90-92
    refuse, 98
    run backwards, 89, 98, 184, 196
    rear, 98, 165, 198
    stand stock-still, when being loaded into transport, 189
    turn hindquarters, when being loaded into transport, 187
Bag, folded for tying up, 59, 60
Bags of sand, tying to, 57
Bit, feel the bit as the horse feels it, 133
    fitting the snaffle, 74
    removing the bit from the mouth, 74
    taking the bit into the mouth, 71-72
Biting and kicking, dealing with, 28-30, 90
Bowline knot, 64, 193
    how to tie, 65
Bridling (see Ch. 8), 69
Bringing in after resting, 14
Bullock carts at Kirkee, 142

Canter, the (see Ch. 17), 15, 127, 155-163
    "Figure 8", 159-162
    footfalls, 146
    leading leg, 105, 146, 157-162
    on the lunge, 105, 123
    positioning for, 147
    simple change of leg, 161
Cavesson headstall, 80-82
Colliver, Miss Lynda, 98
Control, rider begins to take, 122-124, 130-136

Dally, use of, 61-65
Discipline begins before mounting, 27-30
    the "Imp", 28
Distraction —
    can help, 109, 111
    can be a nuisance, 82
Driving from over the saddle, 114, 125
    (and see back Dustcover)

Ears, passing bridle over, 71
Education begins before breaking-in, 13, 18
Encouragement (see Ch. 1), 1-5, 95
End-of-Lesson, Training Procedure (see Chs. 1 and 2), 1-5, 6-9, 94, 102
Exercise, run loose daily if possible, 128

Farrier, preparations for, 108-112
Fear and anger, 11, 99
Feeding, 15, 128
Feet, handling, 108, 111
Fillis, James, 7
Fitzgerald, Danny, 46, 73, 78, 82, 106, 162
Footfalls — walk, 146
           — trot, 146
           — canter, 147
Force, horses resist, 23, 70, 89, 184, 193
Force, how little can we use, 64, 166, 173

Gentling your young horse, 16
Girth, accustoming to, 83
    can cause trouble, 107
Gloves, prevent rope burns, 35
"Go-Forward Lesson" (see Ch. 10), 86
    benefits incalculable, 97
    leads into lunging, 99-102
    precedes Loading Lesson, 184
Good hands (see 'Hands')

Habits (see 'Bad')
Halter, special for foal, 19-21
  halter-bridle, 72
  breaking the, 66
  teaching to accept, 20
  when leaving on, 68
Handling
  general, preparatory to riding and shoeing, 106-112
  safety precautions (see Ch. 5), 31
  the feet, 108
  the foal (see Chs. 3 and 4), 12, 17, 44, 52
  the head (see Ch. 8), 18, 69
  the young horse (see Chs. 4 and 11), 19, 106, 111
  use a small yard (see Ch. 5), 31
Hands, good (see Ch. 14), 22, 130
  heavy, 23, 156
  light in hand, 26-27
  'limited' resistance, 134
  'relatively still', 23-27, 190
  still — resistant, 132
Heyer, Herman Mr. — author "Reflections on the Art of Horsemanship"... see 'Acknowledgements'
Holding, from the ground (see Ch. 6), 19, 41
  neck as lever, 42, 45, 56
Horse-sense, use, 77

Injury to mouth, check for, 54
Imp the, example in discipline, 28
Impulsion, definition (see Ch. 19), 175

Jeffery's "Magic Lunj", 43, 46
Jig-jog (see 'Bad Habits')
Jumping, any, 15

Kicking (see 'Biting and')

Lameness, suspected, 14
Lateral effects should always be followed by forward movement, 170, 177, 178
Leading forward, sideways, and backwards: teach before mounting (see Ch. 4), 21
Leg, leading (see 'Canter')
Legs, nursing the, 12-15
Legs, rider's use of (see also 'Aids') 86, 128, 130
  — see Ch. 19 'Impulsion' 175
Lesson, what is a (see Ch. 2), 6
  end-of-lesson (see 'End')
Loading Lesson, the (see Ch. 20), 181-204
Long rein driving, 113
Loose rein, work on a, 126, 141, 151, 162

Lunge rein, use recommended, 19, 35-38
  danger of loops, 37
  how to coil correctly, 37
Lunge — teaching your horse to, (see Ch. 11), 99-112
Lunging and mounting (Ch. 12) 113
  still a lunging lesson (see Ch. 13 — "First Few Days under the Rider") 121

Manege, avoid long periods in, 125
McGillivray, Mr D., 46
  bag tie prevents hurt to horse, 58-63
  Round Yard, construction of, 39-40
McKelvey, Mr. Webb, 46-51
  method of conditioning nylon rope, 35
  use of a "dally", 61-62
Mouthing, 84, 99, 114
Mouthing Gear, 82, 107
  can put back on, 124
Mounting (see Ch. 12) 113, 121
  and dismounting, 118

Neck as a lever, use, 42-46, 56, 167

Off-loading from transport, 194
"Old Hat", Training Procedure (see Ch. 1), 1-5, 124

Paces, the
  walk and trot (see Ch. 16), 127, 145
  canter (see Ch. 17), 155
  varying the, 127, 135
Pain, (see also Author's first book, 'Horse Control and the Bit')
  provokes troubles, 10, 54-56, 130-140, 160
Pearce, Capt. J. J., 176
Positioning, 147, 152, 162
Pull — don't, 23
  think "Go no Further", 132
Pulling is not impulsion, 175
Punishment, not a normal procedure, 2-3, 11, 97, 177

Quiet Persistence, Training Procedure (see Ch. 1), 1-5
Quintilla, Police Mare, 172

Rarey, "Gentling" method, exhibitions, 46
Readhead, Mr. C. C., 46
Rearing, can be caused, 84
    can be corrected, 97, 198
Reed, Mr. W. V., 60, 63
Relatively still hand (see Ch. 4), 23-27, 190
Rein back, to step back, 24-27
Rein effects (see Ch. 18), 164, 179-180
Reins, yielding to, 21-28, 115
    use with caution, 157-8
    weight on reins when mouthing, 83
Resistance, limited, (see Ch. 14), 134
Reward and Punishment — superseded (see Ch. 1, Training Procedures) 1-5
Rogers, Colin and Yvonne, 57-9
Rope, Bowline knot, 64-5
    burns, wear gloves, 34
    nylon — to 'condition', 35
    recommended length, general, 19, 36
    when tying up, 55
    where and how to tie in transport, 193

Saddling, preparations for, 106-7, 113
    badly fitting gear provokes troubles (see also "Horse Control and the Bit"), 10, 82
Safety precautions (see Ch. 5), 31, 193
Shying and 'spookiness' (see Ch. 15), 125, 138-144
Shoeing, need for, 14-15
    preparations for 108-112
Side reins, 80-84, 134
Simple change of leg, 161
Snap hooks, not generally recommended, 68
Snubbing post, 55
Stirrup irons, recommended, 34, 113
    what to do if foot caught in, 35
Stop lightly rather than quickly at first, 8, 93, 116, 122, 128, 131
    on the lunge, 102, 104

Teach or introduce only one thing at a time, 8-9, 106, 128
    repeat rather than prolong, 124
Teaching Teacher, 94-98

"That will profit you — that will profit you not", Training Procedure, (see Ch. 1), 1-5
Tie-up the, different methods used (see Ch. 7), 52
Tongue-over-the-bit habit, to prevent (see also "Horse Control and the Bit"), 78
Traffic (see Ch. 15), 125, 138
Training Procedures —
    End-of-lesson
    Old Hat
    Quiet Persistance
    That will profit you — that will profit you not
    Use of the voice,
    (see Ch. 1), 1-5
Transport, teaching the horse to load into, (see Ch. 20), 181-198
Trot (see Ch. 16), 151-154
    and diagonals, 146
    footfalls, 146
    sitting, 153
    to run away at, 157

Voice, use of (Training Procedures, see Ch. 1), 1-5, 102, 104

Walk, the (see Ch. 16), 121-3, 145-151
    aids for, 148
    controlled, 148
    footfalls, 146
    lengthening the stride, 149
Whip, about, 88, 103, 178
    can become sharper, 95-6
    means 'forward' and only 'forward' ("Go-Forward Lesson, see Ch. 10), 86, 97, 177, 189
    restraint in use of 97, 140, 176-9
Wilton, Mr. J. D.
    author "The Horse and his Education", 46
Wright, Mr. Maurice
    and the 'Jeffery Method', 43, 46

Yard, suitable, 19, 31, 45
    Round Yard, how to construct, 39
Yielding the quarters, 162
Yielding to the rein (see 'Reins')